TWILIGHT
of
TRUTH

TWILIGHT
of
TRUTH

Chamberlain, Appeasement
and the Manipulation
of the Press

RICHARD COCKETT

St. Martin's Press
New York

© 1989 Richard Cockett

All rights reserved. For information, write:
Scholarly and Reference Division,
St. Martin's Press, Inc., 175 Fifth Avenue, New York, NY 10010

First published in the United States of America in 1989

Printed in Great Britain

ISBN 0–312–03140–8

Library of Congress Cataloging-in-Publiction Data

Cockett, Richard.
    Twilight of truth: Chamberlain, appeasement, and the manipulation
of the press / Richard Cockett.
        p.   cm.
    Bibliography: p.
    Includes index.
    ISBN 0–312–03140–8
    1. Great Britain—Foreign relations—Germany. 2. Great Britain—Foreign
relations—1936–1945. 3. Great Britain—Politics and
government—1936–1945. 4. Germany—Foreign relations—Great
Britain. 5. Chamberlain, Neville, 1869–1940. 6. Government and the
press—Great Britain—History—20th century. I. Title.
DA47.2.C59   1989
327.41043—dc19   89–4108
                                                              CIP

Contents

Illustrations

Acknowledgements

This work started life as a Ph.D thesis for the University of London and I would like to record my debt to my supervisor, Dr John Turner, for keeping faith in what was initially a very sketchy idea. My examiners, Dr John Ramsden and Peter Hennessy, not only passed me but also proffered excellent advice from which this book has greatly benefited. I am also indebted to Mr Kenneth Harris for his guidance and faith in my work. I am grateful to my editors at Weidenfeld and Nicolson, Juliet Gardiner, Peter James and Benjamin Buchan, for their support and scrupulous work on my manuscript.

I also had the benefit of personal interviews with Sir John Colville, Sir John Lawrence, Douglas Jay, Iverach McDonald and Mrs Jackie Alford. David Astor not only granted me several substantial and fascinating interviews but also suggested several telling improvements in the manuscript. I am also grateful to Sir Tom Hopkinson, Peter Brooke MP and Professor Alfred Gollin for furnishing me with valuable written contributions. I owe a great debt to Miss Anne King-Hall in London and Peter Wright in Washington for allowing me access to their fathers' papers at my leisure in their own homes and for their permission to quote from their fathers' correspondence. My research in America was only made possible by the kindness of Standish and Sarah Meacham in Austin, Texas and the efficiency and helpfulness of the staff at the Harry Ranson Humanities Research Center in Austin.

The Central Research Fund of the University of London contributed invaluable financial assistance to my work, and the administrators of the Helen Cam Fund of Royal Holloway and Bedford New College helped to put me on a plane to America. Mrs Cynthia Hutchins was a supremely fast and accurate typist who was also blessed with the gift of being able to read my handwriting. Finally, I would like to record my great debt to my parents for their unfailing support.

Needless to say, the opinions and conclusions contained in this book are mine entirely.

Richard Cockett, London 1988

Introduction

The support that the press gave to Chamberlain and the politics of appeasement from 1937 to 1940 has always been a matter of controversy and notoriety. Yet the behaviour of the press during these vital years has remained one of the most enduring puzzles in what is now a well-documented if discredited chapter of British history.

Indeed, so intriguing was this question considered to be that a Royal Commission on the press was set up after the war (reporting to Parliament in 1949) which was partly charged with finding an answer to this very question. The widespread contemporary assumption was that the capitalist press owners, the celebrated 'press barons', had supported a policy that was conducive to a profitable and stable trading atmosphere that would attract advertising revenue to their papers. After exhaustive study, the Commission could find no solid evidence of this, and concluded, much to the disgust of the socialist journalists who had called for the Commission, that advertising pressure on newspapers had been negligible. But the initial question remained. Subsequent Commissions and academic studies have done little to enlighten us.

This book sets out to answer the question why the press supported Chamberlain and appeasement, and to do so it looks at the problem as much from the government side as from the side of the press. It is the contention of this study that due to the incestuous relationship between Whitehall and the press that had developed during the 1930s, the press in fact could do nothing but help Chamberlain pursue appeasement, as the 'free' and 'independent' press of Britain is at best merely a partisan political weapon controlled by politicians for their own purposes, and at worst a mere arena at the disposal of Whitehall to play out a game of interdepartmental warfare. The reasons for this

1

have little to do with advertising or commercial gain, but have more to do with those 'informal' contacts that are such a hallmark of the English way of life and the peculiar and uniquely English relationship that exists between the government and the press in the dissemination of government news.

This relationship was always to the advantage of government, and it exists to this day. The genesis of this relationship is discussed in Chapter 1. It was during the 1930s that the peculiarly English customs and habits that had governed the relationship between the government and the press became institutionalized by Whitehall to the permanent advantage of the incumbent government. Chamberlain was thus only exploiting a system; he became autocratic and undemocratic because the system allowed him the liberty of doing so. This study is as much a study of the system as it is of Chamberlain and appeasement.

Part of this system is that network of personal and informal contacts that permeate so much of English life. George Steward, Chamberlain's Downing Street Press Officer, was to prey on what he called the 'human element' in the service of his master. This informal pattern of links between the government and the press had already been seen to work to good effect during the Abdication crisis of 1936, when the King and the government had effectively preserved a blanket censorship on the press about a matter that was front-page news in almost every other country for weeks before the storm broke in Britain. This unity of silence was volunteered by the press to the government, and it was a foretaste of what was to come during appeasement. Although one might despair at the level of control government was able to exert over the press during these years, it is nonetheless true that it could do so only with the willing connivance of journalists, editors and newspaper proprietors. It is a sad fact that the press was just as much responsible for surrendering its freedom during the years of appeasement as the government was responsible for consciously trying to subvert editorial independence.

1

Whitehall and the Press: The State of Play in 1937

The national governments of 1931 to 1937 had overseen striking developments in Whitehall's techniques of disseminating information to the press, and when Neville Chamberlain became Prime Minister in May 1937 he was inheriting a system with which he, as a senior member of those national governments, was thoroughly familiar. The development of Whitehall's techniques for both giving information to the press and seeking to influence it was focused on the two principal centres of Whitehall power, the Foreign Office and Downing Street. In an era when the ubiquitous Whitehall press officer was still a comparatively rare breed, the Foreign Office News Department and the Press Office of 10 Downing Street had a free rein as the official spokesmen for the government. Chamberlain had paid careful attention to the development of the Press Office in Downing Street and it had, by 1937, become virtually his personal fiefdom; it was from this office that he sought to direct the press and its view of appeasement. The Foreign Office News Department had developed independently under the vigorous direction of Reginald ('Rex') Leeper. These two centres of information seemed to have had very little contact with each other throughout the 1930s, a point that was to prove vital in the period after Chamberlain's accession to the premiership. However, what distinguished both departments by 1937 was the fact that they had built up a clientele of pliant journalists throughout the 1930s who were eager to do the bidding of the relevant department. But to see how this state of affairs had arisen it is necessary to describe briefly the genesis and influence of these two rival practitioners of press manipulation.

The origins of the Press Office at 10 Downing Street are very obscure, because no files of that office survive. Any official portrait of the man variously described as Chamberlain's 'Press Adviser', 'Press Chief' or 'Press Officer', namely George Steward, is thus impossible to construct – whilst those who had less formal links with the Press Office in Downing Street, such as Major Sir Joseph Ball, have covered their tracks equally well. However, it is evident that George Steward's post was created in 1929 by Ramsay MacDonald in an attempt to counteract the influence of the all-pervasive Conservative press barons, who would be hostile to the new Labour regime. The purpose of having a press officer at Downing Street was thus to build up an alternative route of access to the newspapers by establishing a close relationship with the group of political correspondents known as the Lobby, and this is precisely what George Steward very successfully did. As one writer has observed of this development, 'Labour Prime Ministers have been especially helpful to Lobby correspondents – hoping presumably, by extending access to the correspondents, to counter the Conservative preponderance of the owners.'[1] In a conversation with A. P. Waterfield, a Treasury official, in the summer of 1939, George Steward described how the government looked at the press:

> the Press representatives may be divided into three groups; first the editors; secondly the specialists, such as the political, diplomatic, parliamentary, naval or military etc. correspondents; and finally the reporters. The first group will never deal with anyone except Ministers or very high officials whom they meet in clubs or special ministerial conferences. The second group, who are the real backbone of a paper, will always claim the right to go to the permanent departments where they will talk not only to the Press Relations Officer but with individual Civil Servants who they have got to know personally. Finally, in the third class there are the reporters who receive the handouts (a thing which the second class

would never condescend to do) and distribute them to the paper and to members of class two.[2]

Steward, as the permanent Press Relations Officer of 10 Downing Street, cultivated his own class of specialist political correspondents, known as the Lobby. The Lobby, as a group of select political journalists with special access to the Palace of Westminster, had existed since 1885 and its functions and duties had hardly changed during the course of the next forty years. But, with the arrival of Steward at Downing Street, the traditional functioning of the Lobby changed in a way that few appreciated at the time. The unique privilege of a Lobby journalist was that he had free and unfettered access to any Member of Parliament or Minister who wished to speak confidentially to the press. On the face of it, the appointment of Steward looked like an attempt to help the press in its search for information, but in retrospect the Lobby journalists realized that Steward was merely erecting a barrier between the press and the government. The old system had worked on the basis of competing journalists constantly in search of contacts and stories. But with the arrival of Steward, as James Margach, a young Lobby journalist at the time, has written, 'the change of power and status was implicit, the old-style competitive outsiders were converted into a fraternity of organized insiders'.[3] Steward organized a series of meetings at which he would brief the press, and by restricting the journalists' access to other Whitehall departments he ensured that this Lobby briefing was the primary source of a political correspondent's news.

At first, the Lobby refused to accept this change in their working habits and they were particularly wary of Steward's attempts to centralize all dissemination of government news in his own hands. The Lobby's annual report for 1930 records the inauguration of these Lobby briefings: 'definite times were arranged for conferences and rooms were provided at Number 10 for meetings'. This, as Margach observes, saw 'the beginning of the end for the old system, and the introduction of a new formula for the organized group meetings and corporate briefings which would meet twice a day'. In 1933, Steward went further towards centralizing the flow of information in his own hands by explaining to the Lobby that 'although he was formally appointed to act for the Prime Minister and the Treasury, he was also required to act for the government as a whole in all matters of a general character'. Although this attempt to channel all journalistic enquiries to the government through him was initially resisted by the Lobby, Steward seems to have been very adept at ensuring that this is exactly what happened. The Lobby recorded its suspicions of his centralizing tendencies and observed that this system 'carries certain dangers' as 'it may become too much a personal service of Prime Ministers'.[4]

However, not only Steward addressed the Lobby; by the mid-1930s ministers were coming to be so impressed by Steward's creation that they too began to brief it. Chamberlain in particular was very quick to see the potential of Steward's Lobby system for influencing the press; during Baldwin's premiership Chamberlain, as Chancellor of the Exchequer, regularly took the Lobby meetings and indeed resented any attempts by other ministers to 'muscle in on his regular briefings of Lobby correspondents'.[5] Even before he became Prime Minister himself, Chamberlain was regarding the Lobby as his personal service and was careful to court the fifty or sixty British correspondents who formed the most substantial element of the Lobby. Sir Samuel Hoare was another minister who fostered excellent relations with the Lobby, and it was with great regret that the Secretary of the Lobby journalists bade him farewell in May 1940 and thanked him for his 'invaluable guidance in the past', which had 'constituted ... a really distinctive period in the history of the Lobby'.[6] What made the system so advantageous to the ministers was that all these briefings were confidential or off the record, so Steward and the ministers could not be named as the sources. The rules of collective lobbying allowed that 'members of the Lobby are under an obligation to keep secret the fact that such meetings are held and to avoid revealing the sources of their information'.[7] This system enabled the government to release information or inspire stories without being publicly responsible for them – only the *aficionados* of Whitehallspeak could trace the attribution of 'an authoritative source' to the appropriate minister or official. They could thus set the tone for political reporting without being responsible for their actions. A modern Cabinet Secretary, Sir Robert Armstrong, has described this system of unattributable briefings as an attempt to 'seek to influence opinion without accepting responsibility'.[8]

However, this system could only work to the benefit of the government if the Lobby journalists were prepared to act as the passive receptacles of government briefings and suspend their critical faculties for the greater duty of writing what they had been invited to write at the Lobby meetings. When Chamberlain was Prime Minister, some of his Lobby briefings were to be so patently contrary to all other existing evidence that many civil servants were at a loss to understand why the Lobby journalists were prepared to transcribe what he had to say without any independent evaluation or critique of the veracity of his comments. The main reason for the collusion between Chamberlain and the Lobby was not so much the fact that he was adept at handling the Lobby, although this was a contributing factor, as that the Lobby journalists themselves were so ready to regard themselves, in James Margach's words, as 'honorary members of a power establishment and ex-officio members of a political system ... as allies, legmen and buddies'.[9] Margach observed as a young Lobby journalist how years of close association with ministers within the furtive confines of the Lobby system led to an incestuous relationship between the government and the members of the Lobby in which the journalists' intellectual independence was eroded, and the healthy 'adversarial relationship' which the journalist was supposed to enjoy with a minister was replaced with a relationship that was 'too cosy and comfortable'.[10] By 1939, Steward and Chamberlain had been briefing the Lobby for years, and what Harold Macmillan scathingly remarked of the Tory backbenchers of this period could be equally well applied to the Lobby journalists: 'if Chamberlain says that black is white, the Tories applaud his brilliance. If a week later he says that black is black after all, they applaud his realism. Never has there been such servility.'[11]

For the journalists, the system had the manifold advantage of involving less work and effort, as they knew they could safely rely on the twice-daily Lobby pronouncements to fulfil their editors' journalistic demands for political copy. As well as paying particular attention to the Lobby in general, Chamberlain was also very careful to court three or four 'true-blue Lobby correspondents' from Conservative papers whom he would honour with 'private meetings and extra information'.[12] As Chamberlain's premiership progressed, he became increasingly aggressive towards the journalists and openly manipu-

7

lative, refusing, for instance, to answer off-the-cuff questions and insisting that any question should be submitted four hours in advance if the journalist were to expect a reply. James Margach records that any dissent was greeted with 'a cold arrogance and intolerance', and journalists who expressed suspicions about Hitler's or Mussolini's intentions that differed from Chamberlain's own views would be answered with the stock reprise that 'he was surprised that such an experienced journalist was susceptible to Jewish–Communist propaganda'.[13] This revealed Chamberlain's ambivalent attitude towards the press: he was happy to court it in order to win its support for his policies, yet he treated individual journalists with utter disdain. As one writer has observed, 'on the one hand he religiously scrutinized the papers to determine how his actions were reported and doted on favourable comments, while on the other hand he held the Press in scarcely concealed contempt'.[14] Unusually for a Conservative Prime Minister, he had very little contact with either editors or proprietors and the only journalist whom he consulted or whose opinion he valued was W. W. Hadley, Editor of the *Sunday Times*. This was principally because, out of a largely doting press, Hadley was by far the most consistent and extravagant in his praise of Chamberlain, and their relationship is indicative of Chamberlain's whole attitude towards the press. He believed that its sole function was to echo his own views and support his own policies and was prepared to go to great lengths, as with the Lobby, to ensure that the press did not depart from the role he had assigned to it.

A more insidious aspect of the Press Office of Downing Street was the way in which the boundaries between the government and the Conservative Party were successfully blurred through the system of non-attribution that the Lobby rules enforced. This meant that although George Steward, a government civil servant, normally briefed the Lobby, under the Lobby rules Conservative Party officials could also brief the Lobby in an extremely partisan spirit, without being identified or held responsible for their actions. The select 'true-blue correspondents' would frequently be briefed at St Stephen's Club opposite Westminster Bridge, where the host would be Sir Robert Topping, the Director-General of Conservative Central Office – thus, to James Margach's mind, 'ensuring that Chamberlain's simultaneous control over government and party networks remained tight'.[15] On these occasions, if the Lobby was not briefed by Chamberlain himself, it was briefed by Sir Joseph Ball.

In Sir Joseph Ball, Chamberlain found a fervent Conservative who was particularly interested in the control of the press. Lord Blake has correctly described Ball as 'a quintessential éminence grise', whose influence on affairs, like George Steward's, cannot 'be measured by the brevity of the printed references to him'.[16] His career is thus appropriately obscure, but it is clear that he was recruited by the Conservative Party Chairman, J. C. C. Davidson, in 1924 from MI5, where he had been head of the Investigation branch. Ball was initially responsible for running a 'little intelligence service'[17] as an independent service for the main Conservative Central Office organization. This included using the same techniques that MI5 had employed to infiltrate the Communist Party to infiltrate Labour Party headquarters. Christopher Andrew has written of Ball that throughout his term of service under Chamberlain with the Conservative Party he 'maintained informal links with some of his former intelligence colleagues'.[18] In 1930, he became the first Director of the new Conservative Research Department and became Chamberlain's closest and most indispensable political adviser. The historian of the Conservative Research Department has written that 'Ball and his staff were especially keen to help Chamberlain not only because they were working to his instructions, but because he represented their link with the top of the party hierarchy; the enhancement of Chamberlain's influence on policy was also the enhancement of their own.'[19] Chamberlain inspired an extraordinary degree of adulation and fierce personal loyalty amongst his coterie of closest personal advisers, and of no one was this more true than Ball. He and Chamberlain enjoyed probably the closest friendship that Chamberlain was capable of enjoying with anyone and they spent several fishing holidays together during the later 1930s – indeed, Chamberlain was fly-fishing with Ball in March 1939 when he heard of Hitler's invasion of Prague.

Ball was useful to Chamberlain in two ways. His experience 'in the seamy side of life and the handling of crooks', gained in his MI5 work, enabled him to indulge in 'domestic political intelligence work ...',[20] which included, for instance, tapping the telephones of the Eden Group and its sympathetic journalistic supporters in 1939. Secondly, he took a close interest in the presentation of the Conservative Party

9

and its policies and in particular the careful presentation of Chamberlain himself to the press. His involvement with the Lobby and his briefings at St Stephen's Club were only one aspect of this work. In the 1935 election campaign Ball busied himself with writing articles for ministers to plant in various newspapers and was assiduous in writing to sympathetic newspapers to draw their attention to the attractive features of the national government's policies. He was also instrumental in setting up the National Publicity Bureau to advertise the ideals of the national government for the 1935 election. However, despite these activities, Ball remained dissatisfied with the lack of acquiescence that he saw in the press, writing to Baldwin that 'the Daily Mail and the Daily Express attack us more frequently than they support us, while, although The Times and the Daily Telegraph are admirable newspapers and give us their full support, their circulations are so small ... that their influence among the masses is almost negligible'. To overcome this problem, Ball advocated the acquisition of a 'suitable weekly publication, and ... to build up a staff of really good young writers capable of exposing effectively the fallacies upon which the public is being regularly fed'.[21] The weekly publication that Ball acquired was the old radical publication *Truth*, which had been founded by Henry Labouchere in 1877. In June 1936, the shares in *Truth* were bought by Lord Luke of Pavenham, who was a prominent Conservative businessman and Chairman of the Business Committee of the National Publicity Bureau. All the files for these organizations have, like Ball's own papers, been destroyed, but Sir Robert Vansittart commissioned a private enquiry into *Truth* in 1941 which revealed the previously unknown connection between Ball, the Conservative Party and the newspaper. Ball was very closely connected with Lord Luke and was a director of three companies in which Lord Luke's family held large interests. Horace Samuel, who conducted the enquiry for Vansittart, concluded that it was 'almost inevitable that the bulk of the money with which the control of the paper was secured was put up by the National Publicity Bureau.... it seems that ... Ball had been able to exercise considerable influence over *Truth* through his connection with its Chairman. In fact, he actually admitted it in conversation with an old acquaintance of his in June 1941.'[22] The paper's association with the National Publicity Bureau was artfully camouflaged through a series of small shareholdings, and so secretly was this done that other members of the Business Committee of the National Publicity Bureau, whose funds were used for this transaction, were unaware that *Truth* was being secretly run by a member of their own Committee. Given Ball's close and regular contact with Chamberlain, it is impossible to escape the conclusion that Chamberlain was fully aware of the paper's policy, even if he did not directly orchestrate it himself. Indeed, Chamberlain's letters to his sisters demonstrate that he closely followed *Truth* and delighted in the fact, for instance, that in July 1939 *Truth* published a couple of 'witty articles' making 'fun of the suggestion that he [Churchill] would help matters in the Cabinet ...', and in the same letter he confided to his sister that *Truth* was 'secretly controlled by Sir Joseph Ball'.[23]

Truth was used by Ball to discredit Chamberlain's political opponents in a way that the rest of the press would shy away from. As Vansittart's report concluded, *Truth* represented the 'hard Munich core of the Conservative Party ...',[24] and after spring 1939 Ball and Chamberlain used *Truth* to try and sabotage the policies that they were now being forced to adopt as they saw their appeasement policies crumbling before them. *Truth* became stridently anti-Churchill, anti-Semitic, anti-American and pacifist: and as such accurately reflected the real state of Ball's and Chamberlain's minds from 1939 onwards. Some of Chamberlain's political opponents were genuinely offended by the attacks on them in *Truth*; one such was Leslie Hore-Belisha, who was deeply hurt by a venomous, anti-Semitic attack on him in the issue of 4 January 1940 after his resignation from Chamberlain's Cabinet. Numerous copies of this particular issue were posted to prominent persons during the ensuing week, presumably to counter the rapturous reception that Hore-Belisha had received on his resignation from large sections of the press. Harold Nicolson, however, received the strictures of *Truth* with sardonic resignation, confiding to his diary that the 'rude article about me in Truth saying that I have the "mincing manner of a French salon", that I lack virility and should retire from public life and bury myself in books ... was all rather true, I suppose ...'.[25] Even with Chamberlain on his death bed, Ball pledged his undying devotion to the Chamberlainite cause and in remembering the 'great work' of 'countering numerous intrigues in the press and in the party ...' during his service to Chamberlain, he nonetheless reminded the ailing politician that they had made 'many unscrupulous

11

enemies during the course of his work'. However, Ball declared that he had no intention of 'giving them best', and was fully determined to deploy all his ability in the matters of 'political controversy and propaganda' to exposing 'Chamberlain's enemies', and to tell the 'full truth' about the ex-Premier's 'sustained effort to save the peace of the world'.[26] Never one to shrink from such an undertaking, Ball continued to use *Truth* to campaign against the personnel and policies of the wartime government well into the war.

Through Ball and George Steward, Chamberlain was able to run an entirely unattributable news campaign. Via the obliging Lobby, he could set the tone of political reporting every morning, and through *Truth*, he could publish personal or political details that might discredit his political opponents. Chamberlain could also use his Cabinet colleagues' personal relations with editors and proprietors to persuade editorial opinion to follow, or positively aid, his policies. The inner Cabinet of Chamberlain himself, Sir John Simon, Sir Samuel Hoare and Lord Halifax was particularly rich in such contacts, especially Hoare with Lord Beaverbrook and Halifax with Geoffrey Dawson, Editor of *The Times*.

The close relationship between Lord Beaverbrook (proprietor of the *Daily Express, Sunday Express* and *Evening Standard*) and Sir Samuel Hoare will be discussed in the next chapter. The closest liaison between a journalist and a government minister was, however, that between Lord Halifax and Geoffrey Dawson. The two men shared a very similar background: Eton (where they both sat on the Governing Body), All Souls College, Oxford (of which they were both Fellows), North Yorkshire (where they both lived and shot) and a spirit of high Anglicanism in matters religious. Dawson's diary testifies to the almost daily visits to see Lord Halifax when the latter had become Foreign Secretary in February 1938. It was through Halifax that Dawson had also grown close to Neville Chamberlain – just as Dawson had also been a keen admirer, confidant and advocate of Chamberlain's predecessor, Stanley Baldwin. Indeed, throughout the 1930s it can be said that Dawson was privy to more Cabinet thinking and secrets than most members of the government, whether the Prime Minister was MacDonald, Baldwin or Chamberlain. Dawson's role during appeasement was to bear this out all too well. It was not for nothing that *The Times* was thus taken to be the semi-official conduit of the British government's thinking abroad, and every nuance of its long and elegant leaders was scrupulously scrutinized in the chancelleries and embassies of the world. It was a charge that was always strenuously denied by both *The Times* and the government, but it was one which was, nonetheless, fundamentally true – as the actions of Dawson during the appeasement years were to demonstrate.

Chamberlain himself was on close terms only with Lord Kemsley (the proprietor of the *Sunday Times*, the *Daily Sketch* and a plethora of provincial papers); indeed, Kemsley was the only newspaper proprietor that Chamberlain confided in and trusted. Lord Astor (proprietor of the *Observer*) and his wife Nancy Astor were also keen admirers of Neville Chamberlain during the 1930s, seeing in him the strand of progressive Conservatism that Lord Astor had entered politics to support. Members of the government and fellow newspaper proprietors and editors would often be invited to the Astor country seat at Cliveden, on the Thames near Taplow and conveniently near to London. These informal weekend gatherings were to take on an altogether more sinister aspect as British politics became ever more partisan in the late 1930s – although the Astor guest list was a good deal more catholic than has since been alleged by some of the Astors' more energetic detractors.

Oddly enough, it was the proprietor of the *Daily Telegraph*, Lord Kemsley's brother Lord Camrose, who seemed to have the least personal contact with members of Baldwin's and Chamberlain's governments. Traditionally the bastion of mainstream Conservatism, the *Daily Telegraph* nonetheless found itself eclipsed by the traditionally more independent-minded *Times* as the most enthusiastic editorial supporter of Chamberlain's policies during the late 1930s. Part of the credit (or blame) for this must go down to Lord Camrose himself, although he remains a relatively enigmatic figure in the history of the 1930s, awaiting a biographer to penetrate some of the mystery surrounding him. However, what is clear is that of all the press proprietors of that decade he was the only one (apart from the mercurial Beaverbrook) who maintained a close friendship with Winston Churchill, which might serve to explain why the *Daily Telegraph* was the only national paper with Conservative loyalties to treat Chamberlain and appeasement with a modicum of caution.

The way in which these personal contacts and associations could be used by the Cabinet – or other elements within His Majesty's government – to support a particular policy had already been amply demonstrated in the autumn and winter of 1936 during the Abdication crisis. Indeed, the close collusion between certain elements of the press and the government on the one hand and the King on the other can be seen as a precursor for the much more damaging and long-term control of the press that was to occur between 1937 and 1940. This is not the place to give a detailed account of the Abdication crisis and the role that the press played in it,* but it is instructive to note that while the American press was saturated with gossip and comment about Edward VIII's relationship with Mrs Simpson for months before the Abdication actually took place, the press in Britain maintained a discreet silence about the whole affair until only a week before the King finally abdicated. That this extraordinary feat of collective silence on behalf of the journalistic profession was possible at all was due to the personal requests for silence both from the King – to Esmond Harmsworth (son of Lord Rothermere, proprietor of the *Daily Mail*) and Lord Beaverbrook, who then enlisted the help of Sir Walter Layton of the *News Chronicle* – and from the Cabinet, who prevailed upon Geoffrey Dawson and Lord Kemsley to keep the scandal out of their papers. Dawson and *The Times* were crucial, as on the whole the rest of the press looked to *The Times* for a lead on such a matter of grave constitutional propriety. Nonetheless, it is striking that the almost complete silence that the British press maintained on a subject which was, by all accounts, the only topic of conversation in the rest of the western world was preserved exclusively by a clandestine system of 'gentleman's agreements'. It was a quintessential example of that amorphous British entity 'the Establishment' at work. No newspaper broke ranks and finally, on 3 December 1936, the Abdication crisis can be said to have 'broken' on a largely unsuspecting British public when the press collectively abandoned its self-restraint on the same day. It is very pertinent to the study of the press and appeasement that, with the notable exceptions of Baldwin and Edward VIII, almost exactly the same members of His Majesty's government were to call on the press for the same spirit of self-restraint over Germany and Italy: confident, perhaps, in the knowledge that what they had suc-

---

* The best account can be found in the biography of *Baldwin* by Keith Middlemas and John Barnes (Weidenfeld & Nicolson, London, 1969), ch. 34.

ceeded in doing during the Abdication crisis could be repeated with the foreign policy of Britain.

Sir Horace Wilson, the government's Chief Industrial Adviser and, more importantly, Chamberlain's own personal choice as his chief adviser on foreign affairs (a position for which Wilson was ill-qualified), was also used by Chamberlain as his own personal emissary to editors and proprietors. It is impossible to tell how much he co-ordinated his activities with George Steward or Sir Joseph Ball. The principal advantage of Chamberlain's press control was that it came to be entirely centralized in his own hands, so news management could almost be raised to the level of an exact science. Moreover, if the Germans ever doubted the true source of any of the appeasing news articles or editorials that appeared in the press, George Steward was always on hand at the German Embassy in London to put them right. His clandestine contact at the German Embassy was the German correspondent and Press Attaché, Dr Hesse, who was described by the German Ambassador as 'a rather close friend of Steward'.[27] Whenever there seemed to be any confusion about the source of any press news story or editorial, such as the notorious *Times* leader of 7 September 1938, Steward was always able to clarify the source as Downing Street or to disclaim responsibility for the article altogether. Steward's liaison with the German Embassy was, to say the least, strictly against his code of conduct as a civil servant. It is impossible to tell whether he acted on his own initiative or whether he was acting on instructions from Chamberlain, Wilson or Ball. If he was acting on his own initiative, then his activities were frankly treasonable and if he was acting to orders his behaviour could at best be described as furtive. In any case, his comments to the Germans always represented, as will be seen, the 'Chamberlainite' view of affairs.

As Chamberlain's pursuance of appeasement became more vigorous and single-minded, he was eager to centralize all government press briefings at Downing Street so as effectively to silence any sounds of dissent in Whitehall. This attitude was perfectly consistent with his general autocratic approach to politics. As a Conservative colleague observed, 'he knew his own mind and saw to it that he had his own way. An autocrat with all the courage of his convictions right or wrong.'[28] Contemplating Chamberlain's succession to Baldwin as Prime Minister, the Conservative Research Department was anxious that Chamberlain should first 'say something about his belief in democracy', as they were conscious of a 'widespread feeling among people that Mr Chamberlain is an autocrat, and that if he would take Mr Baldwin's place as P.M. we should be taking a step away from democracy'. However, although Chamberlain did indeed say something at the 1936 party conference to 'diminish the popular impression that he is an authoritarian at heart',[29] this did nothing to alter his real character, which was essentially, as his own Research Department suggested, 'authoritarian'. In no field of government was this better illustrated than in his dealings with the press. James Margach reflected bitterly that 'from the moment he entered Number 10 in 1937 he sought to manipulate the Press into supporting his policy of appeasing the dictators'.[30]

The only obstacle to the absolute control of the news in Whitehall by Steward, Ball and Chamberlain was the Foreign Office News Department on the opposite side of Downing Street. The origins of the News Department have been ably described by Philip Taylor* but the Department only really began to grow in importance and numbers with the arrival of Rex Leeper, who became head of the Department in 1935. Just as George Steward was responsible for centralizing the corporate Lobby system at Downing Street, so Leeper was responsible for centralizing the flow of diplomatic news through his own coterie of specialist reporters, the diplomatic correspondents. In doing this, Leeper set himself the gargantuan task of altering the traditional Foreign Office view of journalists, which was one of barely disguised contempt, in order to make the Foreign Office understand how journalists could be used to further the aims and policies of the Foreign Office. He realized that with a certain degree of openness and flattery diplomatic correspondents could be welded into a cohesive body who could be relied upon always to put the Foreign Office point of view in the press. The measure of his success is that by 1937 he had built up a set of diplomatic correspondents who were as loyal to him as the Lobby correspondents were to Steward and Chamberlain.

Leeper crystallized the standard Foreign Office view of journalists when he informed his colleagues, 'I trust it will cause no offence if I

* Philip Taylor, *The Projection of Britain: British Overseas Publicity and Propaganda* (Cambridge University Press, 1981), ch. 1.

say that by many in our service the journalist is regarded as a potential enemy rather than as a willing collaborator.'[31] The profession of journalism, with its onus on investigation and exposure, was seen as wholly incompatible with the exercise of diplomacy, which thrived on secrecy, confidentiality and trust. Leeper saw, however, that if the journalist could be turned into a 'willing collaborator' rather than remaining as a suspicious outsider, it could only be to the benefit of the Foreign Office. Thus, for Leeper, the duty of the News Department was 'Not only the supply of day to day news, but to educate the different organs of publicity along the lines of the foreign policy pursued by the Government'.[32] Thus Leeper rested his policy on the assumption that the more correspondents were let into the News Department's confidence, the more willing they would be to adopt the Foreign Office view. He tried to spread this philosophy throughout the Foreign Office, incorporating his views in a circular to all British missions abroad that it was 'thus a highly important duty of His Majesty's missions to assist British correspondents'.[33]

Leeper was never successful in achieving his aims throughout the Foreign Service. Typical of a wider attitude were the comments of Ivone Kirkpatrick, who complained in 1938 from the Embassy in Berlin that apart from 'The Times and the Reuter's correspondents', who were 'often useful scouts and touts of the Embassy, the remaining correspondents are a liability rather than an asset. They never obtain any news worth having, they waste the time of the staff, and often cause embarrassment by sending silly messages. . . .'[34] Sir Eric Phipps, Ambassador to Germany, had little sympathy with the journalists who managed to get themselves expelled by the Nazis, and remarked that 'both tact and intelligence are essential to journalists in Germany, although he admitted that these were qualities which commanded a high salary which many newspapers could not afford'.[35] Leeper himself held a specific view of 'our free press', as he felt that it 'often . . . degenerated into the freedom to abuse others instead of exercising its proper function – freedom to understand and interpret both ourselves and others'. Eden, the Secretary of State at the time, was suitably impressed by the wisdom of this remark and minuted in the margin of Leeper's document, 'this is very sound'.[36]

Leeper's aim was thus to give out news which was appropriate to getting Foreign Office policy soundly interpreted. Furthermore, in this

17

he was closely supported by the Permanent Under-Secretary from 1931 to 1937, Sir Robert Vansittart, who was very impressed by the loyal band of diplomatic correspondents which Leeper had built up – a band which, on occasions, he used himself to place secret information in the public domain. Leeper's most privileged diplomatic correspondents were F. A. Voigt of the *Manchester Guardian*, Victor Gordon-Lennox of the *Daily Telegraph*, Norman Ewer of the *Daily Herald*, Charles Tower of the *Yorkshire Post*, and Vernon Bartlett of the *News Chronicle*. Iverach McDonald, diplomatic correspondent of *The Times* from 1938, has given a glimpse of the methods of the News Department as the officials 'would read long passages to me, sometimes for publication when duly paraphrased, more often for private guidance, and I was only one who they saw day by day. It was a point of professional etiquette and pride not to take any notes in these long private talks: a daily exercise in memory training for us.'[37]

One correspondent who noticed the development of the News Department's sophisticated handling of the diplomatic correspondents, and who was very critical of it, was Robert Dell, the *Manchester Guardian*'s veteran correspondent in Geneva. He had an opportunity not only of observing the general workings of the News Department, but of seeing at close quarters how his paper's own diplomatic correspondent (F. A. Voigt) became, in his own words, 'the mouthspeak of the F.O. ...'. Dell dated the attempts at manipulation of the diplomatic correspondents from 1929, but saw that Leeper was the first 'Press agent, or whatever he is called, from the F.O. that we have had ... who has tried openly to tune the Press'. Observing Leeper at work with the British delegation to the League of Nations in Geneva, Dell noticed that 'Leeper gives information only to his tame pets', and rightly suspected that he gave his pets 'full information and tells them what they are to use and what to suppress'. Dell concluded that the diplomatic correspondents of the London papers were 'just mouth pieces of the F.O. which has successfully introduced the system of accredited journalists of the Quai D'Orsay. The only difference is that the diplomatics are not paid by the F.O. ... I think they should be.'[38] Dell's main objection to this system was not only that as all the diplomatic correspondents got their information from the same mouth, so a deliberate attempt was 'being made to get the whole British Press to say the same thing', but also that, due to the same non-attributable rules that applied to the Lobby, the Foreign Office could tune the press without taking any responsibility for doing so. Dell presented the journalistic quandary in this system: 'unless a diplomatic correspondent gives the Foreign Office information as his own, he runs the clear risk of not getting it and ... if he made it clear that he was giving official information for which he took no responsibility he would not remain on good terms with the F.O.'. It was Leeper's job to ensure that it was always worth the correspondent's while to remain on good terms with the FO; as Dell noted, 'nowadays we are given too much information' by Leeper, thus enticing the correspondents into retaining their links with the News Department. For Dell, the consequence of this system as developed by Leeper was that 'the independence of the British Press will be destroyed, and so, as far as Foreign policy is concerned, it will become merely a gramophone repeating the F.O. dope ...'.[39]

Dell blamed the Foreign Office and the journalists in equal measure for this state of affairs, as he considered it important that although 'we ought to know what the F.O. says, we ought never to believe it without verification'.[40] Dell saw that as the system became increasingly centralized around Leeper, who was apparently so eager to disseminate information and help the journalists, so the inducements to check other sources and hunt for more information became seemingly less important and certainly less attractive. Much as James Margach saw the Lobby system compromising the healthy antagonistic relations between government and the press, so Dell concluded that rather than succumb to Leeper's system of news management it was 'better for a paper not to be on good terms with the F.O.'.[41] From 1935 onwards, Dell waged his own private campaign against the Foreign Office News Department, both in lectures to young correspondents in Geneva and in print. It was thus not surprising that the unfortunate Voigt in London bore the brunt of Leeper's displeasure at Dell's activities, and Voigt noted with masterful tact in 1938 that 'The relations between Dell and the News Department have been a little strained ...' and that this was prejudicing the 'good terms ... that the Department has always been on ... with the M.G.'.[42] Although Dell initially exempted Voigt from his scornful survey of diplomatic correspondents, by 1935 he had managed to convince the Editor of the *Manchester Guardian*, W. P. Crozier, that Voigt was 'surprisingly ready to act as a mouthpiece of the F.O.'. Crozier accepted the principal drawback of this, because he lamented, like Dell, that although what the FO had to say 'was certainly news ... the pity is that we cannot say point blank that these views and assertions are the result of close contact with the F.O.'.[43]

Voigt, however, reacted sharply to such criticism, and extolled the virtues of the News Department, on the grounds not only that it provided him with a flow of information, but also that the personnel of the News Department were very good as 'reliable sources of information ...' and that 'they were incapable of telling a lie' – a quality which, in his view, would be much reduced 'if they had to give official information only ...'.[44] From the journalist's point of view, of course, this was the great merit of the system, as the officials could say as much as they wanted, confident of the fact that since it was all off the record their utterances could not be traced. Dell himself frequently took advantage of this system, and confided to Crozier that during Sir John Simon's visit to Berlin in 1935, Leeper frequently 'shows me Phipps' reports ...' as guidance.[45] Voigt was used on numerous occasions to publish information that Leeper wanted drawn to the public's attention – as was Gordon-Lennox of the *Daily Telegraph*.

One example of this relationship at work has been left by Ian Colvin, a journalist with the *News Chronicle*. Leeper and Vansittart were the two Foreign Office officials who came to be most opposed to the policy of appeasement, and Colvin has described how in 1935 they leaked information to Gordon-Lennox in order to alert the nation to the dangers of the growing German air strength. In conversation with Hitler on 19 March 1935, the Foreign Secretary, Sir John Simon, was told that Germany had gained air parity with Great Britain. This admission was included in Simon's formal record of the conversation, but was not revealed in the account which he gave to the House of Commons on his return. Vansittart had been disappointed with the government's White Paper on defence of the previous March, which had sanctioned an increase of spending of only £10 million, and he obviously saw Simon's public omission as a way of justifying this, to his mind, low figure. The case for a higher figure, would, of course, be vindicated if this sin of omission on Simon's part in the House of Commons was made good and so Leeper was instructed by Vansittart to inform selected correspondents of Hitler's claim to air parity. The report duly appeared in the *Daily Telegraph* on 29 March that 'Herr

Hitler is said to have admitted that the German airforce is already as large or slightly larger than the R.A.F.'. Simon had to confess the accuracy of this report in the House of Commons. He then called in Leeper, who admitted that the press would 'have gathered this in conversation with me'. But Leeper boldly justified himself on the ground that he was merely trying to refute rumours circulating abroad that Simon had been having discussions with Hitler 'behind the back of Mr Eden'. (Eden was then Simon's deputy and Minister of State for the League of Nations). So 'it was necessary to inform the Press about what really happened'. We are assured by Ian Colvin that Simon was so 'visibly taken aback by that rejoinder that ... the Foreign Secretary made not the slightest further allusion to the matter'.[46] On 26 April, the *Daily Telegraph* published under the byline of the Diplomatic Correspondent another article on German air strength, this time claiming that the German air force was already equipped with 'practically double the number of first-line military aircraft available in this country ... for purposes of home defence'. Winston Churchill was one politician who picked up on these reports, basing a 'forceful memo on these figures', secure in the knowledge that they 'evidently came from some official source'.[47] Thus through these devious means was Churchill launched on another trenchant criticism of the government's lacklustre defence policy.

As Voigt freely admitted, the Foreign Office was his principal source of information and it became virtually the exclusive official source for such as Gordon-Lennox, Ewer and Bartlett. There was no doubt that Dell was right to the extent that Leeper had adroitly reared his tame pets so that they faithfully presented the Foreign Office view on government foreign policy. The News Department was thus a powerful competitor with Downing Street for the dissemination of Whitehall news and in exerting influence over the press – but this dual system became menacingly fractious when the political policies pursued by the Foreign Office and Downing Street parted company.

One of the great virtues of Leeper and his fellow News Department officials such as Charles Peake and C. F. A. Warner was, as Voigt observed, that they had 'a very individual view and will air their own doubts with regard to Government policy'.[48] Leeper shared the views of Sir Robert Vansittart on foreign policy and in particular his attitude to Germany. He would act in tandem with Vansittart to pursue the latter's policy of reconciliation with Italy as a counterweight to what was viewed as an aggressively hostile Germany; this is the policy that Leeper and Vansittart wanted 'soundly interpreted' by the press, and they used the News Department to give out news of conditions in Germany, statistics of German rearmament, reports of German concentration camps to enhance this pessimistic view of Germany – the leak to the *Daily Telegraph* in 1935 was supposed to contribute to this general picture. Vansittart was particularly free with his confidences and encouraged Leeper to take the same attitude in the pursuance of their campaign against appeasement. Ian Colvin relates how 'Rex Leeper sometimes came upon Vansittart in his room at the F.O. in full conversation with Winston Churchill.' The excuse Vansittart gave to Leeper for communicating confidential information to a mere MP was that 'it is so important that a man of Churchill's influence should be properly informed' and so he was quite content to 'tell him whatever I know'.[49]

Vansittart was also particularly open in his communications with F.A. Voigt of the *Manchester Guardian*. Indeed, Voigt was a key member of Vansittart's shadowy 'z Organization', an intelligence service run principally for his own benefit to keep him informed of developments inside Nazi Germany.* It was run with the co-operation of the head of the Secret Intelligence Service (SIS), but otherwise was run clandestinely – unknown to the rest of the staff at SIS headquarters in London. Voigt, as an ex-Berlin correspondent, had particularly valuable contacts and he would meet Vansittart in London on a regular basis. It was probably on account of his usefulness to the z Organization that the Germans tried to assassinate Voigt in Paris during the course of his journey back from Berlin to England. The Gestapo, however, were persistent in their scrutiny of his activities in England, and on one occasion the harassed correspondent learned from one of his z Organization contacts in Gestapo headquarters in Berlin that the Gestapo had almost verbatim transcripts of conversations which he had held with fellow journalists in the Café Royal, Piccadilly – a watering hole that he consequently eschewed in favour of haunts less glamorous, but with more reliable waiters.

* For an account of the z Organization and Vansittart's and Voigt's role in it, see Anthony Read and David Fisher, *Colonel z: The Life and Times of a Master Spy* (Hodder & Stoughton, 1984).

Leeper shared Vansittart's views on the dangers of Nazi Germany and was a keen admirer of Eden, which took him into direct conflict with Neville Chamberlain's policies when the latter became Prime Minister. Sir Alexander Cadogan, who succeeded Vansittart as Permanent Secretary in 1938, 'had a talk with Rex Leeper' in May of that year, only 'to find that he was still "hypnotized" by A [Anthony Eden] and very anti-Chamberlain'. Leeper told Cadogan that he thought Chamberlain was 'splitting the country' with his politics, but Cadogan remained unconvinced and doubtless counted this conversation against Leeper when it came to posting him abroad in 1939.[50]

As well as giving information to the diplomatic correspondents that would confirm their worst suspicions about the build-up of German armaments and generally cast Germany in the gloomiest light possible, Leeper also tried to support Vansittart's policy of appeasing Italy in order to entice her away from the embraces of Nazi Germany. The most obvious expression of this policy was the Hoare-Laval pact, the main architect of which was Vansittart; it was a piece of diplomacy which was largely derided in the editorial column of the newspapers, but which received a good deal of sympathy in the diplomatic columns. When relations with Italy reached their nadir in March 1937 after the final cessation of Britain's obviously futile sanctions policy, Leeper was concerned that there was no one in the British press who was willing 'to be fair to the Italians and to put what seems to be their point of view'. To remedy this situation and to try and arrest the deteriorating state of Anglo-Italian relations which were 'important to the whole of Europe ...', Leeper suggested putting two articles in *The Times* expressing the Italian view, whilst at the same time obeying Eden's strictures not to be too 'apologetic in tone', as Mussolini was 'above all a gangster' who would take a mere apology as a 'sign of weakness'. On this particular occasion, *The Times* refused, but Leeper was assiduous in pacifying the British press as regards their coverage of Mussolini and Italy as he also strove to implement Eden's other suggestion that 'we should strive to ensure that the Press pays less attention to Mussolini – we are doing him too much honour and helping him at home in consequence'.[51]

The effect of Leeper's and Vansittart's briefings on the dangers of Germany varied from correspondent to correspondent. Voigt, for

23

instance, was merely panicked by Leeper into being overawed by the growing German military superiority and thus encouraged W.P. Crozier to take an even more appeasing line than he otherwise might have done. By contrast, Victor Gordon-Lennox of the *Daily Telegraph* was fortified into making that paper uncharacteristically hesitant in its acceptance of the incumbent Conservative Minister's foreign policy. Another person whom Leeper and Vansittart enlisted in their campaign against Germany, and who could be thoroughly relied upon to use their information in the way that they wanted, was Winston Churchill. In a memorandum that Leeper had written for the Foreign Office, and which had been approved by Vansittart, Leeper warned that if Britain was to 're-arm and abandon an attitude of defeatism vis à vis Germany', it was 'insufficient to make a few public speeches or for the News Department of the F.O. to make points with the Press'. Leeper advocated that the programme that he had been following to educate the nation through the News Department should now be 'conceived on wider and bolder lines if it is to bear fruit', and he visited Churchill at his home at Chartwell on 24 April 1936 to encourage him to try and bring together all the various groups who were already concerned about the German danger. This meeting was the genesis of the anti-Nazi council which became known as the Focus Group. This duly tried to rectify what Vansittart had identified as the crucial flaw in Britain's state of readiness: 'the people of this country are receiving no adequate education – indeed practically no concerted education at all – against the impending tests'.[52]

There is no evidence that the Foreign Office News Department ever co-ordinated its activities with George Steward or Downing Street until 1939, although each Department was dimly aware of the other's activities. So Vansittart was prepared to use the News Department to puncture the complacency that Ball, Steward and Chamberlain tried to instil in the press during their Lobby briefings. Moreover, by the time Chamberlain came to power determined to rescue foreign policy from the directionless drift of the Baldwin years, he was fully aware that the Foreign Office was antagonistic towards his policy of achieving a comprehensive settlement with Germany and that it had been leaking for a number of years to undermine the likelihood of any such agreement being reached. On taking power he expressed his strong reservations about the Foreign Office to his sisters; to his mind, it seemed to have 'no imagination and no courage to pursue a settlement with Germany'.[53] He was resolved to embark upon a 'double policy of rearmament and better relations with Germany and Italy which will carry us safely through ...', the only obstacle being the Foreign Office, which he was afraid would not 'play up'. Chamberlain noted that the Foreign Office was 'inclined to be jealous' of what he saw as his personal touch in foreign affairs and on the occasion of his first interview with the Italian Ambassador, Count Grandi, in August 1937, he revelled in the subsequent headlines about 'The Chamberlain Touch' instead of 'The Eden Touch'.[54] His suspicions about the Foreign Office were to be shortly confirmed with catastrophic consequences for both Vansittart and the News Department.

On the other hand, Chamberlain had an influential press which was awaiting his shuffle from Number 11 to Number 10 Downing Street eagerly, as it seemed that only he would rescue the policy of reaching a general settlement with Germany based on a revision of the Treaty of Versailles from the lethargic embrace of Baldwin and infuse it with the necessary vigour. Dawson of *The Times*, Lord Astor, proprietor of the *Observer*, J. L. Garvin, Editor of the *Observer*, Lord Beaverbrook and Lord Rothermere, proprietor of the *Daily Mail*, all shared a sense of urgency on the question of the settlement with Germany and the accession of Chamberlain, whose views were already well known to them.* Thus Garvin, for instance, was writing to Lord Astor

*The following are the circulation figures for the newspapers discussed in this book. All figures are taken from the Political and Economic Planning *Report on the British Press*, published in April 1938 by PEP, London. The papers are grouped together by proprietor:

Daily Express	–	2,329,000	
Sunday Express	–	1,337,000	Lord Beaverbrook
Evening Standard	–	392,000	
Daily Mail	–	1,580,000	Lord Rothermere
Evening News	–	791,000	
Sunday Times	–	270,000	Lord Kemsley
Daily Sketch	–	850,000	
Daily Telegraph	–	637,000	Lord Camrose
Daily Mirror	–	1,367,000	Mirror Group
Sunday Pictorial	–	1,400,000	
Daily Herald	–	'Over 2,000,000'	Odhams (Lord Southwood) TUC
Daily Worker	–	'Over 100,000'	Communist Party of Great Britain

News Chronicle	– 1,324,000	} Cadbury brothers
Star	– 493,000	
Observer	– 214,000	Lord Astor
The Times	– 192,000	Colonel J. J. Astor
Reynolds News	– 500,000	Co-operative Movement
Yorkshire Post	– 29,000	Yorkshire Conservative Newspaper Association
Manchester Guardian	– 56,000	Manchester Guardian Trust

in July 1937 that, just as Chamberlain had always been 'staunch on social reform', so he seemed to have the 'right instinct for the main things in foreign affairs'; Garvin now expected the Premier to follow 'that instinct ... to pull the whole tangle straight so far as this country is concerned'. For Garvin, this right instinct entailed a settlement with Germany that rested on the exclusion of Czechoslovakia and Austria from our 'contingent obligation' and the recognition of the fact that 'the new Reich was destined to be a great Reich and must have a big show somewhere'.[55] Astor was equally enthusiastic about the accession of Chamberlain and was soon urging Garvin to write some articles 'reminding the reader of some of the grosser mistakes of the Versailles and other treaties'.[56] Garvin was also prepared to accept a revision of the colonial side of the Versailles Treaty and wrote to an unconvinced Leo Amery – the veteran Conservative politician who was to become a stalwart anti-appeaser – in March 1938 that he would 'personally give back as part of a firm general settlement [with Germany] ... not only Cameroons and Togoland, but Tanganika as well', and firmly vowed to 'stick to this belief' in his 'usual way',[57] which he did in a number of his famously ascerbic Sunday articles. Garvin wrote what Lord Astor described as a 'splendid' Sunday article to this effect on Germany on 16 May 1937, as he had written a little earlier in the year that the 'only line and sense for Britain is to confine her automatic obligations to a minimum, to obdure all entanglements direct or indirect in Eastern Europe, and to keep out of every conflict into which we are not inevitably drawn'.[58] This was exactly akin to Chamberlain's view, ably summed up by one historian as 'limiting liabilities rather than increasing assets ... as the most realistic method of preventing war'.[59]

At Printing House Square, the home of *The Times*, the historian of

26

the paper has written that 'Chamberlain's policy suited P.H.S. far better [than Baldwin's].' As to the European Situation after 1933, the prospect of 'more rational means of adjustment than war, reached by a conference before the war, instead of after it, had been an axiom of policy in Printing House Square for more than ten years'.[60] By the new year, Beaverbrook was equally enthusiastic, writing to R. S. Bennett that Chamberlain was the 'best P.M. we have had in half a century, excluding A. B. L. . . .'.[61]* So for that section of the press that was controlled by men who were of the same political convictions as Chamberlain, his succession to power on 28 May 1938 was an opportunity to fulfil their plans for a settlement with Germany which they had contemplated independently for years.

At *The Times*, for instance, Dawson found the paper in trouble with the Germans over its accurate report that German planes were involved in the bombing of Guernica in Spain in April 1937, and it was in response to the temporary German ban on his paper as a result of this article that Dawson wrote his notorious letter to H. G. Daniels, their correspondent in Switzerland. Dawson pleaded that he could not understand what 'precisely' had produced this antagonism in Germany as he did his utmost 'night after night, to keep out of the paper anything that might have hurt their susceptibility'. Furthermore, he was convinced that although the Guernica article was accurate there had been no attempts by *The Times* 'to rub it in or to harp upon it'.[62] Both Dawson and Lord Astor had been convinced by their mutual friend Phillip Kerr (later Lord Lothian), lately returned from a visit to Germany in 1937 and a series of personal interviews with all the Nazi leaders, that Hitler was 'genuinely anxious for understanding with the British Empire . . .', but to convince Hitler of British good faith it was essential to 'hold out a hand of friendship or sympathy from this country'.[63] Lord Astor now encouraged Garvin to do the same by writing leaders in praise of the territorial revision of Europe in favour of Germany. From the autumn of 1937 *The Times* began to adopt a tone of friendly optimism along the lines of Phillip Kerr's suggestion. On 28 October 1937, Dawson wrote a leader in antici-pation of Lord Halifax's visit to Berlin in November of that year which asserted that there was 'no support in this country for the view

---

* A.B.L. – Andrew Bonar Law, Conservative Party leader and Prime Minister, had been Beaverbrook's first and most important political mentor.

that the peace of the world would be assured by a mere reversal of the Colonial Settlement of Versailles. The truth is that British public opinion is probably far ahead of the Government in its conviction that a clear understanding with Germany would have consequences more profound and more conducive to a stable peace than any other object of our Foreign Policy.' To reassure the Germans doubly, he ended with Garvinesque certainty that 'there is little sympathy here with the view ... that the proper way to treat Germany is to ring her about with vigilant allied states, sometimes masquerading as the League of Nations'. Given the fact that Dawson and the Chamberlainites in the press were so eager to start negotiating a wide-ranging settlement with Germany, it was not surprising that Chamberlain's long-awaited first step towards achieving this settlement, Lord Halifax's visit to Berlin in November 1938 to talk to the Nazi leaders, should have been treated with a due degree of enthusiasm.

Just as those who supported the principle of a general settlement with Germany were invigorated by Chamberlain's application to the problem of Anglo-German relations, so those opposed to such a settlement were dismayed by the actual course of action that Chamberlain wanted to adopt. They were further dismayed by the choice of the new Ambassador to Berlin, Sir Nevile Henderson, who wrote a memo on his views of the German problem and displayed such a generous sentiment towards that country and its supposed grievances that Sir Robert Vansittart was moved to minute that 'Sir Nevile Henderson's contribution is much more than a bit wide of the mark and it must be thoroughly dissected and shown up as ill-thought out and above all contrary to the policy of H.M.G.' For good measure Vansittart added that Henderson's memo was 'indeed so crude a piece of work that it was not thought worthy of any circulation'.[64] William Strang, the head of the Central Department in the Foreign Office, duly prepared a memo dissecting Sir Nevile Henderson's views, which was sent to both Eden and Halifax before the latter's departure for Germany in November. Eden, Chamberlain's young Foreign Secretary, was equally taken aback by Henderson's extreme appeasing views, and Oliver Harvey, Eden's loyal Private Secretary, recorded that his Minister met Sir Nevile Henderson at Windsor 'and A.E. was rather aghast at the nonsense that he was talking about what he was going to do in Germany'. Harvey comforted himself by reassuring his diary that 'Henderson may steady down when he sees what he is up against,' adding that Henderson had to go anyway as there was 'really not anybody else obvious to send'.[65] On the other hand, when Henderson called at Cliveden, the country seat of Lord Astor, prior to his departure to Germany, Astor found that despite not having 'seen him since Eton', he 'liked him very much'. Furthermore, he wrote to Garvin that Henderson was of the same opinion as himself that 'unless the Germans can come to an understanding with us they will be forced not only to try for an arrangement with Italy but also with Russia – he's convinced that they would prefer to be on good terms with us, but they must know that we shall not attack them in the back if they get involved in a scrap with their eastern neighbours'.[66] Henderson's views as stated in his memorandum were that an understanding with Germany could be reached only if Britain did not stand in the way of an Anschluss (a union with Austria), if Britain recognized Germany's right to own colonies 'and an eventual arrangement whereby some part of say, West Africa is alloted to her', and if Britain would not harbour any 'jealous objections to German economic and even political predominance in East Europe'.[67] This was indeed exactly what J.L. Garvin had been writing and what *The Times* leader pointed to on 28 October 1938 – a leader penned by Dawson as a direct result of Henderson's visit to Cliveden. On 26 October, at Cliveden, Nevile Henderson had confirmed before the assembled company, which included Geoffrey Dawson, that he was 'sticking courageously to his policy of trying to arrive at a settlement between ourselves and Germany' and that to achieve this, for instance, 'the only hope for Czechoslovakia lies in some scheme for devolution ...'.[68] On the following Monday, the 28th, *The Times* leader appeared on exactly these lines, giving the necessary public ventilation to Henderson's private thoughts.

That October weekend saw the genesis of the 'Cliveden set' as a real force in the politics of appeasement. The soubriquet of the 'Cliveden set', invented by Vansittart through the medium of Claud Cockburn, was in fact a geographical misnomer. The people involved, Dawson, the Astors, Henderson, Garvin, Lord Lothian (Phillip Kerr), never assembled at Cliveden specifically to try and direct foreign affairs. Rather, they were individuals of a like-minded outlook, all seeking a revision of the Versailles Treaty, who found themselves in positions of power. They never consciously co-ordinated their activities; neither, except Dawson, did they slavishly follow the dictates of Chamberlain. Individually, however, they were nonetheless to have a crucial effect on the politics of appeasement and particularly the role that the press had to play in it.

The cleavage between Henderson's views and those of Vansittart and other members of the Foreign Office was now quite clear, and Henderson told Lord Astor that ' "Van" is the real obstacle and were he out of the way others, including ministers, would adopt a more reasonable attitude.' Lord Astor thus concluded that ' "Van" has been disastrous.'[69] For his part, Vansittart was now aware of the moves against him and openly told the labour politician Hugh Dalton, who called on him on 4 November 1937, that 'the drive against him was going as strong as ever. Londonderry, Lothian, *The Times* ... it was worse now because lots of people were frightened', but to fortify Dalton, who admitted to similar feelings, Vansittart reminded him that 'It is one thing to have fear in one's heart and quite another to show funk and run away from these people.'[70]

It was clear now that Chamberlain, in league with Henderson, was 'determined to act and in particular fully to probe the practicability of reaching a settlement with Germany'.[71] Eden accepted this fact, and admitted to Oliver Harvey that there was indeed a 'difference as to methods between them' and that he also believed that the 'P.M. au fond had a certain sympathy for dictators whose efficiency appealed to him'.[72] Henderson shared Chamberlain's zeal for efficiency, and he likewise shared his attitude towards the press, which he believed should efficiently be brought into line with government policy. However, before Henderson could get down fully to exploring the practicability of reaching the wide-ranging settlement with Germany that he required, one of Leeper's clique of diplomatic correspondents mysteriously availed himself of Henderson's views and the reaction to them in certain diplomatic circles in Berlin.

Vernon Bartlett of the *News Chronicle*, a newspaper that was virulently opposed to Fascism in any country, prepared an article for the paper in July 1937 which stated that 'despite the fact that Great Britain and Germany find themselves on opposite sides in the Spanish crisis, British efforts to achieve an Anglo-German agreement are continuing. The zeal of the new British Ambassador in Berlin, Sir Nevile Henderson, calls imperatively for a word of warning ... from three separate sources I have received confirmation that the Ambassador's activities are causing uneasiness and on occasion, indignation.' As was his custom, Bartlett informed the News Department that he was going to publish this article, but on this occasion Charles Peake, Leeper's deputy and a less zealous anti-appeaser than his chief, warned Bartlett that he 'sincerely hoped that the *News Chronicle* would refrain from publishing the article' on the ground that such an attack on 'a public servant in such an important position, when he could not reply, would rightly arouse the sympathy of all decent people with him ... and if the charges proved baseless the sole effect would be to render Sir Nevile Henderson's relations with certain of his colleagues more difficult'. Peake claimed that this would be 'prejudicial to the public interest', which was 'surely the last thing that the *News Chronicle* would wish to bring about'.

This was the first time that an appeal was made to the 'public interest' in this way, but it was soon to become a standard refrain in the coming years, and one person who would never cease to be impressed by the gravity of the phrase was Sir Walter Layton, a former civil servant and Editor-in-Chief of the *News Chronicle*, whom Bartlett reported to be 'very excited over this issue'. Bartlett was further warned on the same afternoon, and Peake threatened to take the matter to Sir Robert Vansittart. This, however, proved to be unnecessary as Layton, in his capacity as Director and Editor-in-Chief of the *News Chronicle*, ensured that the article 'would not be published'.[73] Thus Henderson was allowed to continue his work unmolested, and he in turn was to be the most insistent that the press did not upset the policy that he was trying to pursue in Berlin.

This episode also proved to be a trailer for the wider self-censorship that was to come. Even before Lord Halifax went to Berlin in November 1937 to initiate the British policy towards Germany that would come to be known as appeasement, the battle lines within Whitehall and within the press had already been drawn up. The task of the appeasers was to negotiate a lasting settlement with Germany based on a revision of the Treaty of Versailles, which both they and Hitler considered to be unjust to Germany. The policy that Chamberlain now actively pursued towards Germany was designed to win such an agreement before Germany unilaterally, and perhaps violently, revoked the territorial, financial and military clauses of that treaty herself, with potentially disastrous consequences for the peace of Europe. Baldwin might have shared Chamberlain's convictions; Chamberlain was now determined to do something about them. However, as the accepted public policy of the British government was to uphold the Treaty of Versailles (to say nothing of the League of Nations), Chamberlain realized that negotiating such a settlement with Germany would be fraught with danger, especially if the reversal of British policy was to become known to the public prematurely. A close control of the press and a degree of secrecy over his manoeuvrings with Germany was thus to become essential to appeasement. To those opposed to appeasement, the press now had a converse role in alerting the British people to Chamberlain's and Henderson's policy aspirations and, if possible, in stopping them. At the very least, Vansittart and Leeper were concerned that the dangers that such a policy towards a dictator like Hitler invited should be fully realized. The battleground for this conflict between the appeasers and anti-appeasers would be the British press.

2

The Road to Munich: The Personal Touch

The next step forward in reaching a settlement with Germany was to establish some points of contact between Downing Street and Berlin and this was to be achieved by Lord Halifax, the Lord Privy Seal and one of Chamberlain's inner Cabinet of four. In the middle of October 1937 Lord Halifax received through the editors of *The Field* magazine an invitation to attend an international sporting exhibition in Berlin, where he would naturally have a chance to meet and discuss German grievances with the Nazi leaders. Chamberlain was, of course, anxious to achieve a dialogue with Hitler, and so was eager for Halifax to go. However, the Foreign Office reaction to Halifax's invitation to Berlin was somewhat different. Although Eden said he would be 'quite happy about the visit', Vansittart strongly argued that Halifax 'should not go as he would certainly be asked awkward questions'. When Halifax informed Chamberlain of this response, Chamberlain was 'really horrified' and wrote angrily about the Foreign Office wanting 'another opportunity to be thrown away', but he consoled himself with the prospect of taking the opportunity to 'stir it [the FO] up a bit with a long pole'.[1] Despite Vansittart's objections, Chamberlain was determined that the visit should go ahead as he was sure in his own mind that he and Halifax 'understood one another very well'.[2] In Berlin, Henderson was also anxious to smooth Halifax's path and wrote to the Foreign Office about a talk he had had with Dr Goebbels in which the Minister of Propaganda had welcomed Halifax's visit because Hitler's 'instinct was always right and the need for an Anglo-German understanding was one of his instinctive feelings'. During the course of his conversation with Goebbels, Henderson praised the better tone of the German press in the days leading up to the visit as conducive to a 'favourable atmosphere for the visit', and then referred to the British press. He assured Goebbels that it was 'not controlled', yet he hoped it also would say nothing at this juncture to prejudice the atmosphere.[3] At Hitler's request the diplomatic discussions that were to take place in Berlin were to be kept secret, an arrangement that Chamberlain was happy to comply with.

However, Henderson's hopes as regards the British press were not to be fulfilled, for on the evening of the very day that he was speaking to Goebbels the *Evening Standard*, under the headline 'Hitler Ready for an Armistice', revealed what it reported to be the full background for Halifax's visit. The diplomatic correspondent of the paper published a story in which he claimed that Hitler was going to make 'no demands for colonies for ten years if he received a free hand in central Europe'. Since it broke the promised veil of secrecy and mystery surrounding this visit, the effect of this article in Berlin was immediate and tempestuous: Henderson reported that Hitler was 'furious' with the *Evening Standard* 'not only for giving the impression that the Lord President would bring concrete proposals, but also for giving publicity to the visit, the arrangements for which he wanted kept as secret as possible'.[4] Henderson himself was furious, and described the paper's action as 'the height of sensation mongering and of tendentious poisoning of the atmosphere'; he regarded the *Evening Standard*'s attempts to queer the pitch of the visit as an 'almost incredible attempt to poison the atmosphere ... which even the history of western journalism has seldom hitherto approached'. Furthermore he now called for the trip to be postponed; it should take place only 'if the Press in Great Britain ... evinces that calm which is usually called decency and truthfulness in other countries'.[5]

Henderson's wish to postpone the visit was the response desired by the perpetrators of this article, but in an attempt to salvage the situation Chamberlain and Steward in London decided on a rather different path of action to that contemplated by Henderson. On the morning of 15 November, *The Times* and the *Daily Telegraph* published almost identical stories containing what Oliver Harvey in the Foreign Office described as 'the most exaggerated accounts of scope of Halifax's visit'. Chamberlain had in fact turned the situation to his advantage, giving the Lobby a glowing account of the purpose and possibilities of a visit which had horrified the Foreign Office. The stories in *The Times* and the *Daily Telegraph* could only have come from Downing Street: Leeper and Eden were both equally annoyed that the 'note which Rex [Leeper] gave out, emphasizing the informal and limited nature of the visit and the fact that it implied no change in the present policy of H.M.G. was not even referred to, let alone published'.[6] It is evident that having had his hand forced over the visit Chamberlain was determined to make a virtue of necessity and dress up the Halifax visit in as optimistic a light as possible by using the Lobby to propagate such a view. Chamberlain was soon referring to the *Evening Standard* leak as a 'fortunate misfortune' for it now made it possible to reveal the full intentions of the visit in the best light that he was able to give it. Moreover, the rules of anonymity governing the Downing Street briefing meant that the stories seemed to give the 'government view', whereas in fact enthusiasm for such a settlement, and on such terms as were outlined in the *Evening Standard*, was shared by few outside Downing Street itself.

For Chamberlain, battle now 'raged round Halifax's instructions', a battle that was aided by the 'authoritative' reports of the wide scope of the impending talks in *The Times*.[7] Moreover, the stories in *The Times* and the *Daily Telegraph* did indeed have the desired effect in Berlin; Henderson was able to report on the afternoon of 15 November that 'the attitude this morning of the British press, particularly *The Times* and the *Daily Telegraph* are regarded here as very satisfactory and the moderates hope that the Chancellor having ventilated his annoyance will take a calmer view'.[8]

Having used the Lobby to restore the situation, in what was to become a well-tried routine, George Steward called at the German Embassy on 17 November to inform Dr Hesse, his 'close friend', that he was anxious to tell him certain facts privately. Steward emphasized that he 'could not express himself officially with regard to it', but, undeterred, he went on to give a detailed account of Chamberlain's thinking on the matter. He assured Dr Hesse that 'Chamberlain had been exceedingly angry about the article' in the *Evening Standard*. Furthermore, he expressed surprise that the article should 'have created such a sensation in Germany', as it was 'a paper to whose utterances no particular importance was to be attached'. He also advised Hesse not to harbour 'excessive expectations' from Halifax's visit as a rapprochement could 'only be brought about very slowly and gradually'; this he put down to the English character, as 'things sometimes went rather slowly in England and often took years'. But he assured Dr Hesse that such a rapprochement, slowly but surely achieved, 'could also be counted on to last'.[9] Steward also touched on the subject that would now exercise the minds of both Whitehall and Berlin: who had given the news about Halifax's meetings with the Nazi leaders to the *Evening Standard* in the first place. This became a question of urgency, as Henderson's explanation for why the article had aroused so much wrath in Berlin centred on the suspicion held in senior Nazi circles that 'the information had been given to Poliakoff [of the *Evening Standard*] by persons in the Foreign Office who were against the visit'. Henderson reported that as Poliakoff had 'obtained first information of the visit from F.O. he is continuing to receive information from the same persons for the same purpose'.[10] Steward strove to reassure the Germans that this was not the case, and that although 'exhaustive investigations [doubtless by himself and Sir Joseph Ball] had revealed that the author could only be Poliakoff, the article had not been inspired by the Foreign Office, by members of the Cabinet, or by Parliamentary circles'. Steward hinted that the real explanation was that Poliakoff had got his information from the Italian Embassy (an explanation that Vansittart also provided to Sir Nevile Henderson) for 'Poliakoff wrote in the interest of whatever power paid him the most.'[11]

Henderson added unconvincingly to his vigorous exposition of the German view of Foreign Office responsibility for the leak that 'I have done my best to counter these stories,'[12] but Vansittart, probably rightly, detected in Henderson a willingness to believe this story – since Henderson was fully aware that as Vansittart and presumably other members of the Foreign Office had been against the whole visit in the first place it would have been in their interest to execute just such a spoiling trick. Vansittart, however, was quick to put Henderson right on this point and wrote to the sceptical Ambassador that the assumption that Poliakoff had 'obtained from the F.O. first news of Lord Halifax's visit is therefore wholly unjustified', and exhorted Henderson to 'react more sharply against such calumnies'. Furthermore, he went on to add dubiously that 'there are no persons in the F.O. who were against the visit', nor, 'as you are well aware, are these our methods'.[13]

However, despite Vansittart's denial to the contrary, there is strong evidence to suggest that the article was inspired by the Foreign Office. F. A. Voigt (whom Dell was now describing as a 'confirmed hero worshipper of Vansittart who one only had to hear talk ... to know what Vansittart says'),[14] clearly saw the hand of the Foreign Office in this affair. Benefiting from his close contacts with Vansittart and Leeper, Voigt told his editor, W. P. Crozier, that this episode was only part of 'the fight against Halifax's trip', which had 'become desperate about a week ago', and that Vansittart was aware that he 'had had a terrific fight – the pro-Nazis really want to get rid of him...'. Voigt recorded that 'the F.O. rarely resorted to a scheme so desperate (judged by English standards) as to counteract a dangerous political move by making a disclosure to a stunt newspaper. But this is what happened – Poliakoff was told about the German plan so that it would receive stunt publicity and be denied by the Germans.' Voigt discounted the government's and Vansittart's excuse that Poliakoff had got his information from the Italian Embassy; 'he got it from a high official in the F.O. who told him that this was the actual German plan for the talks but did not reveal the fact that the plan had been accepted as a basis for the conversations in Berlin'.[15] The story was confirmed for him by Lord Tyrrell, an ex-Permanent Under-Secretary at the Foreign Office who was close to Vansittart.

The journalist concerned, Poliakoff, was a freelance foreign affairs expert who was also close to Claud Cockburn, Editor of the celebrated and anti-establishment newsletter *The Week* – indeed, it was Poliakoff who gave Cockburn the idea for the term the 'Cliveden set' in November 1937. Patricia Cockburn, Claud's wife, has claimed that Poliakoff obtained his information from Sir Robert Vansittart, who regarded Poliakoff 'as a valuable ally'. Through Poliakoff, 'a line of communication was established with Vansittart', which was 'one of the means by which *The Week* was able to keep itself informed of the proceedings of the Cliveden set'.[16] This would certainly corroborate

Voigt's remarks and point to Vansittart himself as the 'high official in the F.O.'. Indeed, the most enduring propagation of the Cliveden set conspiracy appeared in the same week as the *Evening Standard* article, in *The Week* of 17 November. If Voigt and Patricia Cockburn are to be believed, both articles were thus inspired by Vansittart through Poliakoff to sabotage and discredit the Halifax mission.

Moreover, Lord Tyrrell was, like Eden, distressed at the way *The Times* and the *Daily Telegraph* were used by Chamberlain to turn the situation to his advantage. For Tyrrell *The Times* was in with the Astors and the *Daily Telegraph* was now 'stodgy and accepts dictation from the Government'. He launched into a lamentation about the absence of a 'free Press in England'. Voigt revealed that the long leader in the *Daily Telegraph* of 16 November 1937 was in fact 'inspired by Chamberlain himself'.[17] Eden was infuriated by Chamberlain's attitude generally over this issue, and in particular the fact that he had not been consulted at all about the views of 'The Government' that had appeared in *The Times* and *Daily Telegraph*. Eden was comforted by Chamberlain who apparently told him that he 'deplored exaggerated Press accounts' – which he himself had inspired from Downing Street. It was the first taste of Chamberlain's duplicity in his handling of the press. Furthermore, to reassure Eden he promised that he would undertake to see the two offending papers 'and correct them'.[18] However, this evidently did not dampen their enthusiasm for the Halifax visit, and Beaverbrook, perhaps to make amends for letting his paper leak a story to sabotage an enterprise in which he placed great hope, made amends by writing about Halifax's visit with particular enthusiasm in the *Daily Express*.

The appeasers were glad that the visit, jeopardized by the leak, could now go ahead. Lord Astor assured Garvin that 'fortunately matters have righted themselves'.[19] The long-term consequences for the Foreign Office, however, were to be disastrous, as this episode confirmed for Chamberlain and his entourage all their worst suspicions about the Foreign Office and its News Department. Despite their protestations to the Germans, via Steward, that the sole source for Poliakoff was the Italian Embassy, it is evident that this excuse was principally invented for German consumption to smooth the way for Halifax's visit. In fact, Chamberlain really believed that the Foreign Office was responsible, and was now privately resolved to do something about what he perceived to be a centre of subversion against his own policies. This is certainly the impression that he gave at Cliveden on 15 December, where Dawson of *The Times*, Halifax, Inskip (Minister for the Co-ordination of Defence) and Chamberlain gathered for lunch, during which Lord Astor was told that the 'attempt to spoil the Halifax visit and his work comes from three quarters – certain people in the F.O. – Italy, some French quarters . . .', and that the Prime Minister realized 'the personnel weaknesses in that department [The Foreign Office]. Van is the real obstacle. . . .'[20] Chamberlain's solution to this obstacle was not only to shift Vansittart, but also to neutralize the Foreign Office as a centre for disseminating news. This episode had offered a warning of what was to come – Leeper had for the first time found his own briefing of 14 November discarded in favour of Chamberlain's Lobby briefing at Downing Street. The suppression of Leeper's note stressing the informal, inconsequential nature of Halifax's visit was on this occasion omitted by the editors, probably at Chamberlain's insistence, which allowed his own version of events to dominate in *The Times* and the *Daily Telegraph*. However, Chamberlain was not prepared to leave this sort of decision to editors and proprietors alone, despite his evident success on this occasion. A much more secure way to ensure that Downing Street's version of events would always be given prominence was to cripple the News Department of the Foreign Office by restricting its access to news and barring it from giving out such news as it could lay its hands on. This is exactly what Chamberlain resolved to do in 1938 as the issues became more tendentious and the Foreign Office objections to his policy, particularly Leeper's, steadily mounted.

However, as well as indicating the need to centralize further the flow of news from Whitehall and Downing Street, thus starving the press of alternative news and comments, the Halifax visit also resulted in the first attempts to intimidate the proprietors themselves into adopting a greater degree of self-censorship. For the principal point that Halifax learned during his discussions with Hitler on 19 November and with Dr Goebbels on 21 November was that, if a settlement were to be reached between Britain and Germany, one of the primary preconditions for such a settlement would be the cessation of British press attacks on Hitler. In his talk with Hitler on the 19th, Halifax found that Hitler was absurdly sensitive to adverse press comment, and noted that although during the course of their conversation 'Hitler was on the whole very quiet and restrained,' he did 'get excited now and again over Russia or the Press'. Halifax noted that Hitler distrusted 'democratic methods, to him inefficient, blundering and unsuited to the hard world'. In Hitler's eyes, the essential vices of democracy were that it 'paralysed the capacity to face facts by its love of talk' and fed on a 'distorted view of facts presented to it by a licentious Press'.[21] In the official account of the talk, Hitler was reported as declaring that in the conduct of international affairs 'it was only the part played by the Press which was sinister. Nine tenths of all tension was produced simply and solely by it.' He went on to emphasize that 'a first condition of the calming of international relations was therefore co-operation of all peoples to make an end of journalistic free-booting'. Halifax, surprised perhaps by the virulence of these remarks, if not apparently by their stupidity, 'agreed with the Chancellor's remarks as to the dangerous influence of the Press'.[22] As the main purpose of Halifax's visit was to reduce tension in Anglo-German relations, he understandably took Hitler's words to heart and issued a statement to British correspondents in Berlin on the morning of 21 November 1937 in which he 'alluded to the need for the Press to create the right atmosphere if any real advance were to be made towards a better understanding'.[23]

If Halifax had any doubts about how seriously the Nazis took this matter, they were to be dispelled by his interview with the Minister of Propaganda, Dr Goebbels, on the afternoon of the 21st. Goebbels devoted his entire conversation to the press, as he tried to impress upon Halifax that 'the influence of the Press was under- rather than over-rated. Its power to mould public opinion was greater even than was realized, and if public opinion was moulded wrong incalculable harm could be done since, in the end ... it was public opinion ... which directed policy.' After this preamble, Goebbels got on to the 'one vital and essential point' that he wished to make. He then asked Halifax whether 'something could not be done to put a stop in the British Press to personal criticism of Hitler. Nothing caused more bitter resentment than that. It alienated the Führer ... and Party circles ... which had considerable influence over him.' Goebbels then drew an audacious comparison between Hitler and the British monarchy, and referred to the fact that just as the German press refrained from personal attacks on the British monarch, so the British press should refrain from personal attacks on Hitler. In this connection he referred especially to the cartoons which appeared in some of what he described as the 'left Press'. Goebbels also complained of 'ill-natured and distorted criticism', and quoted the example of Norman Ebbut* of *The Times* and 'the spiteful taint given to him in his reports'. Halifax referred Goebbels to the provincial press, which in general held what he called 'sane views', and reminded Goebbels that in view of the 'complete independence of the British Press', he could not give any guarantee that these attacks would cease, but promised to undertake to 'represent to the P.M. and his colleagues the views which Dr Goebbels had expressed'. In conclusion, Halifax was impressed by the 'earnestness' with which Goebbels promised to support the cause 'of an Anglo-German understanding', but concluded that this support, which was obviously an echo of Hitler's view, would 'not stand the test of disparaging references in the British Press, particularly to Herr Hitler himself'.[24] Thus the Halifax visit not only saw the first skirmish between the Foreign Office and Downing Street in the battle either to sabotage or to pursue appeasement, but it also meant that the question of the British press's attitude towards Germany was now to be central to Chamberlain's plans for appeasement. On his return Halifax wrote to Henderson in a hopeful vein, assuring him that all the recent developments were 'good'. But he ended on the only remaining caveat, 'if only we can get the press in both countries tame'.[25]

Naturally, the person whom Halifax consulted on this question on his return to London was George Steward. As regards the British correspondents in Berlin, who had been the source of unpleasant revelations about the ways and means of Nazism in the past (for example, Norman Ebbut and F. A. Voigt), Steward advised that 'the easiest way of keeping them . . . on the right line . . .' was for Henderson himself to 'keep in close touch with them . . . so that by personal appeals of man to man rather than of ambassador to press correspondent', he 'would prevent them taking lines that might give offence'. Halifax was also assured that as far as the press in Britain was concerned if there

---

*The paper's correspondent in Berlin, expelled from that city in 1936 by the German authorities for his critical reports of the Nazi regime, and in particular the Nazi persecution of the Church.

was cause for complaint it was much preferable to 'adjust the matter privately ... before public action was taken ...'. This private unofficial approach was the hallmark of governmental dealings with the press as developed by Steward and Leeper, and was now to be used with the editors and proprietors as well. Steward argued that 'it is the personal touch that counts'.[26] Henderson agreed with his assessment, but also voiced a note of caution, because although Halifax's and the Prime Minister's personal touch would be most helpful it was the News Department of the FO that could 'do most to help – or to hinder the situation'.[27] Bearing this in mind, Halifax decided to keep his touch strictly personal, and the Foreign Office News Department now found itself excluded from the government's campaign to tame the press.

The personal touch was first extended to Geoffrey Dawson of *The Times*, whom Halifax saw on his return from Germany. To take advantage of the new, optimistic climate in Anglo-German relations that Halifax reported to Dawson, the latter penned a leader which appeared in *The Times* on 29 November 1938 outlining the main German grievances and expressing the general hope of a settlement of the territorial questions. As *The Times* was taken, quite correctly, on the continent as being inspired by the government, Henderson was able to report back to the Foreign Office that 'the Germans were naturally very pleased with *The Times* leading article of November 29th ...' which had 'added to their growing belief that we mean to be realistic'.[28] By the same token, *The Times* leader caused consternation in Prague, for it seemed (together with an article that appeared on the Sudeten German problem on 2 and 3 December) to contemplate an agreement with Germany at the expense of Czechoslovakia. Mr Newton of the British Embassy in Prague reported that Halifax's visit to Germany had been 'regarded with nervousness by the Czechs, who feared that some deal might be afoot that would adversely affect their interests ...' and this justifiable anxiety had been 'vastly increased' by *The Times*.[29] Lord Astor, on the other hand, wrote to Garvin that it was now their task to help Halifax by ensuring that Eden accepted the fruits of Halifax's visit by preventing him from getting on a 'high horse' and rejecting any proposals. Astor calculated that Garvin had to build up Eden to do this, 'to make it easy for Eden to accept Halifax'. Since 'Eden was ... doubtless susceptible to flattery ...' he advised Garvin to repeat the words of praise that he had used in a previous issue of the *Observer*.[30] This was duly done.

However, it was not so much a positive press that the Nazis wanted – which they would now begin to get in ample measure anyway – but a cessation of the negative press, along the lines that Goebbels had indicated. Acting on the personal touch recommended by Steward, Halifax confided to Henderson that he was hoping to see the *Daily Herald* and *News Chronicle* controlling powers himself and had yet to work out a satisfactory approach to get at Low, whose *Evening Standard* cartoons were 'the most troublesome' of all the offensive journalistic pieces that Goebbels had been complaining about.[31] Halifax thus saw Lord Southwood of the *Daily Herald* on 26 November and Sir Walter Layton of the *News Chronicle* on the next day. According to Layton's recollection of this interview, 'after carefully explaining to me that he had no intention of trying to influence me in any way, he merely passed on a message at Goebbels' request addressed to myself and ... other journalists to the effect that Hitler was personally very sensitive to newspaper criticism and unfriendly cartoons and that this made it very difficult for an Englishman to deal with him'.[32] Much the same was doubtless said to Southwood, the chief proprietor of the *Daily Herald*, which was jointly owned by his publishing company Odhams Press and the Trades Union Congress acting for the Labour Party. However, in the latter case, Halifax immediately took up Southwood's offer to approach him privately and wrote to him about a cartoon by Will Dyson in his paper of 1 December which Halifax alleged broke Southwood's undertaking that he wished to see cartoonists 'portraying public characters ... in a temper or humour without cruelty'. Halifax regarded this particular cartoon, though, as exactly the kind of 'unjustly cruel cartoon that did so much to forestall any advance ... in international problems'. Southwood, who admitted to wanting substantially the same as Halifax 'on the big issues that matter', replied that he had not seen Dyson's cartoon before publication but agreed that 'it might have been less grotesque', and he had already told Dyson so. Having done this Southwood informed Halifax of the obvious, that as the paper made its points 'based on the immediate Labour Party policy, ... they were thus bound to differ over methods...', but he assured Halifax they agreed 'on the big issues'.[33] Halifax was evidently satisfied with his response and reported to Henderson in

Berlin that Southwood had been very co-operative and that his replies had been of a 'character which gives me hope that we shall not have reason to complain again on this sort of thing in that quarter at any rate'.[34]

Halifax's approaches evidently had their effect, and Southwood was to become a frequent and pliant visitor to Halifax's rooms at the Foreign Office after Halifax succeeded Eden as Foreign Secretary in February 1938. Hugh Dalton entertained the City Editor of the *Daily Herald*, Douglas Jay, to lunch at Westleighs in June 1938, to find Jay 'rather dissatisfied over recent *Daily Herald* experiences'. Jay confessed that Southwood had 'been sent for several times by Halifax and flattering appeals made to him as great Press magnate' and that there had 'been some reflection of this in pressure to prevent too critical a line on Foreign Policy'.[35] Lord Southwood was not, by all accounts, primarily interested in politics but was more than ready to do anything that would boost the earnings of his papers. As a large part of his revenue was composed of advertising revenue it was obviously of benefit to Southwood and his balance sheets to foster an atmosphere of optimism in international relations which would be conducive to an improvement in international commerce. By favouring the prospects of an Anglo-German rapprochement in his paper he would thus be fostering the economic conditions which would attract advertising to his own paper.

All of Southwood's employees in his publishing empire testified to his essential commercial rapaciousness – this was his governing ethos, to which considerations of politics came second. In this he was atypical, rather than typical, of the press barons of his day. The Astors, Rothermeres and Beaverbrooks were rich men who had bought their newspapers to exert political influence – which they could do very effectively, as we shall see. Southwood, on the other hand, was a commercial publisher through and through, whose entry into partnership with the TUC to run the Labour Party paper the *Daily Herald* was a shrewd move on his part, providing him with an extensive and ready-made canvassing organization in the form of the TUC local committees. War, and the threat of it, was of course the ultimate enemy of successful commerce and so it was not surprising that it was on the *Daily Herald* that journalists were most acutely aware of the pressures to foster an atmosphere of 'business as usual' during the late

1930s. As Douglas Jay has written, 'In the Daily Herald City office in these years I was acutely conscious of the insistent pressure from the City establishment and the Press advertising interests in favour of appeasement, and above all against any suggestion in the press that we perhaps ought to prepare for war.'[36]

The most revealing evidence of Southwood's priorities is provided by the issue of *John Bull* (part of the Southwood publishing empire) of 18 March 1939. On Monday, 13 March, the journalist Robert Fraser had submitted an article strongly in support of Chamberlain's appeasement policy for inclusion in the coming Saturday's edition of *John Bull*. Entitled 'Without Fear or Favour', it mocked what it called the 'know-alls' who had predicted that Hitler would have chosen the preceding weekend of 11/12 March to provoke the next 'crisis, ultimatum, war even...'. Having berated the 'know-alls', *John Bull* then proclaimed a magnificent vision of a tranquil, prosperous Europe: 'But we say that things are not merely better in Europe today, but that they are much better. They are very much better during these weeks when the know-alls predicted with such patronizing confidence that they would be worse.'

The reassuring assertions of *John Bull* were, of course, confounded by Hitler's invasion of Prague and the remnants of Czechoslovakia on Wednesday, 15 March. Robert Fraser naturally took the unfortunate, outdated article to Southwood on the Thursday to point out that it was now irrelevant. But, much to Fraser's surprise, Southwood did not seem to mind that the article had been proven wrong by events and, incredibly, the article duly appeared, as planned, on Saturday, 18 March in *John Bull*. With no hint of irony, the article concluded, 'This paper is no ostrich. All its life it has been digging away at facts, publishing facts, warning people....'[37]

However, as Halifax had earlier predicted, it was more difficult to get at Low, the celebrated cartoonist of the *Evening Standard* and the most vitriolic of all the anti-Fascist cartoonists. Halifax tried to surmount this problem by having lunch with Michael Wardell, Beaverbrook's aide, and Barbara Metcalfe, who had 'suggested this means of approach to get at Low'.[38] The concern over Low's work had already been put to the cartoonist by the *Evening Standard*'s Editor, Percy Cudlipp, on 9 September 1937, probably as a result of Beaverbrook's personal promptings, as he was already aware of the problems of the press vis-à-vis the sensitive German leaders. Low did respond positively to Wardell's subsequent strictures and we are assured by Low's biographers that Low 'played it in a less personal key for a few weeks'.[39]

Halifax also saw Esmond Harmsworth, the son of Lord Rothermere, on the same day as Wardell to convey the same message. The *Daily Mail* became a vociferous supporter of Chamberlain and Hitler throughout early 1938. Indeed, Rothermere had already assured Chamberlain that he had 'instructed his newspapers to lend their full support to the only person who could save the peace'.[40] As part of the same initiative, Halifax advised Eden to have a 'strictly confidential understanding' with Henderson 'whereby he maintained close contacts with the British journalists in Berlin and quietly tried to guide them along the right lines'. But Halifax urged Eden to keep this contact on a personal level, as he advised that it would be 'unwise and indeed dangerous' if any attempts were made to make such an 'arrangement through the Foreign Office' as 'too many people would know of its existence', which probably meant the News Department as much as the general public. Furthermore, he urged Eden himself to have talks with Lord Camrose, Geoffrey Dawson and Lord Astor. The suggestion to talk to the latter two was hardly necessary as Halifax talked almost constantly to them anyway, and Eden made no attempt to. But Halifax did outline the significance of Camrose and Kemsley, owing to the extreme importance of the 'big group of provincial press under Lord Kemsley's direction'.[41] But here again Chamberlain was already in close touch with Kemsley at Downing Street; indeed Kemsley was the most sycophantic of all the Chamberlain press supporters. Chamberlain and his inner Cabinet were now confident that the press could be at least damped down, and Chamberlain was optimistic that the prospects for a settlement with Germany, based on a solution to the colonial issue, could be achieved. In the words of one historian, Chamberlain 'believed that the barriers to success were not insurmountable if only the Press and the Commons would play along and allow the delicate negotiations to proceed quietly at their own pace'.[42]

However, this confidence was punctured on 7 December when Henderson wrote an angry despatch to Halifax, complaining of the 'immense harm'[43] which had been done in Berlin by two articles written by Victor Gordon-Lennox in the *Daily Telegraph* of 2 and 3 December which both painted fairly alarming pictures of the German claims on the colonial question. Halifax sympathized with Henderson and assured him that he had written to Eden to exhort him 'to come as near as possible to wringing Gordon-Lennox's neck as he can'.[44] Henderson, mindful of the circumstances surrounding the *Evening Standard* leak in November, hinted meaningfully that Gordon-Lennox was 'in close touch with the News Department of the F.O. . . .', thus affirming the opinion that now existed in the minds of the Chamberlainites that any press article that did not allow the delicate process of appeasement to proceed quietly at its own pace emanated from the Foreign Office News Department. Eden, a personal friend of Gordon-Lennox, stood by the errant correspondent and revealed that in fact Gordon-Lennox had been prevailed upon by the News Department 'to tone down . . . considerably what he had previously said'.[45]

However, there were those who refused to be convinced. Eden began to be viewed by Chamberlain and the inner Cabinet as dangerously over-influenced by Vansittart and the News Department. Sir Samuel Hoare privately noted that Eden was 'not impressive in Cabinet . . . jealous of interference . . . The epitome of F.A. [Foreign Affairs] superiority'. Hoare was more than ready to attribute Eden's unfortunate attitude to the view that the 'Press Department of the F.O. [was] running him' and that he was 'too much in hands of a clique'.[46] Hoare's ungenerous sentiments were fairly representative of the wider Chamberlainite view of Eden; as Eden proved to be more resistant to the direction in which the Chamberlainites wanted foreign policy to go, before the year was out they were starting a whispering campaign amongst their closest journalistic supporters directed against the increasingly beleaguered Foreign Secretary. Ronald Cartland, Barbara Cartland's brother and the most promising of the coming generation of younger Conservative MPs who clustered around Eden, related how Beverley Baxter, the author of Atticus in the *Sunday Times* and Chamberlain's most loyal scribe in the Sunday press, 'had been visited by both Simon and Hoare separately to explain that A.E.'s 'flu was the beginning of the end . . . that the strain was too great and he would soon go'.[47]

However, a more practical step for the Chamberlainites to take than forcing Eden's resignation was to move against the 'clique' in the Foreign Office that supposedly controlled him. This, of course, principally meant Vansittart. In December 1937, it was decided to promote him to be the government's Chief Diplomatic Adviser, a grandiose title that in fact removed him from the day-to-day running of foreign policy. It was a great coup for Chamberlain, for by technically promoting Vansittart it looked as though the latter's influence had increased – whilst the cognoscenti knew that in fact the exact opposite was true. Vansittart was replaced as Permanent Under-Secretary by the less emotional and less prejudiced Sir Alexander Cadogan. Chamberlain hoped that 'the change will make a great difference in the F.O. and that when Anthony can work out his ideas with a sane man like Alec Cadogan he will be much steadier'. He added that by removing Vansittart from 'active direction of F.O. policy' he rightly suspected that 'in Rome and Berlin the rejoicings will be loud and deep'.[48]

The irony of the situation was that it was Eden, when he had arrived at the Foreign Office, who had first protested about Vansittart's peculiarly strident working methods and personality. He resented the older man's patrician and over-bearing ways 'and did not think he was any longer in a fit state of health for his work'.[49]

Eden could thus hardly object to Vansittart's removal. This was exquisitely handled by Chamberlain to betray as little as possible about the real reasons surrounding the 'promotion'. The announcement was delayed throughout December until Parliament had broken up for the Christmas recess, thus sparing the government any awkward questions in the House of Commons. When the announcement did come out, on 1 January 1938, Vansittart's apparent promotion was received with great acclamation in the press. Oliver Harvey noted with pleasure that 'a tremendous puff of him appeared in the Press', which he thought 'Van' had 'worked himself'. However, Harvey could not have been more wrong, as he went on to remark with dismay that 'no one so much as hints at the truth which is that he has been side tracked'. In fact, so strong was the impression in the press that Vansittart had been effectively promoted that Harvey felt that 'something must be done through the Press to restore the balance'.[50] Chamberlain had succeeded, through his influence at Downing Street, in persuading the press that Whitehall was united behind his policy and that Vansittart was being promoted for excellent service to the government. Even those who were beginning to realize the depth of the cleavage within the government were misled by the press effusions. W. P. Crozier was not the only editor who took Vansittart's promotion as a victory for the Eden group – although the *Manchester Guardian* refrained from speculating on the situation.

With the left-wing press now showing greater caution towards the dictators, and now that relations with Germany were evidently improving in the wake of Halifax's visit, Chamberlain turned his attention to the Italians. There had been very little contact since his talks with Count Grandi the previous August, and so the best way to establish an optimistic environment in which such contacts might be resumed was to inspire a press campaign fostering an atmosphere of Anglo-Italian goodwill. On the morning of 9 February 1938 Oliver Harvey duly found the morning papers carrying stories 'crying up the prospects of early and complete agreement between us and the Italians'. Like the Chamberlain-inspired articles of 15 November 1937 about Halifax's visit to Germany, these stories took Eden, who was 'very annoyed', and the Foreign Office by surprise. On checking with the News Department Oliver Harvey was told that this campaign could 'only have come from Number 10 and that it had been initiated by articles in the Daily Mail'. Despite denials to this effect by Chamberlain, which were confirmed by Horace Wilson, Rex Leeper still maintained that this must have been so, and confided that he had 'circumstantial evidence from journalists that they did come from N.C. at any rate'.[51] The answer was that this campaign had indeed come from N.C. (Neville Chamberlain) – but not from the civil servants in Downing Street, for Harvey learned a few days later that the 'press campaign about Italy was given out by Sir Joseph Ball at Conservative Head Office, not from Number 10'.[52] Thus, technically, Chamberlain had been scrupulously correct in his treatment of Eden, since the story had indeed not come from Number 10. As in the previous November, Chamberlain was using his own coterie of Lobby journalists to run a campaign against the better judgement of the Foreign Office, and was then disclaiming all responsibility for it, knowing that the Lobby rule of non-attribution would camouflage his scheme. The *Daily Mail* was one of the true-blue papers that Sir Joseph Ball and Chamberlain gave their private briefings to, together with the Kemsley press, represented by James Margach, who later described these discreet meetings at St Stephen's Club. The reason why Eden and Oliver Harvey deplored these optimistic reports, later to be termed 'rainbow stories', was that this was 'exactly the way to arouse exaggerated hopes and to make the Italians difficult, because they will think we are so eager we will try anything for agreement'.[53] This duplicity on Chamberlain's part brought to a head the differences between the Prime Minister and his Foreign Secretary, and now precipitated Eden's resignation.

Eden and Chamberlain were already in profound disagreement over Roosevelt's offer of co-ordinated talks to ameliorate the European situation (which Chamberlain had rejected out of hand, without consulting Eden), and on top of that there was now evidence that Chamberlain was running his own foreign policy behind the backs of the Foreign Office via the press. To try and salvage the situation, Eden managed to secure a promise from Chamberlain that there should be 'contact between Rex L. and Horace W. [Wilson] ... to co-ordinate the Government's dissemination of information'. Sir Alexander Cadogan thought this an 'excellent arrangement',[54] which, on the surface, it was; but for Chamberlain it was an easy concession to make since Horace Wilson had very little to do with the press Lobby briefings that so infuriated Eden and the Foreign Office.

Chamberlain's aim throughout this affair was to minimize the apparent differences within his government over foreign affairs in exactly the same way as he had successfully obscured the meaning of Sir Robert Vansittart's promotion. The Edenites believed that it was 'a good thing that [the country] ... should realize that there are two minds in the Government itself'.[55] Chamberlain's and Steward's task was, by contrast, to ensure that the country regarded the government as acting with one mind – that being Chamberlain's mind. To quash rumours of the split between himself and Eden which were percolating through to the press, Chamberlain used W. W. Hadley of the *Sunday Times*, Chamberlain's most loyal editorial supporter, to print a formal *démenti* of the speculation in the paper. The article duly appeared, written by a 'political correspondent', which was in this case Hadley himself. The headline announced 'Political Canard. Premier and Mr Eden in complete agreement', based on information 'from the highest authority'. The Edenites assured themselves that no one would believe this, but the ensuing days saw an unusual calm descend on Fleet Street over what would normally have been a period of widespread speculation.

In the course of the next week, as it became clear that Eden could not continue under Chamberlain, the Prime Minister realized that it was not so much a case of persuading his Foreign Secretary to continue in office as of how to demonstrate to the country via the press that Eden had resigned over technicalities rather than over profound differences in the conduct of foreign affairs. Sir Joseph Ball was very active in this process; he wrote to Chamberlain on the day after Eden's resignation to report that he had taken 'certain steps privately' to destroy 'the cases of Eden and Cranbourne'* in the Conservative press.[56] What these private steps were cannot now be exactly adduced, but both Ronald Cartland and Oliver Harvey heard that 'the sly people' in the government had put round the story that Eden had resigned out of 'personal pique' and that 'poor Anthony was completely exhausted by the strain . . . and had lost his grip and judgement'. Oliver Harvey sombrely remarked on the morning after Eden's resignation that 'The Government took every possible step to secure the London papers. The Times, of course, was on their side already. The Telegraph came heavily in against A.E. . . .'; and he noted that Victor Gordon-Lennox, the diplomatic correspondent of that paper and a personal friend of Eden, 'was in tears at the way his paper had behaved'.[57] Crozier had been convinced for some time that Eden might have to resign, but when the day actually arrived Crozier was taken aback by the deafening silence that surrounded the event in the press, as he had been waiting for the eruption of public discussion over what many people now saw as the government's dangerous foreign policy. On 24 February, the *Manchester Guardian* observed in its leader column that 'the Government Press presented . . . a curiously distorted picture . . . and for the most part . . . preserved a unity of silence that could hardly be bettered in a totalitarian state'. Sir Joseph Ball filed this last quotation amongst his cuttings – 'presumably as a tribute to his own work'.[58] As Eden's biographer has remarked, 'with great skill

---

* Lord Cranbourne, later the 5th Marquess of Salisbury, was Eden's deputy at the Foreign Office. Cranbourne was a staunch supporter of Eden throughout the latter's career; he resigned with Eden in 1938 and later served under Eden at the Foreign Office during the war.

and cold calculation, Chamberlain had made it appear as though his differences with Eden were really quite trivial, and certainly were not of principle'.[59] But for the efforts of Chamberlain's inner Cabinet and entourage (Ball and Steward), the questions asked about Eden's resignation would have been that much more penetrating.

With the removal of Vansittart and the resignation of Eden, the opposition to Chamberlain within the government and Whitehall was gradually being removed; this left Leeper at the News Department of the Foreign Office dangerously exposed. At the same time as Eden was leaving the Foreign Office, Sir Nevile Henderson in Berlin was warming to his chosen theme of constantly conveying Hitler's sensitiveness over the British press. Throughout January, February and March 1938, Henderson sent a stream of telegrams to the Foreign Office arguing that if the British were to expect a positive sequel to the Halifax visit it was essential that a 'propaganda-truce' should be preserved during the next few months to allow the ensuing negotiations to follow in a calm and confidential atmosphere. Henderson was particularly keen on sending reports from the German press on the subject of the 'vilification of Germany in the foreign press', a vilification that was led by papers such as the *News Chronicle* and the *Manchester Guardian*, which, the Germans complained, were 'Jewish newspapers with journalists connected in one way or another with Soviet Bolshevism'.[60] Charles Peake of the News Department tried to correct this impression, assuring the rest of the Foreign Office and Henderson that the proprietors of the *Manchester Guardian* were 'entirely Aryan', whilst the *News Chronicle* was 'free from all Jewish influences'.[61]

The cumulative pressure of these telegrams did, however, persuade the new Foreign Secretary, Lord Halifax, to take action once again to curb the abuses of the British press. On 28 February Rex Leeper was summoned by Halifax to discuss 'the steps which might be taken to moderate the tone of the BBC and the Press'. Leeper suggested persevering with the personal touch that had worked so well with Halifax before, urging Halifax to see both the press and John Reith of the BBC to persuade them 'to avoid provocation against Germany and Italy ... and to have a sense of National responsibility'. Leeper was resolutely against informing the German government or Sir Nevile Henderson that such approaches had been made, on the ground, as he put it to Halifax, that these were 'very delicate matters, and to inform the German Government of them would increase the chances of leakage, and therefore of trouble in the House of Commons'. In private, however, Leeper must have been aware that such an admission to Hitler would only encourage his belief that Britain was now prepared to sacrifice cherished principles as well as territory in order to run after him. But Cadogan ruled that Henderson should be allowed to tell Hitler 'in confidence of Halifax's interviews with the BBC and the press'.[62]

Acting on this advice, Halifax first saw Reith, with the result that a series of talks on the German colonial problem was dropped – but the BBC, due to its direct government funding, had, in the view of one historian, already been 'firmly on the leash since 1936'.[63] Halifax saw representatives of the press on 8 March to tell them that although we lived in 'the happy state of affairs' of having a 'free country with a free press', the fact was that just as this 'freedom implies freedom to criticize so it also implied responsibility'. Halifax warned darkly that 'unguarded criticism of other countries especially ... the Heads of States' would only make the present European situation 'worse by needless provocation'. The text of Halifax's message was then communicated to Hitler by Henderson, and the Prime Ministers of the Commonwealth were contemporaneously assured that this confidential communication was evidence of the fact that His Majesty's government 'had done all in their power and had indeed taken an unusual step, in order to show their sincere desire to improve the atmosphere and to facilitate conversations with the German Government'.[64]

For those opposed to appeasement, this was a distressing step. Leeper now felt, with the robust support of Vansittart and the political protection of Eden gone, that he would have to conform more with Chamberlain's policy – which meant, in effect, that the information to the diplomatic correspondents from the News Department now began to dry up. F. A. Voigt noticed this, and wrote gloomily to W. P. Crozier about 'the "twilight" creeping over the foreign policy and about the silent censorship, the stopping of channels of news'. He warned that the ' F.O. people indicate that there is going to be a stopper on news, talks with the press ...',[65] thus curtailing the work of the News Department. If Leeper's new attitude of self-restraint was a necessary reaction to the new atmosphere at the Foreign Office, it was soon to be underlined by Chamberlain's express interference. All this was, of course, grist to Henderson's mill in Berlin and he was able to report that the cancellation of the BBC talks on the colonial question was taken there as 'a sign of improvement in the future . . .'. He added with scarcely concealed enthusiasm that the London correspondent of the *Berliner Teggerblat* had hinted that '. . . Mr Voigt has been complaining that sources of information he used to possess are now closed to him . . .'.[66]

The fears of the anti-appeasers were increased when the Germans pre-empted the negotiations for a possible Austrian plebiscite to decide that country's future by an armed invasion of Austria on 11 March 1938. The initial reaction of the press was one of universal condemnation of the German method of achieving the Anschluss, a condemnation led by *The Times*, which attacked the naked use of force. However, after the dust had settled over the weekend, *The Times* felt it could return to a more sober assessment of the situation. The Assistant Editor, Rupert Barrington-Ward, wrote a leader (which appeared on 14 March) entitled 'March and a Moral', in which he observed that 'Herr Hitler has enjoyed two days of triumphal progress from the Austrian frontier. Our correspondent leaves no room for doubt about the public jubilation with which he and his army were greeted everywhere . . . but the higher the value that is placed on their demonstrations the more extraordinary it must seem that it was thought necessary to surround so spontaneous a welcome with all the paraphernalia of tanks . . . and marching infantry.' Given *The Times*' previous commitment to an Anschluss, it was to be expected that the paper should avoid any criticism of the result of the German action, even if it might condemn the method. Furthermore, *The Times* published despatches from its own correspondent in Vienna which to a large extent contradicted Dawson's analysis of the jubilant atmosphere in Austria. Dawson also chose to ignore the warnings from the same correspondent who wrote from Austria to his editor to say that 'In my wildest nightmares, I had not foreseen anything so perfectly organized, so brutal, so ruthless, so strong. . . . The vital thing to remember is that the ultimate object is precisely the destruction of England.'[67] *The Times* correspondent in Prague counselled Dawson in similar terms, but the Editor was not moved by either opinion.

Another editor who took much the same view as Dawson was W. P. Crozier, who was increasingly out of step with his European correspondents and ignored their advice in favour of his own firmly held opinion. Robert Dell had written in February to inform Crozier that in his opinion the diplomacy of Britain and France was 'completely bankrupt'.[68] On the very day that Hitler invaded Austria, Crozier went to see Vansittart, whom he found 'obviously gloomy, depressed and bitter. He said that the methods and intentions of Hitler were now at last openly disclosed and he hoped that people ... would now at least pay some attention to what he had all along been telling them.' As Crozier was leaving, Vansittart 'repeated his view about the Hitler method and in particular that the time will come when we would receive one of the ultimatums'.[69] Alexander Werth, the *Manchester Guardian*'s correspondent in Paris, similarly advised Crozier and wrote to his editor that Chamberlain's appeasement policy 'merely acted as an encouragement to Hitler to go ahead ...'.[70] Despite all these warnings, however, Crozier stuck to his preferred course of placating Germany in the hope that, by settling the thorny territorial disputes, she would eventually see reason. The disregard of the editors for the reports of their own correspondents was one of the more remarkable features of their conduct during this period – and shows how much someone like Dawson was prepared to use his paper to help the government pursue appeasement at the cost of ignoring his own staff.

Naturally, the first question that arose after the Anschluss was the future of Czechoslovakia. To the appeasers, it was evident that with the dismantling of an independent Austria the plight of Czechoslovakia was now hopeless. Leo Kennedy, *The Times* chief leader writer on foreign affairs, was in Prague on 15 March when, as a representative of *The Times*, he was shown a despatch by Basil Newton of the British Embassy to 'H.M.G. summing up his impressions after the German coup in Austria'. Kennedy recorded in his journal that Newton was 'against making any sort of promise to help Czechoslovakia. He regards the place as unworkable. Its strategic position is hopeless now that the Austrian and German armies will form one. He thinks it will be much the best if these people make the best terms with Germany that they can and as soon as they can.' Armed with this candid opinion, Kennedy went to see the President, Dr Beneš, on 16 March and on being told that any 'agreement [with Germany] means surrender', Kennedy replied that Britain would be more prepared to give a guarantee of Czechoslovakia's future 'if the Czechoslovak Government has first made a resolute attempt to come to an agreement direct with the German Government'. He found Beneš' pessimism a 'rather startling view', but nonetheless tried to imply that a British guarantee such as Beneš wanted was 'improbable'. Kennedy observed that 'pathetically, the one thing he wants is a British guarantee', and his wish to dispel such hopes from the mind of the hapless Czech President on 16 March was only to be a rehearsal for the policy of *The Times* up to its notorious leader of 7 September. On 18 March, Kennedy met Geoffrey Ward Price of the *Daily Mail*, 'a Nazi heart and soul', freshly arrived from 'Hitler's entourage in Vienna'. Ward Price proceeded to accuse Czechoslovakia of being 'about to plunge civilization into war because she was so obstinate about the Sudetenland' – 'pretty stiff!' remarked *The Times* man. In conclusion, he told Basil Newton that he did 'not see a long existence for' Czechoslovakia. The only hope he could now see was for the Czechoslovaks to let the 'Sudetens join Germany', and after his return to London it was this general attitude that was to dominate the considerations at Printing House Square.[71] Others were equally unimpressed by the claims of Czechoslovakia.

Ward Price's views reflected those of Lord Rothermere, and no encouragement for the beleaguered state could be found in that quarter. The support that Beaverbrook now gave to Chamberlain was highly valued by the latter and Beaverbrook was equally happy to be drawn into the world of government again by secretly placing his newspapers at the government's disposal. As will be seen, under Chamberlain's guidance Beaverbrook was to be both advocate and exponent of appeasement, to an extent shared only by Geoffrey Dawson of *The Times*. Whenever an approach was made to him by the government between 1938 and 1940, Beaverbrook was eager to oblige, reminding Halifax in November 1938 that 'my newspapers will do anything to help you in your difficult negotiations with the central European countries, or indeed in any direction. Besides, I am in agreement with your policy and I can give you the strongest support.'[72] The politics of appeasement consumed Beaverbrook's newspapers to an extent that few imagined possible – which is why even Beaverbrook's severest detractors had to seek the reason for his newspapers' excesses in the years 1938 to 1940 in the more understandable field of commercial motivation.

But as well as finding the appeasement policies of Neville Chamberlain politically to his taste, Beaverbrook also had a more personal reason for lending his support to the government's policies. Beaverbrook championed lost causes, and he found a lost cause of flesh and blood in the Home Secretary Sir Samuel Hoare – one of the inner circle of four ministers who steered the government's appeasement policies, a man who had occupied a number of important offices under MacDonald, Baldwin and Chamberlain. After the death of his first and foremost political hero, his fellow Canadian Bonar Law, and the political demise of Lloyd George, Beaverbrook focused his political ambitions on the unlikely figure of Sir Samuel Hoare. For reasons best known to himself, Beaverbrook found in Hoare the blend of sagacity and political experience required of a future Prime Minister and, despite the mounting evidence to the contrary, Beaverbrook maintained his faith in him right to the bitter end.

Beaverbrook had a journalist's interest in personalities and, just as there was a 'white list' of names which could not be mentioned in the *Daily Express*, Sir Samuel Hoare was always assured of that paper's unfailing support. Even during the darkest hours of the Hoare–Laval Pact, the *Daily Express* stood fast and refused to condemn Hoare whilst all the other papers, including the normally faithful *Times*, fell over themselves to accuse Hoare of treachery, dishonour and much more. Hoare's biographer has written that 'His collaboration with Beaverbrook over Ireland from the early summer of 1921 seems to have been the real beginning of what was for Hoare his most important political friendship....'[73] For his part, until 1940 '... Beaverbrook never ceased to look upon Hoare as a potential Prime Minister'.[74] Beaverbrook thus tried to advance Hoare's career in every way possible. Another person who was convinced of Sam Hoare's potential was Sam Hoare himself, and so he was particularly receptive to Beaverbrook's constant flattery. Henry 'Chips' Channon, a Conservative MP and fervent admirer of Chamberlain, was surprised to find that in June 1938 his wife had been asked to dine with Beaverbrook and he confided the results of this dinner to his diary. Beaverbrook had revealed that he was convinced that Chamberlain would die 'in harness' and so:

it is the duty of the Conservative Government to be prepared for such an emergency. Beaverbrook knows that the Baldwin–Whipsroom–Margesson candidate is Inskip, he would prefer Sam Hoare, as I would, who has more personality, drive and charm. Even more convinced than we are that Sam Hoare is the PM's logical successor is Sam Hoare himself, and it appears he asked Max's advice the other day as to how he could become the recognized heir-apparent.[75]

Hoare and Beaverbrook were in constant contact throughout this period and it was principally Beaverbrook who coaxed Hoare back into the political centre-stage after the latter's all too frequent and obvious political gaffes. If Beaverbrook was seeking to exercise the same kind of influence on government that he had had in the days of Bonar Law and Lloyd George, Samuel Hoare was his chosen path to such a position. The bond was irrevocably sealed when Beaverbrook, in response to a begging letter from Lady Hoare in November 1938, started paying Hoare £2,000 per year to keep him in politics. Lady Hoare had cleverly raised the point that due to the time-consuming activities and low pay of the politician, her husband might have to leave politics for more lucrative positions. This elicited an immediate response from Beaverbrook to the effect that he was sending Hoare a 'very small sum ... out of a full pocket ...' and that Hoare could expect 'another dribble of the same size this time next year, and for the rest of Parliament ... if you still decide to stay in office'.[76] Hoare's biographer has identified three payments of £2,000 and observed with commendable understatement that 'had they [the payments] been publicly known at the time the accusation of corruption would undoubtedly have been made'. Although the payments might not have been made 'in the expectation of services to be rendered',[77] services certainly were rendered in the months after these payments were made. Hoare tried to persuade Chamberlain to take Beaverbrook into the government – the office of Minister of Agriculture was usually mentioned. In reply to a letter from Beaverbrook vindicating his stand over appeasement, Hoare recalled in 1943 that 'In the months before the war I ... was constantly trying to push Neville into more resolute action, and particularly, if you remember, to take you into the Government.'[78]

Beaverbrook's connection with Hoare is important not only because it helps to define Beaverbrook's loyalties during the years of appeasement, but also because Hoare was to be the main government link with the press. In this respect, of course, Beaverbrook was only too happy to help him in any way possible. Beaverbrook's unlikely collusion with Hoare let him into the inner circle of government, for which he was quite prepared to let the full range of his papers be used for the pursuance of the government's policy of appeasement.

By the end of May 1938, therefore, the government had let its view of press comment be known on several occasions and the responsibilities of the 'national interest' had been resolutely impressed upon both editors and proprietors. The Foreign Office News Department was now acting in a similar vein of self-restraint, under the veiled threat of the guillotine. This meant that the sources which enabled the diplomatic correspondents to criticize government policy were now drying up, so they exercised less influence on their papers – thus enabling Chamberlain to concentrate still more control over the dissemination of news in Downing Street, or at the Conservative Party offices under the secret guidance of Sir Joseph Ball. The cumulative effect of this constant pressure was such that by the summer of 1938 the British press was either muted in its criticism of Germany and Italy, or positively enthusiastic about the possibilities of a settlement with those two countries. However, newspapers were heterogeneous institutions, encompassing a wide variety of opinions, and as the government put pressure on editors and proprietors, so it was the turn of the editors and proprietors themselves to try and make their newspapers adopt the desired policy of restraint and moderation.

To complicate their task, the press proprietors were faced in the summer of 1938 with a deepening trade depression which papers unanimously attributed to what Sir Walter Layton described as a 'war scare mentality'.[79] Journalists on the *Daily Herald* were certainly under the impression that Lord Southwood, prompted by the government's warnings, was trying to play down a recurring international crisis in order to inculcate greater optimism about the European situation and therefore attract more advertisers. Francis Williams, the Editor of the *Daily Herald*, later testified to the Royal Commission on the press that the anti-Chamberlain line that the staff wanted to follow was intentionally muted because:

there were numerous occasions on which the commercial proprietors of the papers felt that such a policy, if conducted vigorously, was likely to drive away some public support for the newspaper, and some advertising support and there were a number of leading articles, which having been written by myself as editor or by the leader writer under my direction, were subsequently and without consultation ... sub-edited ... by the then Chairman of the commercial board of directors ... on the grounds that the expression of policy was too vigorous.[80]

Douglas Jay, the City Editor, also informed Hugh Dalton that ' "No gloom" has been the Odham slogan. Therefore you may not talk of a slump or emphasize statistics indicating that it has already begun.'[81]

On the *News Chronicle*, Sir Walter Layton had already shown his willingness to help the government, and as a former civil servant and leading luminary in the Liberal Party, to which the *News Chronicle* was informally politically affiliated, he was possessed of what his biographer has termed 'a highly developed sense of responsibility'.[82] As Chamberlain's appeasement policies clarified themselves, Layton increasingly sided with the more Conservative-minded Cadbury brothers, who on the proceeds of their chocolate empire owned the paper, against the more zealously anti-Fascist staff of the *News Chronicle*. The Editor, Gerald Barry, and his most prominent correspondents such as Vernon Bartlett, Philip Jordan and A. J. Cummings had always been inclined to be more radical than either Layton or the Cadburys, and the politics of appeasement further exacerbated these differences. In an effort to exert tighter control over what was often seen as a wayward editor and staff, Layton supported the Cadburys' initiative of starting a series of regular 'policy conferences' at the beginning of 1938, through which the Cadburys could ensure that the paper would remain loyal to what they called its 'Liberal tradition', which had always stood for 'liberty of conscience in the individual and for an anti-militaristic attitude towards international affairs'[83] – or, in the context of the late 1930s, appeasement. Layton was to use his enhanced powers of control to good effect in September 1938, whilst the Cadbury brothers constantly worried about the financial implications of too strongly attacking Chamberlain's appeasement policies, for by 1938 the ailing *News Chronicle* was already in a parlous financial state.

Nor were the mass-market papers the only ones affected by the trade depression, as the *Observer* reported a 20 to 25 per cent loss in advertising revenue over the financial year up to the summer of 1938, a reduction which, as J. L. Garvin indicated, cut off 'the whole of our profit margin'. Thus the paper which had made a profit of £36,729 in 1936–7 made a loss of £22,598 in 1937–8, which Garvin, like Layton, attributed to the 'unprecedented uncertainty respecting peace and war, by the continental alarms'. This is what Garvin called 'the creeping paralysis of confidence; it banishes new enterprise, and kills the City branch of our revenue'. However, despite the gloomy prognosis that it would 'require managerial knowledge and judgement as never yet to keep on the right side of loss', Garvin advocated 'no change'.[84] Various schemes to improve the situation were discussed amongst the Astor clan, but for Garvin there could be no improvement in business conditions 'unless and until the prospect of Anglo-German settlement comes in plain sight'. He was not prepared to allow such considerations to influence his political judgement and was content 'to wait till times improve in respect of company promotions and the buying spirit',[85] whilst Lord Astor was prepared to plunder the substantial family wealth if the alternative meant sacrificing any of the *Observer*'s cherished principles, such as the ban on liquor advertisements. In this sense, Lord Astor was rich enough to be able to afford to run any policy that he liked in the *Observer* – such as the prolonged campaign for air rearmament, which would hardly help an Anglo-German settlement.

The Astor family had bought the *Observer*, just as Lord Beaverbrook had bought the *Daily Express*, to 'propagand'. The concern with the commercial and advertising pressures involved in supporting, or attacking, appeasement thus varied from paper to paper. There is no doubt that the more commercially minded proprietors like Southwood did see the virtues of commercial stability in the strictures of Lord Halifax, but on the whole most proprietors could afford to ignore the obvious commercial gain that might accrue from moderating the tone of the press towards Nazi Germany. In this lay the irony that the papers such as the *Daily Herald* and *News Chronicle* which did not rely exclusively on the great capitalistic wealth of the Astors, Beaverbrooks or Rothermeres were the least able to resist the commercial implications arising out of the European situation in 1937–40.

However, the provincial press was another matter. The attitude of W. P. Crozier of the *Manchester Guardian* has already been noted, but it was the other great provincial newspaper, the *Yorkshire Post*, that quickly attracted the most attention owing to its celebrated stand against appeasement – making it unique amongst the 'quality' press. This was entirely due to the paper's Editor, Arthur Mann, and his courageous stand against Chamberlain and appeasement became a cause célèbre in Conservative circles. The *Yorkshire Post* itself was the bastion of Conservatism in the north of England and was run for the purpose of propagating the party cause by the prosperous banking family of Beckett. During the late 1930s, Rupert Beckett was the Chairman of the Yorkshire Conservative Newspaper Association, a public comany which administered the *Yorkshire Post* and in which the Beckett family had the largest shareholding. There had been very little friction between the Beckett family and the Editor, whom they had purloined from the *Evening Standard* in 1919; Mann had always been fully at home with the ideals of 'progressive conservatism' which the Beckett family regarded as embodying the policy and spirit of the *Yorkshire Post*. The politics of appeasement was to change all that.

Mann was possibly unique amongst the newspaper editors and proprietors of his day in that he not only refused to accept any honours offered to him by Conservative politicians – a singular gesture, since he was ostensibly the Editor of a 'Conservative' newspaper – but he also tended to eschew contact with politicians altogether. In an age when his professional colleagues staggered under the weight of honours bestowed upon them by mercenary politicians eager for their support, Mann had quietly refused two offers of a knighthood from Baldwin in 1923 and 1929. He valued his independence too much to be ensnared in the 'honours system', whereas other editors and proprietors tended to see support for particular governments as a means of advancement up the gilded ladder of the peerage. Mann's attitude towards such chivalrous elevation was reflected in his letter to Baldwin on turning down the Prime Minister's first offer in 1923: 'I feel that a journalist who receives a title, particularly if that title be suggested as a recognition of political services, may ... lessen his power to aid the cause he has at heart.'[86]

As well as resisting the aristocratic embrace that his fellow journalists found so hard to resist, Mann was also highly aware of the other danger to his editorial and political freedom and independence – being on too familiar social terms with politicians in or out of government. This he saw as the most dangerous pitfall of the journalistic profession and he became the most trenchant critic of that familiarity between journalists, proprietors and the politicians which, in his view, led to collusion between the journalist and the politician rather than a healthy adversarial relationship. With a rich irony, in the midst of such collusion on an unparalleled scale, Mann broadcast on this subject in January 1939, expressing the hope that 'most editors follow a golden rule not to be in close social relationships with Ministers of the Crown ... for as journalists they may be called upon to criticize them in their representational capacity'.[87] For an editor like Geoffrey Dawson, for instance, the lack of knighthood or ermine was adequately compensated for by his personal friendship and almost daily contact with Lord Halifax, which rendered Dawson all but incapable of criticizing a government of which Halifax was part. For Mann, his duty was to 'put what I truly believe to be the national interest first ...'[88], just as he was determined to do his own thinking, rather than let the politicians do it for him. It was his independence of thought that swiftly brought Mann into conflict with the Conservative Party and the party's journalistic adjunct in the north of England, the Yorkshire Conservative Newspaper Association.

Mann had already severely censured the government's weak response to the German invasion of the Rhineland in 1936, but his attack on the Germans over the Anschluss and his strongly worded leaders warning of the dangers inherent in Chamberlain's policy only started to attract the disapproval of the Chairman and directors of the Yorkshire Conservative Newspaper Association in March 1938. On 23 March, Rupert Beckett, the Chairman, was at last moved to write to him to say that he had read 'with growing concern day-by-day the Y.P. leaders devoted to foreign policy'. Beckett deduced from Mann's leaders that he would like to see Chamberlain 'replaced', but he warned that he did 'not wish the Y.P. involved in any plan or manoeuvring whereby such object may be furthered'.[89] Arthur Mann had a chance to express his doubts about the wisdom of the government's policies in an interview with Chamberlain himself on 27

March 1938, in which he appealed to Chamberlain for a 'declaration now that would rally the democratic world and avert war'. Chamberlain, looking upon him 'with no friendly eye', refused to respond and left Mann with the impression that he was 'obstinately and feverishly determined to do nothing that will be bold and farseeing'.[90] Major Stanley Pearson, a director of the *Yorkshire Post*, attacked Mann over the paper's policy in early March, though curiously Beckett leaped to Mann's defence. This action was to be symptomatic of Beckett's attitude over the course of the next two years, as he would chastise Mann in private but defend his editorial freedom in public. He was very willing to raise the supposed commercial implication of the paper's foreign policy with Mann and in October 1939 reminded him that the paper's financial misfortunes were regarded by 'some' as having arisen out of the paper's anti-government policy.[91] It is evident that Beckett counted himself amongst the 'some'. His pressure on Mann was to grow considerably after Munich. Beckett was a well-known figure in national Conservative circles and would have been in contact with Conservative Central Office throughout the crisis months.

Newspaper policy was thus being directed by a small body of men at the top imposing their directions, taken from the Chamberlainites, upon journalists who often dissented from these political directions. By the summer of 1938, the papers were therefore coming dangerously adrift from a majority view of their own staff, let alone public opinion. This was the burden of Mann's complaint to Chamberlain, as he tried to put his case to the Premier as 'one in touch with public opinion'.[92] Garvin and Lord Astor shared Mann's misgivings and Garvin voiced his fears on this subject to Astor in August, writing that 'the Daily Press no longer gives any true idea of the feeling of this country. There is at last – wide anxiety – a slow, eating anxiety, though silent and feeling helpless. There is not one particle of sympathy any more with Germany. Not an atom. That's dead.... the Germans could not possibly have been clumsier ... more egotistical.'[93] Astor likewise warned Sir Horace Wilson on 6 May that 'although the newspapers might have been silenced now ... there was widespread uneasiness and that this was likely to show itself soon'.[94] The same sentiment was expressed by Rex Leeper the very next day, as Cadogan records in his diary that Leeper thought 'Chamberlain is splitting the country.'[95] Even a paper such as *The Times*, which constantly seemed to present a solid front of support for Chamberlain, was in fact ridden with dissent. After a conversation with Iverach McDonald just after Munich, Barrington-Ward confessed to his diary that 'most of the office is against Dawson and me!'[96] There is no adequate measure of public opinion to test these feelings, but if both pro-Chamberlain and anti-Chamberlain sections of the press felt that their newspapers were no longer reflecting the true state of national feeling it is unlikely that the country was anywhere as united as Chamberlain fondly believed and as the press continued to suggest. Large sections of the press had now quite clearly abandoned their role of articulating public opinion in favour of a religiously partisan support for Chamberlain. The press was thus quite consciously spurning its popular mantle of the 'watchdog of government' (the historic role of Macaulay's fourth estate), and was instead seduced by the glittering prize of political power. Papers like *The Times* and the *Daily Express* became mere ciphers for Chamberlain's policies, whilst camouflaging their partisanship in the guise of a democratic 'free press'.

Disquiet also began to be expressed in Parliament about the level of government interference with the press. Major Milner MP was the first to raise the subject in March 1938. In considering a response to Major Milner's queries, Leeper considered that if the question referred to any 'private conversations with editors of newspapers who support the Government but who are perfectly free to give or withhold support as they think fit, the question seems ... to be quite improper'. On the basis that such conversations were 'quite legitimate', Leeper advised against revealing Halifax's conversations with newspaper proprietors and editors, as they had been conducted in a private and unofficial capacity. Halifax's written reply to Milner, given on 23 March, took a robustly innocent line, asserting that 'no attempt had been made by instruction, request or suggestion to prevent newspapers from expressing their considered views'.[97] The personal touch could thus go wholly undetected. This answer was, at the very least, being economical with the truth.

One official who did dissent from the growing consensus within the government in its efforts to control the press as much as possible was Sir Robert Vansittart, who found the government's increasing readiness to put pressure on the press a farcical policy. He argued that the reason Hitler protested that he did not understand the working of the British press and their apparent freedom to criticize him was because 'Sir Nevile Henderson has not been emphatic enough. Hitler can understand a raised voice.' He minuted that he was 'entirely dissatisfied' with the situation, 'as it was time that this ill-founded and futile recrimination about the Press should stop, as it will impair Anglo-German relations more than the alleged disease'. Vansittart expressed the fond hope that Henderson would be instructed to bring an end to the Anglo-German exchanges on the subject of the press by adopting 'a really rigorous attitude', concluding that 'we have reached a point where this correspondence must now cease'.[98] However, the lack of any change in the government's attitude either in London or in Berlin only provided further evidence of Vansittart's new-found impotence as the Chief Diplomatic Adviser to the government.

Chamberlain began to prepare the ground for the impending negotiations on the future of Czechoslovakia by further centralizing the dissemination of news-flow from Whitehall at Downing Street, thus completing a process that had been going on ever since he came to power. He had wanted to silence the Foreign Office News Department for some time, and at the end of July he gagged it as a prelude to silencing it altogether. The reason for his move is obscure, but it was probably the consequence of another frustrating leak from the diplomatic correspondents, this time in the *Daily Herald*. On 19 July 1938 that paper carried a story about the secret visit to Britain of Captain Wiedemann, a close friend of Hitler's, and his subsequent conversations with Halifax at the Foreign Office. In such a tense atmosphere, this was a striking revelation. Chamberlain, in particular, was greatly annoyed and wrote bitterly that the press had been 'completely irresponsible' in its willingness to reveal the substance of confidential negotiations.[99] On 24 July Leeper had to inform Orme Sargent, Assistant Under-Secretary of State at the Foreign Office, that he had been instructed 'by the Prime Minister' himself that the News Department was 'to say nothing whatever at any cost' about the impending British mission to Czechoslovakia led by Lord Runciman which was to try and mediate between the Germans and the Czech government; thus it was no longer possible 'to give any guidance' on the European situation.[100] In doing this Chamberlain had finally gagged the News Department, allowing the Downing Street Press

Office and the inner Cabinet to monopolize the dissemination of news from Whitehall and to influence the press with their very own personal touch.

Steward was soon exercising his personal touch at the German Embassy, where he assured the Germans that the 'British Government were prepared to demand the most far-reaching sacrifices from Czechoslovakia if only Germany would adhere to peaceful methods in settling the Czech question'. This was Steward's method of paving the way for Runciman's 'mediatory' mission, as 'he knew for a certainty that Chamberlain had an intense desire to start conversations on the Czech question ... and the British Government had no interest whatever in Czechoslovakia, other than the affair should not end in Germany's using force'. Furthermore, 'speaking as a specialist', he suggested that Germany's 'propaganda was extraordinarily bad', as it only succeeded in making the world 'more and more uneasy'.[101] Besides Steward's specialist techniques, German propaganda did, indeed, sometimes look extremely clumsy.

The silencing of the News Department came as a grave blow to the diplomatic correspondents, and Gordon-Lennox, Voigt and Charles Tower (of the *Yorkshire Post*) asked for, and obtained on 3 August, an immediate interview with Halifax on the subject. In a memo prepared for the Foreign Secretary, they stressed that in the 'intensive period of diplomatic activity' that clearly lay ahead it would be of 'vital importance that the British Press should be kept correctly advised of facts etc'. They praised the News Department for giving 'a coolly detached view' in its 'day-to-day guidance', but then noted that 'unfortunately of late, it had been increasingly apparent that the News Department was no longer in the same advantageous position.... correspondents have been bewildered to be told that the Department had nothing to say on some matters'. Notwithstanding Halifax's 'sympathetic interest' nothing was done – despite Gordon-Lennox's soothing reminder a few days later that the old form of contact with the News Department was 'mutually beneficial'.[102] The official from the News Department who was present at this interview, C. F. A. Warner, 'bore out everything' that the journalists claimed, according to Voigt's account, and 'did not hesitate to emphasize the contrast between the present regime and Eden's as far as the Press was concerned'.[103] The 'silent censorship' that Voigt had talked of was now complete and the diplomatic correspondents found themselves isolated and uninformed. Leeper was invited to take a holiday at the beginning of August: his 'coolly detached view' was no longer good enough.

The Times led the way for Chamberlain over the thorny problem of Czechoslovakia with a series of leaders in June and July that anticipated much of what was to happen in September. On 3 June, *The Times* leader surveyed the problem in an optimistic tone, declaring that as the 'rigid application of the principle of self-determination everywhere is obviously impractical', so 'the Sudeten Germans have an undoubted case'. It thus counselled the Czech government that 'if they could see their way to it [that is, a plebiscite] and to granting a similar choice to the other minorities, Hungarian and Polish, the rulers of Czechoslovakia might in the long run be the gainers in having an homogeneous and contented people. ... it would be a drastic remedy for the present unrest, but something drastic may be needed'. *The Times*' proposal drew a swift *démenti* from the Foreign Office: the Foreign Secretary telegraphed to Prague that *The Times* 'in no way' represented the policy of His Majesty's government on the Czechoslovakian question. As was to happen in September, however, Dr Hesse, the Press Attaché at the German Embassy, was able to report to Berlin on 9 June with a greater degree of certainty that *The Times*' leading article was in fact 'based on Chamberlain's interview with representatives of the British Press on Wednesday evening' (1 June). Dr Hesse, whose normal confidant in these matters was George Steward, was able to tell the German Foreign Ministry that despite the official *démenti* from the Foreign Office 'no part of the article has been disavowed' by Chamberlain.[104] Not for the last time, a Foreign Office denial was fatally undermined by the Press Office at Downing Street. Safe in the knowledge that it was articulating the views of Chamberlain, *The Times* persisted and declared on 14 June that 'it would really be the bankruptcy of European statesmanship if this question of the future of something over three million German Czech subjects were allowed to plunge a continent into devastating war. ... what remains to be done is to rectify that error of 1919, and to allow the Sudeten Germans peacefully to express their own views as to the future'. Even John Walter, the paper's Manager and usually silent paternal custodian, felt bound to remonstrate with Dawson over the 3 June article. He put the real burden of *The Times'* case very well when he wrote that it came as a great shock to find the paper advocating 'the cause of the wolf against the lamb, on the grounds of justice'.[105]

There was still greater consternation at this article in the Foreign Office, but once again, and this time fatally, *The Times* received conflicting signals. Leo Kennedy, who had decided in Prague as early as March that Czechoslovakia was an unviable territorial proposition, was shown a private letter from Halifax to Dawson on the subject of *The Times*' attitude apropos the Czech–German dispute. In this letter Halifax noted that he regarded the paper's advocacy of a plebiscite as being unhelpful at that time. But, according to Kennedy, Halifax added that he himself might come round 'to supporting the idea of the plebiscite himself; but asks to go slow'. Thus Halifax seemed to be tacitly condoning the attitude of *The Times* and this impression was strengthened in July when Dawson was sent the official FO memorandum on the subject of a plebiscite for the Sudetan Germans; the memo was strongly critical of such a step. Kennedy observed that 'we (T.T.) had advocated it, hence this counterblast, evidently by Vansittart'. But once again the effect of this counterblast was undermined by a 'private note by H. to G. D.', in which the former said that the Vansittart memorandum was 'not necessarily the last word'.[106] Halifax, who was seeing Dawson on almost a daily basis at this time, would have clarified any doubts that the latter might have held on the subject and it was this two-faced attitude of Halifax, running counter to the expressed Foreign Office view, that laid the seeds for the celebrated leader of 7 September which was to recommend authoritatively the complete dismemberment of Czechoslovakia. Vansittart, dejectedly surveying these effusions from *The Times* leader writers, told journalists that he thought the paper 'most irresponsible';[107] Orme Sargent complained of the paper's 'various inaccuracies' and pleaded with Leeper to keep 'the gentlemen on the right lines'.[108] Leeper, of course, was unable to help him as he was no longer at liberty to give guidance to *The Times*, or any other paper.

On the *Manchester Guardian*, despite the warnings from Vansittart, Dell and Werth and the oscillating opinions of Voigt, Crozier now too set himself on a course of accepting a Czechoslovak surrender. From May onwards, he adopted the government's desired course of omitting any information likely to inflame the international situation, which included reports on 22 May of German plans to invade Czechoslovakia and Voigt's description of the calling up of German recruits in July as 'it looked extremely threatening'.[109] Crozier's rationale for his news selection had thus been totally turned on its head – any unusual or disturbing news was now being left out of the paper! He also held over a Voigt message in which the latter referred to Czech independence as a 'vital interest' for Britain, on the ground that Voigt had previously referred to Czech independence only as 'an interest'. He further argued that 'for that reason we ought not to fight if Czech independence were attacked'.[110] This was Crozier's view exactly, and so it was not surprising that he should welcome the Runciman mission, which attempted to mediate between the Germans and the Czechs. The *Manchester Guardian* remained restrained in its leader comment, as Crozier did not want to queer Runciman's pitch. Meanwhile, the *News Chronicle* became daily more suspicious of events, and by September Layton was poised to silence these suspicions to help the Chamberlain government.

Against this enveloping silence, Vansittart now endeavoured to do something to puncture the sense of 'false optimism' that he saw engulfing the press, which he informed Crozier was 'misleading the people'. He pointed to a column in *The Times* of 11 August, and its assertion that the spirit of the Foreign Office was one of 'cautious optimism'. Vansittart 'did not know where they got that from, but it did not represent anything he knew in the F.O.'.[111] The next day, Vansittart was able to inform Charles Tower of the *Yorkshire Post* that after the diplomatic correspondents' discussion with Halifax and Warner on 3 August instructions had been given that, as far as the four newspapers described as 'responsible' were concerned, there was to be 'no attempt to withhold any information necessary for guidance'.[112] Where these instructions came from is impossible to tell, but as Vansittart indicated that the purpose of this was to prevent the four papers (*The Times*, the *Daily Telegraph*, the *Manchester Guardian* and the *Yorkshire Post*) from displaying 'a false optimism', which was his own individual diagnosis of the situation, it is reasonable to presume that Vansittart took advantage of Cadogan's August holiday to unshackle the News Department. As an example of this false optimism, on 31 August *The Times* published a communication from its diplomatic correspondent which said that 'there appears to be no reason to doubt Herr Hitler's own declaration of peaceful aims'. This false note startled Vansittart, who found it 'completely misleading', and this added to his fear that 'this unfounded optimism ... can only create a false impression among our own people'.[113]

Unknown to the press, the Cabinet was recalled for a special crisis session on 30 August, which marked the end of any real hope that the Runciman mission could persuade the Germans to accept a mere plebiscite for the Sudetens; it was now obvious that German demands for immediate secession of the Czechoslovak Sudeten lands to Germany would soon be backed up by military force. The one person in the press who was privy to this change of perception in the Cabinet, on Chamberlain's and Halifax's part in particular, was inevitably Geoffrey Dawson, acting in his capacity as what amounted to an *ex officio* member of the Cabinet. Leo Kennedy, reflecting in his journal in October on the genesis of *The Times* leader of 7 September, was quite clear that by early September 'feelings were running so high that separation without a plebiscite seemed the only solution, as Lord Runciman himself came to agree'. Kennedy also stated that *The Times* had come to know that Chamberlain was 'ready to consider secession of the Sudeten land to Germany' as a solution because the Premier had stated that he 'would not refuse to consider it' at a luncheon given by Lord Astor to American journalists in May.[114] It was Dawson himself who added the fatal lines to the leader of 7 September that it might 'be worthwhile for the Czechoslovak Government to consider whether they should exclude altogether the project, which has found favour in some quarters, of making Czechoslovakia a more homogeneous state by the secession of alien populations who are contiguous to the nation with which they are united by race'. Kennedy, who had composed most of the offending leader, was quite right to point to the fact that Halifax himself had indicated in his private letter to Dawson in July that he 'personally by no means ruled a plebiscite out as an ultimate solution' – knowing full well that a plebiscite would mean the secession of the Sudeten Germans. So here *The Times* was privy to government thinking of which the Foreign Office was unaware. On seeing the article of 7 September, J. M. Roberts of the News Department minuted that the 's. of s.* privately sent to Mr G Dawson a copy of an F.O. memo showing the objections to a plebiscite, so *The Times* can hardly plead ignorance or lack of guidance.' But he, and everyone

* The Secretary of State, i.e. Lord Halifax.

else in the office, was totally unaware that Halifax himself had fatally undermined the force of this memo by insisting that he *personally* did not rule the plebiscite out 'as an ultimate solution'.[115]

Thus *The Times* was floating a *ballon d'essai* on behalf of the inner Cabinet in Downing Street, against the considered judgement of the Foreign Office. It was probably the most famous, and certainly the most controversial leader ever to appear in a British newspaper. Furthermore, *The Times* gave the impression that secession was now a generally agreed solution within the government; there was no way for the ordinary reader to tell that the 'some quarters' of the leading article were in fact the tiny cabal of Chamberlain, Halifax and Dawson. Under its traditional rules of anonymity, *The Times* could thus give a totally misleading impression of a united government moving towards a considered conclusion, obscuring the reality of a Prime Minister and Foreign Secretary acting against the wishes of the Foreign Office, of many other permanent advisers and of the bulk of their Cabinet colleagues. The Foreign Office immediately issued a *démenti* that the article 'in no way' represented the view of His Majesty's government – exactly as it had done on 3 June. The Foreign Office officials unanimously condemned the article, led by Vansittart, who wrote to Halifax on 7 September to complain that *The Times*' leading article was 'calamitous', as his fear had always been that 'when we had got Beneš to make the necessary offers, the extremists in Germany would turn it down. *The Times* leading article definitely encourages them to turn it down and leads to a most dangerous misconception of the British attitude.' He returned to this theme later in the day after consulting his sources in Berlin, concluding that 'from our point of view the consequences of *The Times* leading article this morning have been disastrous, since it gives the impression that His Majesty's Government is on the run'.[116] The Czech government was not reassured by the Foreign Office *démenti*, and Jan Masaryk wrote to Halifax on that day to confess that the Foreign Office's belief in *The Times*' independence 'is not shared by a very large section of the population abroad'.[117] He could not have been more right.

Everyone was suspicious of the official *démenti*. Ivan Maisky, the Russian Ambassador, called on Halifax on 8 September to inform him that in his judgement 'the article had had the worst possible effect'. Halifax assured him that he 'did not in any way disagree with his judgement in this matter, and added that he would no doubt have noticed the official démenti of any Government connection'. On being pressed by Maisky to endorse this by a 'personal démenti', Halifax briskly observed that 'it was not our habit to repeat contradictions'.[118] As well he might, for what Halifax was saying in the Foreign Office and what he was telling *The Times* were two very different things – as Dawson recorded in his diary when he lunched with Halifax at the Travellers' Club on 7 September. The former wrote that 'there was a hubbub, as I fully expected, over the morning leader'. The one person, however, according to Dawson who seemed immune from this consternation was Halifax: 'not so however, the Foreign Secretary, who came and ... had a long talk' and who apparently expressed no reservations about *The Times* leader.[119] Dawson later assured Barrington-Ward that Halifax 'does not dissent privately from the suggestion that any solution, even the secession of the German minorities should be brought into free negotiation at Prague'.[120] This is very different from what Halifax was saying to Maisky or to Oliver Harvey in the Foreign Office; the latter recorded in his diary that Halifax had told 'that little defeatist Dawson' at lunch on the 7th about the 'untimely and unfortunate nature' of the article – whilst in fact he had done no such thing.[121]

So, once again, Halifax and the Foreign Office were giving out conflicting signals and it was the course of Halifax and thus Chamberlain that Dawson was following. *The Times* was in fact being used by Halifax and Chamberlain as it had been during the summer, to circumvent their own permanent officials. Chips Channon, who was closely connected to the Chamberlainites, was one who learned that Halifax had dined with Dawson on the 5th to inspire the article 'to see how the public would react, and to prepare them for the Runciman report'.[122] Whether Halifax actually invited Dawson to make the suggestion in his article can never be known, but it is evident that Dawson had correctly interpreted the minds and executed the wishes of Halifax and Chamberlain. To clear away any doubts that the Germans might have entertained about the meaning and import of the leader, George Steward must have called at the German Embassy again, for the German Chargé d'Affaires, Thedore Kordt, reported to Berlin that 'according to reliable information, *The Times* article was certainly not inspired by the Foreign Office. The possibility exists, however, that it derives from a suggestion which reached *The Times* editorial staff from the Prime Minister's entourage.'[123] The Germans certainly drew this inference from the leader article, and their review of the Czechoslovak crisis assumed that while 'it was not the Foreign Office' that had inspired the article, 'it was very probably the office of the Prime Minister at Number 10 Downing Street, which, if it did not actually approve that publication, nevertheless permitted it'.[124] Through Steward, the Germans were thus a great deal better informed about policy-making in Downing Street than the Foreign Office. Dawson and *The Times* were no longer independent in any sense of the word; the paper was placed at Chamberlain's disposal to circumvent not only the Foreign Office but large sections of his own Cabinet and party as well.

At a meeting of the inner Cabinet with the French on 18 September, the decision was indeed taken, as put forward by *The Times*, to recommend to Beneš that immediate secession of the Sudetenland was the only way forward. Although this, and the implementation of Plan Z (Chamberlain's proposal to fly to Germany to negotiate directly with Hitler) was to be kept secret, much of the press as a whole was in a state of indignation over the possibility of surrender to Germany over Czechoslovakia. The *News Chronicle* began to be increasingly shrill in its condemnation of the Nazis, as did the *Daily Herald*, and even the *Daily Telegraph* now began to register its suspicions about the impending government action. Once again, Chamberlainite suspicion was focused on Leeper and the News Department for supplying the gloomy prognostications of Chamberlain's imminent action to the press. On 16 September, Cadogan met Sam Hoare at the door of the Foreign Office, who informed him of 'complaints that Ewer, V Bartlett and V Gordon-Lennox are the darlings of the News Department'. Cadogan admitted that he 'believed this to be true: I am afraid I am becoming sick of R. Leeper. Saw him at eleven and gave him strong hint.'[125] But in case Leeper did not take the hint, Downing Street was glad to act on an alternative proposal from a press proprietor, Lord Beaverbrook.

Beaverbrook had become one of the most vociferous supporters of the inner Cabinet's policies, of which he was now very well informed by Sir Samuel Hoare. On 16 September Beaverbrook wrote to assure

Halifax that the newspapers were 'all anxious to help the Prime Minister and to help you. But they are greatly in need of guidance.' He urged the delegation of a minister 'authorized to have direct contact with the newspaper proprietors individually and personally . . . as great benefits would flow from the decision'. For Beaverbrook, the purpose of these meetings would be to 'guide the newspapers in their policy, to strike out errors and to crush rumours'.[126] To Chamberlain, he suggested that the Minister given this duty should be Hoare, asserting that the Minister he was running for the Premiership had the necessary 'balance, judgement and prestige'. Beaverbrook assured the Prime Minister that given 'guidance . . . the newspapers of the right and the left will go with you in your decisions'.[127] The speed with which this plan was put into action and the readiness of Hoare to acquiesce in it must have depended to a certain extent on the conclusions already reached by the Chamberlainites and Hoare: namely that, as Hoare had told Cadogan, the News Department of the Foreign Office was trying to sabotage government policy again and had to be counter-acted. As a result of this initiative, Hoare began to hold daily meetings with proprietors and editors, which became more frequent as the crisis worsened. The purpose of these conversations with the press was to ensure secrecy and calm, which was the desired atmosphere in which to negotiate with Hitler. Hoare also urged the press to take a conciliatory attitude in order to make Hitler more amenable to negotiation. On 17 September, the American Ambassador, Joseph Kennedy, cabled home that 'when I saw Sir Samuel Hoare he had just finished seeing the editor of the *Daily Herald* and Sir Walter Layton, Chairman of the *News Chronicle*, and he was trying to persuade them to have the paper strong on the side of peace. I judge he had been spending the last two and a half hours seeing all the newspaper men to urge peace. He felt that the *Herald* would play ball. He hoped that Layton would but was not quite sure yet.'[128] The desire for secrecy in the cause of the 'national interest' was bound to be beneficial to the Chamberlainite cause, as there would thus be no news of the Anglo-French pressure put on Prague nor of any opposition to the negotiations in Whitehall. The intense diplomatic pressure exerted on the Czechs to surrender to Germany thus went almost entirely unnoticed at the time, so it appeared to the public that the Czechs must have been willing par-ticipants in the dismemberment of their own country.

Vansittart had done his utmost to puncture the enveloping wall of silence – and this contributed to the desirability of using Hoare to counter the isolated but vocal Chief Diplomatic Adviser. The press as a whole was now in an acute dilemma: it was conscious of the government's appeal to the national interest *not* to exacerbate the situation by printing anything that would provoke Hitler, even though many journalists rightly suspected that the only thing Hitler would listen to was what Vansittart had described as a raised voice. Yet the anti-appeasers were also aware that by keeping quiet they were vastly helping Chamberlain by demonstrating that the press was willing to do this in order to reach an accommodation with Hitler. The News Department was also aware of this dilemma, and so despite vigorously enforcing the government's appeals for calm, Leeper also knew that by doing so he was hiding from Hitler the firm resolve or willingness to fight that the press should have been showing and which many journalists wanted to show. This state of affairs had prevailed throughout July and August, and it intensified in September. Thus the public was entirely unaware of how critical the situation was. The intense war scare of 22 May had been dutifully played down on 23 May; the announcement of the fact that Hitler was holding the army manoeuvres at the start of August was dutifully 'written down ... as much as possible so as not to create a sudden panic'.[129] Now, in September, the adoption of the secession option and the prospective concessions to Germany were to be shrouded in mystery.

Arthur Mann epitomized this anguished silence when he wrote to Churchill on 1 September to confess that although he had come away from an interview with Halifax feeling that the dangers of the European situation were not fully appreciated, he realized that for 'patriotic reasons we may not say so'. Despite this Mann was still certain that 'great numbers ... are of the opinion that menace has been invited by Mr Chamberlain's pursuit of appeasement without any true regard for the realities of the European situation'.[130] Mann was also now writing his leaders with one eye on his growing pile of cautionary letters from Rupert Beckett, the Chairman of the *Yorkshire Post*. *The Times* office was becoming similarly divided, but similarly silent. Colin Coote, a leader writer, was very disappointed at the paper's attitude and told Harold Nicolson that he was 'appalled by the lack of responsible guidance in PHS. Nobody seemed to realize the amount of damage which such an article [on the 7th] would cause.'[131]

On the *Manchester Guardian*, Crozier stuck faithfully to supporting Chamberlain's efforts for peace amongst a rising chorus of objections from his own correspondents. Crozier's main aim was to help Chamberlain's efforts in any way that he could, so he rejected a message from Werth in Paris on the grounds that as it had purported to show that the French were divided on the issue of the immediate secession of the Sudetenland it would be seen as 'downright and discouraging [*sic*] . . . and would have looked very bad on the day of Chamberlain's departure' for Berchtesgaden on the 16th for his first meeting with Hitler.[132] Crozier rejected Voigt's despatch for publication on the eve of Chamberlain's first flight to Germany as he did not want to do anything that would seem 'to crab his visit in advance'.[133] Garvin was also conscious of writing under great restraint, which needed 'iron control': he also warned Astor that due to the way the negotiations over the months had been conducted the 'hideous dilemma' was 'far worse than is yet suspected outside of few'. Much of what he warned Astor about could not be said or 'hinted at in print'.[134] The editors and proprietors were thus freely engaging in a conspiracy of silence based on a policy of self-censorship – a policy in which they were being daily encouraged by Sir Samuel Hoare.

However, this state of suspended animation changed on 20 September when it became obvious that something more than a mere plebiscite was being contemplated, and *The Times* admitted of the secession plans now put forward by Chamberlain that 'the general character of the terms submitted to the Czechoslovak Government could not, in the nature of things, be expected to make a strong prima facie appeal to them'. This was a hollow understatement that even moved one of Harold Nicolson's breakfast guests that morning to be sick in the lavatory. Nicolson described this leader, to Barrington-Ward's face, as 'a masterpiece of unctuous ambiguity', and the press now started to break ranks and support the Czech cause.[135] As Chamberlain flew off for his second meeting with Hitler at Godesberg on the 22nd, the press was hardening against what were now seen as unjust and unreasonable German demands. The *Daily Telegraph* in particular, owing to Camrose's doubts and Gordon-Lennox's convictions, now became openly critical of the government's stance. Churchill was writing in the *Daily Telegraph* to stiffen the British and Czech resolve, and on 15 September he had assured his readers that inside Czechoslovakia there was 'an absolute determination to fight for life and freedom'. As a response to this growing chorus of disapproval, Halifax was moved to send Chamberlain at Godesberg a telegram on the 23rd warning him that 'public opinion as expressed in Press and elsewhere' was 'mistrustful of our plan but prepared perhaps to accept it with reluctance as alternative to war. Great mass of public opinion seems to be hardening in sense of feeling that we have gone to limit of concession and that it is up to the Chancellor [Hitler] to make some contribution.'[136]

However, Chamberlain's response to this revolt in public opinion, which was clearly indicated in the press, was not to bow to it but to quell it. Hoare was once more detached to see 'the big Press men'. In his own notes for these interviews, Hoare recorded that his job was made necessary by the fact that the 'Duff party'* in Cabinet had been 'very incensed about . . . Neville's weakness in conversations. – Stoked up by F.O. Press Department.' It was Hoare's belief that he was seeing the proprietors himself as 'a result of the F.O. Press Department'; it was the inner Cabinet's belief that opposition to the capitulation to Hitler's terms now rested entirely in the Foreign Office News Department, and it was only that department's influence that was making the press 'revolt'. The fact that the Chamberlainites could attribute opposition to their plan solely to the machinations of an emasculated Foreign Office News Department demonstrates how entranced they had become by the Whitehall games of news control. They could no longer even entertain the idea that there might be real public opposition to their plans; they were trapped in a twilight world of self-delusion that was largely of their own creation. Increasingly, Chamberlain and the inner Cabinet were becoming victims of their own tight control of news; any criticism was now freely attributed not to genuine conviction but to bureaucratic in-fighting. According to his notes, Hoare was seeing Camrose, 'snow white and the seven dwarfs [Southwood] and Max . . .' as well as Sir Walter Layton.[137] Rothermere had been as shocked as anyone else by the intemperance of Hitler's demands at Godesberg for the prompt and complete

---

*Alfred Duff Cooper, later 1st Viscount Norwich, was First Lord of the Admiralty in Chamberlain's Cabinet and the Cabinet's most consistent critic of appeasement. He was later to resign over the Munich agreement.

secession of the Sudeten land to Germany, and had telegraphed to Churchill that he had been 'staggered by Germany's further demands after what looked like a settlement'.[138] But the *Daily Mail* nonetheless came round to complete support for Chamberlain's efforts.

However, the most spectacular success that Hoare achieved in his efforts with the press was with Sir Walter Layton, whom he saw on the 17th and again three times between 19 and 23 September. All through this period, as his biographer remarked, Layton 'behaved more in his old role of Government adviser than as a newspaper man'.[139] Layton's intervention at the *News Chronicle* was the cause of much bitterness, which boiled over in later years. The *News Chronicle* had been outspoken in its denunciation of Hitler's terms up to 27 September, after which date Layton intervened. On the 28th he held over a leaflet that had been brought back from Prague by Jonathan Griffin, purporting to show Germany's timetable for the conquest of Europe (including Czechoslovakia in autumn 1938), which had been issued by Henlein, the leader of the Sudeten Germans. Layton prevented publication and instead sent it to the Prime Minister. Although he promised the *News Chronicle* staff to publish it in twenty-four hours' time, he did not in fact do so until March 1939. For this, he was privately thanked by Hoare. Gerald Barry recalled that Layton had 'caused a much modified leader to be written' which was to replace a more anti-Chamberlain one written by him: all done without the editor's knowledge. On the day that Chamberlain returned from his third and final meeting with Hitler at Munich on 30 September, William Forrest had written an article entitled 'From Madrid to Munich', outlining the march of Hitler's conquests – but this was stopped by Layton when it was 'set up in type' and 'hung for many subsequent weeks in the features department'. Layton did this on the grounds that as the Prime Minister 'had received a great national welcome, we must be careful etc'. On the night that the news of the Munich agreement itself came in, the *News Chronicle* also received a message from Vernon Bartlett, who had been specially sent out to cover developments in Prague. This message described the Munich agreement as 'an almost complete capitulation to Hitler'. Layton, though, questioned the accuracy of this report and requested Barry 'to whittle it down' until the latter suggested that it would 'lose all its validity', at which point it was agreed that rather than 'garble' it

completely it would be best to leave the story out of the paper altogether. Barry also criticized the leader of that morning which had
been composed under the direction of Layton; this leader talked of
'profound thankfulness' and ended by saying that the agreement had
saved 'great numbers of innocent Czechs from war'.[140]

Barry was not the only editor who found the editorial process
interrupted at this juncture. Arthur Mann also found himself under
great pressure to support the Munich agreement, which he personally
bitterly opposed. Beckett sent him a telegram from London, where
he was in touch with 'Conservative opinion', instructing him that
Chamberlain's policy was one of 'success so far' and the 'Munich
agreement must now govern the policy of this country and it is our
duty loyally to support this policy and to cease personal criticisms
which alienate Conservative opinion and with which I do not agree.'[141]
Mann bowed to Beckett's demands at this point and, whilst dutifully
praising Chamberlain's efforts, reserved his judgement by stating that
'we have yet to fathom all the consequences'.[142] The *Daily Herald* was
also supportive of Chamberlain's efforts, in particular his flights to
talk to Hitler. How much of this attitude was due to the cumulative
effect of Southwood's discussions with Halifax and Hoare is impossible to tell, but it was far removed from the tenor of that paper's
reporting up to 1938. The Editor later testified how he had been forced
to moderate his anti-Chamberlain views, and he might have echoed
Gerald Barry's statement that his 'recollection and that of my colleagues [on the *News Chronicle*] is that during the critical days of that
humiliating period we were obliged to hold in our horses and, if I mix
metaphors – back-pedal'.[143]

However, if the government and Hoare were very successful in
squaring those newspapers which might have been expected to oppose
the Munich agreement, they were equally successful in securing the
unrestrained adulation of the rest of the press. Lord Rothermere, who
had been so shocked at the Godesberg terms of the 26th, telegraphed
to Chamberlain on 1 October to inform the Premier that 'you are
wonderful'.[144] The *Daily Mail* duly gushed, on the same day, that the
Premier had returned from Munich 'with peace at the summit of his
valiant endeavours'. However, the most ecstatic and optimistic paper
was the *Daily Express* as Beaverbrook, through his close liaison with
Hoare, put his papers totally at the service of the government. Hoare

informed him of the stiffening of resistance from Duff Cooper and some of his colleagues in the Cabinet meeting on the 25th and urged Beaverbrook to disregard their criticisms and to 'stick at present to supporting the P.M. as about the only hope of peace'.[145] On 1 September 1938, Beaverbrook's *Daily Express* first printed the headline 'There Will Be No European War', and throughout September the paper struck a very pro-Chamberlain and optimistic note. In celebration of Munich on 30 September, the same paper printed its notorious streamer 'Britain will not be involved in a European war this year or next year either' and it repeated the former phrase in the ensuing days, hailing the Munich agreement as an outright success. In a short memorandum prepared by Beaverbrook at a later date he confessed that the 'newspaper was invited by the Government itself to make these declarations, the purpose being to influence opinion favourably so that there might be delay and time for consideration'.[146] Beaverbrook recorded that his papers completely 'supported the Government throughout the months of crisis'.

This optimism and sense of vindication was prepared with the co-operation of Hoare and Downing Street and was the high point of the dubious collaboration between the Home Secretary and Beaverbrook, who soon after began to finance Hoare's political career. The attitude expressed in the *Daily Express* was one that was designed to unite the nation behind Chamberlain in the cause of peace as much as it was designed to create as optimistic an atmosphere as possible in which Chamberlain's talks could proceed. The Foreign Office News Department noted that the optimistic stories printed in the *Daily Express* were in fact going 'considerably further than we have been authorized to go'. Peake commented on the *Daily Express*'s 'There Will Be No European War' headline on 5 October that it bore 'all the marks of official inspiration from Number 10', and contrasted the apparent willingness of the 'P.M.'s secretariat' to talk to certain papers about 'the future policy of H.M. Government' through their own 'special channels of communication with the Press' with the Foreign Office News Department, which had 'not had over much material to use'. A senior official commented on Peake's minute, 'What a pathetic state of affairs.'[147]

For the Foreign Office it was indeed a 'pathetic state of affairs', as Downing Street, through Halifax, Steward and no doubt Ball, had managed not only to exaggerate vastly the positive aspects of Munich and emphasize Hitler's commitment to peace in papers like the *Daily Express*, but also to persuade the proprietors of the *Daily Herald*, the *News Chronicle* and the *Yorkshire Post* to still their criticism and praise Chamberlain's achievements – against the wishes of all their editors and staff. The situation was even repeated on *The Times*, as Barrington-Ward and Dawson increasingly found themselves isolated in their extreme support for Chamberlain and Munich. The Foreign Office had failed in its last gambit of 26 September, when, in view of the more extreme demands made by Hitler at Godesberg and announced to the Cabinet on the 25th, Halifax had sanctioned the issuing of a communiqué drafted by Leeper on the 26th stating that the Russians were ready to stand beside the French and the British in defence of Czechoslovakia – thus sending the first clear signal of intent to Germany that a military alliance would come into being against her if she did invade Czechoslovakia. Once again, two distinct policies were now being disseminated. Hoare wrote later with masterful under-statement that this communiqué caused 'some trouble in Downing Street', and was one of the factors that persuaded him to intensify his contacts with the press proprietors after the Godesberg meeting.[148] *The Times*, however, in its last vital contribution to the Munich agreement, did not publish this Leeper communiqué, so it was never authoritatively advertised around Europe, thus nullifying its effectiveness as a deterrent to Hitler. Leeper's act of the 26th was seen as virtually treasonable by Downing Street and after Munich he was telephoned by Sir Horace Wilson 'to say that some of the Cabinet thought him disloyal and a posting abroad would be best'.[149] If the first casualty of Munich was Czechoslovakia, the second was the News Department of the Foreign Office, and the editorial freedom of the press.

In the wake of Munich, Garvin was forced to watch in impotent rage as the rest of the press acquiesced in Chamberlain's plan and celebrated his statesmanship. In his notebook, however, he cynically assessed the 'hysterical raptures for Chamberlain' as 'the saviour of peace ... a debauch of delusion about things and consequences ...' and saw the government attitude towards the press as a 'smokescreen of hypocrisy'. Writing of the press reaction to Munich of 1 October he commented that 'Fleet Street might have been bombed this Saturday' and acknowledged that 'we have written under the strictest reserve'. That this was true was seen in his own public comment on Munich in the *Observer* of 2 October – in which he expressed none of his true feelings on the subject owing to his considerations for the national interest, which to his mind dictated that 'comment on many aspects must be rigorously postponed'.[150] As Lord Astor recognized, Garvin's obfuscations in this article were at least more realistic than the 'inspired dope in the *Sunday Times*'.[151]

There is no doubt that by reading the press comment on Munich one would have gained the impression that, as W. W. Hadley later claimed, 'the free press of this country has never been nearer to complete unity than in the chorus of praise and thanksgiving which followed ... Munich'.[152] This has, indeed, always been one of the major justifications for the Munich agreement in the eyes of the Chamberlainites, that it had the overwhelming support of the British public, as demonstrated by the press. But what Chamberlain, through his consistent and secret cultivation of the personal touch with the press, managed to achieve was to mask the real divisions that lay at the heart of government and society. Through the government's insistent courting of the proprietors, editors and political journalists, it managed to achieve an appearance of national unity – whereas in fact on most papers this appearance was achieved against the wishes and views of most of the staff. It is significant that the only paper which positively denounced the Munich agreement, *Reynolds News* (the paper of the Co-operative Movement) was the one paper that had absolutely no contact with the government – so was truly 'free' to come to its own editorial decisions.

3

Munich to War: October 1938 to September 1939

In the immediate aftermath of Munich Chamberlain took advantage of his apparently impregnable position as the national saviour to eliminate finally the Foreign Office News Department as a source of anti-appeasement in Whitehall. The primary object of his wrath was Rex Leeper, not only for his inopportune communiqué of 26 September, but also for his supposed record of betrayal and dissent stretching back to Lord Halifax's visit to Berlin in November 1937. Sir Horace Wilson, who had rung Leeper up after Munich to tell him that some members of the Cabinet thought him to be disloyal,* saw Cadogan about Leeper on 4 October, after which Cadogan recorded that 'R. Leeper must, I fear, go.'[1] Cadogan had already lost confidence in Leeper, and in November he had to inform Halifax that 'since Anthony's departure ... I have had constant complaints from Number 10 on the handling of the Press by our News Department. Blame has been particularly attached to Leeper....'[2] So Leeper was now taken away from the daily task of dealing with the press correspondents in the News Department and put in charge of the more amorphous and pressing task of propaganda. He was further removed from any position of interference in Downing Street's policies by his posting

* For Leeper's own account of what Wilson said to him, see *Halifax: The Life of Lord Halifax* by the Earl of Birkenhead (Hamish Hamilton, London, 1965), pp. 424–5.

abroad in the early summer of 1939 to Bucharest. Not content with removing Leeper, the creation of a shadow Ministry of Information in the summer of 1939 gave Downing Street an opportunity to super-sede the Foreign Office News Department and Vansittart's recently formed Committee on overseas propaganda by the creation of the Foreign Publicity Bureau (FPB), which was to be run from the Foreign Office by Lord Perth in his capacity as Director-General Designate of the embryonic Ministry of Information. The FPB cut into the power of the News Department and largely usurped the more recent work of Leeper and Vansittart in the field of foreign propaganda, and was viewed by the Foreign Office as an unjustified encroachment on its own areas of excellence. The anti-appeasers in the office were especially suspicious of the FPB, and saw it as a 'ramp of Sam Hoare and Horace Wilson to further the control of Downing Street over foreign policy'. Harvey, for one, thought that the treatment of Leeper was 'dis-graceful'.[3]

The removal of Leeper from the News Department and the partial emasculation of that department represented Chamberlain's final and triumphant effort to make Downing Street the sole distributor of news from Whitehall. The News Department had always been the most prominent Whitehall obstacle to Chamberlain's increasingly cen-tralized control of government and in Sir Samuel Hoare's words, 'he was so sure that his plan was right ... that his singleness of urgent purpose made him impatient of obstacles and indifferent to incidental risks'.[4] George Steward duly explained the background to the Prime Minister's actions in great detail to Dr Hesse at the German Embassy, who was told that during the recent crisis the Prime Minister had not 'received assistance or support of any kind from the Foreign Office, who on the contrary had strived ... to sabotage his plans and commit Great Britain to warlike actions against Germany', due to the 'extremely bitter feelings against Germany that existed in the Foreign Office'. Steward confirmed what Hesse had already deduced, that Chamberlain had thus been circumventing the Foreign Office by various means, so the final satisfactory outcome at Munich was 'exclusively due to Chamberlain'. Steward also informed Dr Hesse that Chamberlain had achieved this only by 'ignoring the provisions of the British Constitution and customary Cabinet usage',[5] which may have been added to convince Hitler that Chamberlain was indeed keen to discard the tiresome democratic practices that the Führer so vocally objected to as a barrier to peace.

As it turned out, this was to be the last of George Steward's communications with Dr Hesse, as an MI5 source inside the German Embassy alerted the Foreign Office to the liaison between Hesse and Steward in November. Cadogan, confronted with this information, was at first reluctant to inform Halifax for fear that it might prompt his resignation, but eventually he did so. Halifax raised the matter with Chamberlain on 29 November and the latter apparently appeared 'aghast at the news'. Halifax was convinced that Steward had been acting independently but Cadogan correctly suspected that Steward was acting on behalf of Sir Joseph Ball, thus inferring that Chamberlain had lied about the matter to his own Foreign Secretary. As Chamberlain had already employed the same tactic over Sir Joseph Ball's Lobby briefing on 9 February with Eden, it is probable that Cadogan's suspicions were correct. Indeed, the fact that Steward remained at his post in Downing Street until May 1940 suggests that he had not done anything untoward in Chamberlain's eyes. Steward's interpretation of the Prime Ministerial mind had, as we have seen, always been very accurate and prescient; he had always been a very reliable guide to the Germans about what represented Chamberlain's private views in the British press. In this capacity, Steward's liaison with the German Embassy had been invaluable to Chamberlain, as it had allowed him to prepare the ground for his appeasement policies by inspiring press articles or editorials and to have them correctly and accurately described as such to the Germans through Steward – whilst at the same time Chamberlain himself remained strictly anonymous as the source. However, after this episode it was seen as prudent to stop Steward's connection and Cadogan's private wish that his action might 'put a brake on them all' was apparently fulfilled, since Steward does not appear in the volumes of the German foreign policy documents after November 1938.[6] The curtailment of Steward's furtive relationship with the German Embassy could be viewed as a partial compensation to the anti-appeasers for the removal of Leeper, as Chamberlain no longer had anyone who could interpret the nuances of the British press to the Germans. But Steward nonetheless stayed at Downing Street and, cheered no doubt by Leeper's removal, the Press Office in fact became more blatant and manipulative in its handling of the press during the ensuing months.

If Chamberlain was somewhat more than discreet about his conduct of the Downing Street Press Office to his own ministers and civil servants, he was even more guarded with Parliament and the public in his account of the government's contacts with the press leading up to Munich. Naturally, due to the extensive contacts between Halifax, Hoare and the press proprietors and editors in the month before Munich, rumours had begun to circulate that the government had brought pressure to bear upon the press to write about foreign affairs in a manner favourable to the government's policy objectives in that field. Indeed, as we have seen, this matter had already been the subject of a parliamentary question in March 1938. On 23 November, the question cropped up again in Parliament as an MP asked Chamberlain 'to what extent recent advice has been officially tended by members of the Government towards owners of newspapers as to what attitude they should take up on the subject of foreign policy'. Chamberlain himself answered this question to the effect that no such advice had been tendered. The MP gave the Prime Minister a chance to rephrase his answer by asking him if the advice had been given 'unofficially', but Chamberlain persisted with his statement to the effect that 'no such advice had been tendered ... neither officially or unofficially'.[7] If Chamberlain had merely been economical with the truth in March, he was now telling an outright lie.

Indeed, this was symptomatic of an increasingly cavalier attitude that the Premier now showed towards the press as, flushed by his success at Munich, he came to regard any criticism as tantamount to treason and went to increasingly exaggerated lengths to guard against it. Many journalists and politicians were moved to voice their concern at the obvious pusillanimity of the press in the face of Chamberlain's censorious treatment of them. Eden, for instance, had a chance to contrast the American press with the British papers during his visit to the United States in December and remarked that 'he was much struck by the greater freedom and frankness of the press about Germany and Italy as compared with our damped-down organs'.[8]

Arthur Mann, who had been forced to stifle his denunciation of Munich by Rupert Beckett, shared Eden's concern about the damped-down organs, and his correspondence with Beckett became gradually more acrimonious in the months after Munich as he continued to defy

Beckett's instructions and to revert to occasional but strongly worded attacks on Chamberlain and his foreign policy. Mann privately denounced those who would have him be silent on account of the sentiment that the *Yorkshire Post*, by fomenting distrust of the Chamberlain government, was 'increasing disunity and therefore although we may be right in the view we have taken, we should maintain silence as to our doubts and fears'. For Mann, this was a dishonest policy and he focused his vitriol on Chamberlain himself, whom he saw as putting the 'making of political capital for the party over the greater national interest.... the situation would never have become so grave but for blindness as to Chamberlain's incapacity due to party loyalty. And by the same token those who would spread the truth and restore sanity are now asked to be silent!'[9]

Evidence of the inner Cabinet's involvement in the efforts to silence Mann through the medium of the Yorkshire Conservative Newspaper Association came in late December when Mann learned that Sir Samuel Hoare had persuaded one of the directors of the paper, Sir Stanley Jackson, to protest to him about the attitude of the paper towards Chamberlain's foreign policy. For Mann, this offered further proof to the 'scores of proofs' that 'an effective censorship may operate through subtler channels – for instance, through social contacts between newspaper proprietors and persons highly placed in Government circles'.[10] In the *Yorkshire Post* itself on 5 December, Mann compared this subtler form of censorship to the more usual 'prohibitions' imposed in other countries. He warned that the exercise of this kind of censorship whereby local 'expression of opinion is muzzled by orders received from London ... not to deviate from the strict party line' meant that the channels through which public opinion could express itself were being closed. For journalists to be able to report 'what people are saying and thinking in the districts ... newspapers must be able to publish their findings without fear or favour' and it was this freedom that Mann now saw as being denied. Mann was, however, alone in being prepared to endure a debilitating and acrimonious correspondence with his Chairman and directors in order to expound this point of view. In the new year this pressure began to tell as he evinced signs of physical weakness arising out of the stress that he was now under. Of the other papers, either the editors were happy to collude with the government in this silent censorship out of political or business expediency or the journalists were oppressed by the proprietor or editors-in-chief, as happened on the *News Chronicle*. As a result, what misgivings were felt about the situation were left to Mann to express in comparative obscurity.

On the other hand, the degree of control that Chamberlain and the inner Cabinet found themselves able to exercise over the press merely seemed to whet their appetite for greater control over the damped-down organs. Chamberlain in particular was growing increasingly intolerant of criticism and increasingly partial to praise, especially when he could read it in a newspaper. This desire for printed adulation was barely satisfied by the continually fawning attitude of certain sections of the press which competed to outdo each other in their chorus of acclaim. Hadley of the *Sunday Times* wrote to Chamberlain to tell him that the *Daily Sketch*, his daily sister newspaper, had offered its readers a photograph of Mr and Mrs Chamberlain at Downing Street after Munich and that the paper had already received 90,000 applications – 'they had never known anything like it'.[11] Dawson, Beaverbrook and Rothermere were all lavish in their private and printed praise of Chamberlain. Privately, the Premier now regarded any criticism as 'foolish' and confided to his sister that the 'only distress that criticism or obstruction can cause me is if it prevents my purpose'.[12] Fortified, however, by this volume of praise he vowed not to 'sit and bask in this popularity while it lasted'[13] but to press on with his wider objective of securing the general settlement with Germany and Italy of which the Munich agreement was only a part. Having reached an agreement with Germany it was thus with this purpose in mind that he set off for Rome in January 1939.

In his hardening hostility to criticism, Chamberlain had been much taken aback to read of boos in the streets of Paris during the course of his visit to that city in November to see Premier Daladier in the wake of Munich. Harvey, who accompanied Chamberlain on this visit, recorded how the PM was 'annoyed with the papers' for reporting 'the boos in the street',[14] and this unfortunate occurrence made Chamberlain determined to secure a more flattering press for his journey to Italy that he was to undertake with Lord Halifax to meet Mussolini in January 1939. It was with this object in mind that the Press Office in Downing Street and the less antagonistic Leeper-less News Department at the Foreign Office orchestrated the most complete setpiece of news manipulation yet attempted by a British government. Yet it can also be seen as the logical outcome of the accumulated skills and techniques that both the Foreign Office and Downing Street had acquired during the 1930s and especially under Chamberlain's guidance as Prime Minister. With the confidence bred of an outstanding record of success, the government now plotted to ensure that Chamberlain's meeting with Mussolini was the success that the Prime Minister required it to be.

The immediate cause of the detailed planning that was to go into the Italian visit was the request of Vernon Bartlett to travel as a special correspondent with the Prime Minister's party. Since Bartlett's celebrated victory at the Bridgwater by-election on an anti-Munich platform, he had become a torch-bearer for the anti-Chamberlainites. His daily reports in the *News Chronicle* would obviously be somewhat less than sympathetic to the visit and yet the News Department realized that if he were to be refused admission by the Italians the result 'might be unfortunate' owing to his being a Member of Parliament and because he was 'popular among his fellow journalists'. Furthermore, the News Department was aware that the 'News Chronicle would not be ill-pleased if the Italian Government declined to allow him into Italy . . . as a refusal on the part of the Italian authorities to allow him in could with little difficulty be worked up into a press campaign here'. Since Layton's interventions in September, the *News Chronicle* had found its most abusive tone again and had in particular aroused German feelings with a series of articles by H. G. Wells early in January 1939 during the course of which he had described the Nazi leadership as 'certifiable lunatics'. During the course of a bitter interview with the German Ambassador, Herbert von Dirksen, over these articles Halifax admitted that they constituted 'the most shocking insult to the Führer', whilst attempting to mitigate this insult by assuring the unconvinced Ambassador that such articles 'were primarily written for reasons connected with domestic politics in order to attack the Government'.[15] With the *News Chronicle* in this sort of mood, there was obviously just as great a risk in letting Vernon Bartlett go to Italy as there was in risking an Italian bar to his entry. This also applied to Norman Ewer of the *Daily Herald*, who was likewise vulnerable to refusal of entry by the Italians.

Lord Perth, the British Ambassador in Rome (prior to his appointment as Director-General designate of the nascent Ministry of Information), thus took the matter up with the Italian Foreign Minister, Count Ciano, and gained an assurance that the 'definite ban of Bartlett in Italy would be lifted', thus avoiding a press campaign in Britain over a refusal to admit him. This done, Charles Peake, Leeper's successor as Head of the News Department, turned his mind to finding the best way in which such recalcitrant correspondents as Bartlett and Ewer could be controlled while in Rome. It was clear to him that 'we must make every effort to get the British Press to accept our point of view during these conversations and do all we can to prevent the special correspondents sending messages of which we do not approve'. Whilst admitting privately that this would be 'no easy task since some of them are very anti-Italian', Peake set out to employ methods similar to those which Leeper had often used to tune the press to his liking – except on this occasion he sought and could rely on the co-operation of not only the Press Office at Downing Street but the Ministry of Popular Culture in Rome itself. His desire was to accommodate all the British correspondents at the same hotel, where they would be under his own supervision. This is what Leeper had managed to do successfully in Geneva and elsewhere and it was this which had first alerted Dell to the incestuous nature of Leeper's relationship with the diplomatic correspondents. Furthermore, Peake sought the help of the Italians to show the correspondents 'some attention' as it was clear that if the frantically busy journalists could be returned to the hotels by the early evening 'exhausted by a round of sight-seeing under official auspices' their weary minds would be likely to be 'more receptive' to what he had to say and 'less eager to plumb undesirable sources of information'. Peake presented an unattractive alternative of bored correspondents 'lounging about the hotel waiting for news all day which would induce a restless and critical state of mind'. The solution was to ask the Italians to arrange for a little 'programme of entertainment which would last for 24 hours'. Sir Alexander Cadogan thought that Peake's ideas on the subject were 'very sound' and instructed him to put them into effect. On 15 December, Peake was able to report that he had aroused great enthusiasm at Downing Street for his proposals and that 'Mr. Steward ... was anxious to elaborate the scheme which I myself proposed in my minute.' The elaborations on the original scheme now included a suggestion that more 'descriptive writers' should be sent as well as the diplomatic correspondents, to 'give good publicity' to the material that would be provided by the Ministry for Popular Culture. Ward-Price of the *Daily Mail* was given as an example of a 'descriptive writer'. Cadogan and S. H. Wilson of the British Embassy in Rome were both agreed that the scheme of Peake and Steward might be 'likely to produce results the Prime Minister had in mind'. This first formal co-operation between the News Department and the Press Office at Downing Street was to demonstrate how formidable an instrument for the control of the press such a united front could provide.

Cadogan took up Peake's and Steward's proposals and asked Lord Perth in Rome to approach the Ministry of Popular Culture to offer the British journalists 'some attention ... and some hospitality' to satisfy the political appetite of those journalists who might otherwise be 'tempted to indulge in speculation and imaginative writing which ... may do harm to Anglo-Italian relations'. Cadogan also pledged that if such a promise of help was extracted from the Italians, 'well-known descriptive writers' could be sent who would be relied upon to dwell on the 'social and spectacular aspects of the visit' and who would serve to 'put the conversations in the second place from the publicity point of view which would be all to the good'.[16] Not surprisingly, Percy Lorraine of the British Embassy in Rome was sure that the Italian government would be delighted to show such attention and hospitality if it could be directed to this end. Lorraine outlined a programme of events which included an invitation to the initial formal reception of the British visitors at the Palazzo Venezia, a visit to the opera, a visit to two exhibitions (a scientific exhibition and the second reclamation exhibition of the Pontine Marshes), 'a visit to recent excavations could be arranged ... and a look at the work going on for the exhibition of 1942'. Amidst this enthusiasm for exhibitions, Lorraine inserted a note of warning that if the programme was 'too heavy' or took up 'too much time' the press representatives 'will say that they are being captured and kept from their sleuth work'. To guard against any such sentiments, the Ministry of Popular Culture thus laid on cars for the correspondents as 'guests of the Italian Government'. A paper such as the *Yorkshire Post*, which might have proved unsympathetic to the visit, was accorded 'most favoured nation treatment' in respect of the issue of official news by Charles Peake, and the paper's special correspondent for the visit, John Dundas, a cousin of Lord Halifax, was allowed to stay at a private address whilst the other correspondents had to stay at the Hotel Flora.[17]

With such attention to detail and with the co-operation of the Italians, the visit was portrayed as a great popular triumph for Chamberlain. The press did indeed write enthusiastically about the large crowds and popular acclaim for the British Prime Minister and the Italians also received a great deal of coverage for their various exhibitions. There was no doubt that, in terms of popularity at home in Britain, the visit was a welcome success for Chamberlain, whose star had begun to wane since his triumph in September. Iverach McDonald, *The Times* correspondent assigned to the Italian trip, has admitted that 'So many sideshows were there to distract our attention.' On his return, a friend, having read his daily despatches to London, could only remark, 'I didn't see anything in *The Times* that looked as if it had been written by you.'[18]

Geoffrey Dawson, who was privy to the preparations and immediate results of the Italian visit, went to see Halifax about the trip immediately before his departure. The result was a glowing leader in *The Times* on the virtues and expectations of the visit on the day of the party's departure. It is indicative of the close relationship that now existed between Chamberlain, Halifax and Dawson that the latter was called to see Chamberlain about the visit the day after his return. In contrast to Chamberlain's visit to France in November, the Prime Minister was obviously exhilarated by the results of his Italian trip and the very positive publicity for both him personally and Mussolini that had accrued from it. Dawson recorded of his interview with him on the 15th that he looked 'amazingly fit, bronzed and cheerful – said that he had done all that he had set out to do ... and had had a wonderful popular reception wherever he went'.[19] Dawson suggested to Chamberlain that the latter had 'evidently impressed his personality on the Italian people', to which Chamberlain agreed and related how Mussolini 'himself grew steadily more friendly during the visit and the people clapped Halifax and me wherever we went'.[20] It is remarkable how susceptible Chamberlain was to the orchestrated demonstrations favoured by the dictators.

Whilst Chamberlain, with the new-found support of the News Department at the Foreign Office, strove to enhance the European success of his visit, the pro-Chamberlain press continued to moderate its comment on foreign affairs and to maintain the high degree of self-restraint and self-censorship that it had been practising since the summer. The Foreign Office News Department kept its customary eye on the press for anything that might offend the Germans or Italians, and the case of the H. G. Wells articles in the *News Chronicle* which drew complaints from Berlin saw another attempt to induce Layton to moderate his paper's attacks on Hitler. Vansittart was deputed to interview Layton on this occasion, but by the time this could be arranged the Chief Diplomatic Adviser's view was that the H. G. Wells articles were 'ancient history and could be forgotten'.[21]

At the same time, the most pro-Chamberlain papers assiduously continued to help the government in any way possible. Rothermere was particularly sensitive to German complaints about the British press – possibly because it added so much to his self-esteem as a 'press baron'. On 3 October, he was cabling to Halifax that 'in official circles in Berlin it is freely stated that the London newspapers ... with their cartoons and comments will provoke war between Britain and Germany'. He asked Halifax, 'Can nothing be done?', to which the Foreign Secretary calmly replied that he had often warned the press of the danger of the 'liberty of the press developing into licence'.[22] Rothermere exercised a rigorous control over his own papers, and the *Daily Mail* was trumpeting Chamberlain and refusing to publish any condemnation of the Fascist powers even as its circulation started to fall sharply. Beaverbrook was particularly eager to act as a guardian of the government's political interests and was quick to act if there was anything in the *Daily Express* that might offend the sensibilities of any foreign governments that Halifax and Chamberlain were eager to please. Knowing that Sir Samuel Hoare was Beaverbrook's main contact with the government, Halifax invited Hoare in October to ask Beaverbrook to desist from publishing a series of articles on the 'Disposal of colonies in Africa' after a request to do so had been put to him by the Portuguese Ambassador. Halifax was afraid that a scheme would be propounded in the *Daily Express* for the amalgamation of Portuguese, French and Belgian colonial possessions in Central Africa into a kind of commercial company, the majority of whose shares would be in the hands of Germany. This would obviously distress Britain's three principal and oldest allies, namely France, Belgium and Portugal. Hoare duly reported that he had seen Beaverbrook and had told him that the government did not want to 'irritate the Portuguese at the moment'. Beaverbrook denied that he was 'contemplating any immediate campaign on the subject', but the word of warning was prescient for he did admit that he was strongly in favour of the colonial scheme that Halifax had been afraid of.[23] In the event, no such series of articles was subsequently published in the *Daily Express*.

In November 1938, Halifax wrote directly to Beaverbrook to request him to keep any 'past misdemeanours of King Carol of Roumania' out of his paper in view of that monarch's impending visit to Britain, because Halifax was anxious to do all that he could to 'ensure that this visit to our King of the Monarch of a friendly country should not be marred by raking up the past or by any reflections on the private life of the King's guest'. Beaverbrook promptly replied to assure Halifax that King Carol would have 'absolute immunity in my newspapers' and went on to make the more sweeping declaration that his newspapers would do anything to help Halifax in his 'difficult negotiations with the Central European countries, or indeed, in any direction. Besides, I am in agreement with your policy, and can give you the strongest support.'[24]

With this ringing affirmation of support to guide him, Halifax returned to the matter of the press when he asked Beaverbrook in July 1939 to delete an article in the *Evening Standard* on the secret services of various countries, which Halifax found particularly 'objectionable'. Neither Halifax nor anyone at the Foreign Office had seen the article before the Foreign Secretary communicated his displeasure to Lord Beaverbrook but Beaverbrook still allowed a Foreign Office official to call at the *Evening Standard* to vet it and apply his blue pencil to the offending passages. Even after this, Halifax returned to the attack and asked for the article to be dropped completely as it could only add to the 'nervousness in the country over the international situation, and tension ... is still present'. Halifax warned Beaverbrook that the article would be 'pilloried in the German press' and would thus be likely to increase ill feeling.[25] Despite protestations that such 'indefinite postponement' would be difficult, Beaverbrook did concur and the

95

innocuous and vague article on the espionage systems of Britain and Germany was indefinitely left out of the paper.[26]

Beaverbrook's voluntary self-censorship of material that in the Foreign Office's view would be likely to disturb the calm waters of Anglo-German relations was absolutely in keeping with the political attitude of Beaverbrook during this period, just as he continued the campaign of unguarded optimism which he had started at the invitation of the government in the month before Munich. By instilling an atmosphere of peace and stability he hoped to help the government inculcate in Hitler a sense of trust in Britain's specific and ultimately reasonable intentions which would thereby make the German Chancellor easier to negotiate with. Thus, on 18 January 1939, the *Daily Express* assured its readers that 'neither Germany nor Italy will invade France or seize French territory. Such an enterprise would be madness.' As a caveat to this, Beaverbrook also added that 'Britain has nothing to fear at home or abroad, although our security depends upon increasing our strength by land and sea and in the air.'

Similar acts of self-censorship meant that widely held fears about the course of Chamberlain's policies found no channel of expression despite the fact that editors were well aware that these fears now formed the prevailing mood of the public and the political elite. Barrington-Ward and Dawson were confronted with this on *The Times*; the former discovered after a discussion with some of his staff on 25 October 1938 that 'Most of the office is against Dawson and me!'[27] Barrington-Ward informed Dawson that his impression in the immediate aftermath of Munich was that 'The divisions of opinion over Czechoslovakia are getting rather worse', but he was still not prepared to blame this division on the actual Munich agreement; like Sir Samuel Hoare, he was more inclined to attribute it to the machinations of the News Department of the Foreign Office 'which is really a centre of anti-Government propaganda'.[28] In order to secure a favourable reception for the Munich agreement, Dawson became as cavalier in his treatment of his colleagues as Chamberlain had become in his treatment of the press as a whole. His collusion with Chamberlain to this effect reached its nadir on 3 October 1938 when he altered the text of a note by his parliamentary correspondent on Duff Cooper's resignation speech, replacing Anthony Winn's enthusiastic note with a more satirical comment of his own. The day after this occurred Anthony Winn resigned, informing Dawson of his 'distaste for what I frankly regard as a silly and dangerous policy'.[29] Other members of *The Times* staff contemplated resigning in disgust at Dawson's all-consuming passion for acting as Chamberlain's willing sounding-board. Colin Coote, a leader writer, for instance, was only persuaded by Churchill to stay with *The Times* as the latter preferred 'a friend in the enemy's camp'.[30] Due to this rigorous control, Dawson and Barrington-Ward were able to stifle dissent on *The Times*, although Barrington-Ward was already privately convinced that a greater drive for rearmament was needed and this later became a familiar theme, as it did on the *Observer*.

There was only one paper that attempted to give a true indication of the feeling of the country, and that was the *Yorkshire Post*. Despite his innate Conservatism, the Editor, Arthur Mann, did not suffer from any false sense of loyalty to Chamberlain, nor did he acquiesce in the latter's high-minded identification of himself with the cause of national unity. Uninhibited by the reservations of his journalistic colleagues, Mann attacked Chamberlain personally for misleading the press and endangering the country, and as a result he attracted the scorn not only of Rupert Beckett but of Conservative Central Office as well. After treating the Munich agreement with the respect that Beckett demanded of him, Mann returned to attacking Chamberlain's foreign policy in November and justified himself to Beckett by claiming that he was putting what he believed to be the national interest before the interests of the Conservative Party. Furthermore, he went a good deal further than some other editors in directly identifying Chamberlain as a most serious threat to this national interest, describing him to the horrified Beckett as a 'commonplace politician, and the country calls for statesmanship and leadership'.[31] Mann temporarily allayed Beckett's censure by challenging him to ask for his resignation if he believed him to be wrong in his judgement of the issues, but their truce lasted only until 8 December when Mann published a leader which explicitly attacked Chamberlain. This leader argued that by:

> repeatedly surrendering to force, he has repeatedly encouraged aggression.... our central contention, therefore, is that Mr Chamberlain's policy has throughout been based on a fatal misunderstanding of the psychology of dictatorship and that a

P.M. who is by nature unfitted to deal with dictators has habitually disregarded the advice of those most expertly qualified to correct his private judgement. If the fruits of these methods and the complacency behind them, belonged wholly to the past, we might rightly be urged to refrain from retrospective criticism. It is because we believe that Mr Chamberlain's policy is even now threatening the safety of the realm, and is likely in the near future to threaten it with danger still graver, that we are stating in some detail our case against it.

With this veiled exposé of what Steward had earlier told the Germans was Chamberlain's unconstitutional methods of conducting his policy, the hint of the true state of disarray in the Foreign Office and Whitehall over appeasement and its more direct attack on Chamberlain's misunderstanding of the dictators, Mann incurred the full wrath of Beckett, who wrote to him that after all that he had 'personally' said to Mann over the past months, Mann had 'no right continually to publish these extreme comments against the P.M.'. He ended by inviting Mann to consider his position if he refused to 'write to orders'.[32] He was not only concerned about Mann's denunciations of Chamberlain's foreign policy, but was also fearful that he would not even support Chamberlain in the more immediate test of a national general election 'at no distant date', because to him it seemed that 'day after day the Y.P. takes up an attitude more critical of the Government than any paper calling itself Conservative has any right to adopt'.[33] On 13 December, Beckett called Mann to 'forbid violent attack tomorrow' contained in a pamphlet published by Mann called *Appeasement or Peril?* on the case against Chamberlain.[34] After a meeting of the board of directors, Beckett informed Mann that they, like himself, were 'fed up . . . with this steady spate of personal criticism and recrimination'.[35] More insidiously, however, he jumped on an admission by Mann in the latter's letter to him of 12 December that he now found the task of running the newspaper against the directors 'almost physically impossible' and 'taxing to one's nervous strength'. This frank admission of the nervous pressure involved in his predicament, confided by one friend to another, was seized upon by Beckett in a manner reminiscent of the Whips' whisperings about

Eden the previous November. Beckett attributed Mann's stubbornness over appeasement and Chamberlain to 'the nervous strain' which had 'obscured ... the extent to which [Mann] had gone in this direction' whilst telling Mann that not only he but several of the directors considered 'this nervous strain to be on the increase'. He ended his comments to Mann by writing that 'Your remark of the last page of your letter – "I think Eden might rally the nation, and if it were not for the family connection I would advocate him as leader" – is an exemplification of what I have just written ... of this continuing exploitation of the lurid obsession ... against the P.M. ... [which] is damaging to yourself.'[36]

As well as having his political views attributed to mental and nervous illness, Mann had to defend himself against the unjust charge that he, as editor, was merely a puppet of Eden (with whom he was supposed to be in regular contact but was not)* and so did not arrive at his inconvenient attitudes independently. Under this barrage, Mann raised the issue to one of editorial independence and put it to the directors that the question of greatest importance was 'whether it is in the true interests of a democratic country that honest expression of opinion by editors and experts trained to study public affairs should be stifled by newspaper proprietors who take their inspiration from interested ministers, from their agents or relatives'.[37] He was very conscious of the unprecedented influence that Chamberlain and his government were able to exert over the press and saw in himself and his actions a last line of defence in the battle for editorial independence – a view which he outlined in the leader of 5 December in which he had drawn attention to the 'subtler channels' of censorship which existed. He returned to this theme in a radio broadcast entitled 'The Editor's Job', which went out on 24 January 1939. In this broadcast, he pointedly took the opportunity to affirm the principle that the responsibility for a newspaper's policy must be vested 'in the man who is responsible for its daily conduct'. He also observed in a richly ironical vein that 'I believe most editors follow a golden rule not to be in close social relationships with Ministers of the Crown ... for

---

* Eden was connected to the *Yorkshire Post* by virtue of his marriage to Beatrice Beckett, daughter of Sir Gervase Beckett. There is no evidence that he maintained any political contact with Rupert Beckett or with Arthur Mann. Sir Gervase Beckett was the elder brother of Rupert Beckett.

as journalists they may be called upon to criticize them in their representational capacity.'[38] He observed this rule; it was for the benefit of his fellow journalists that he reiterated it in his broadcast. Mann continued to champion his creed in private to Beckett, and argued in February that 'the suppression of critical thought is a source of weakness to any country; it is a subversion of democracy'.[39]

It was Mann's misfortune that he was the editor of the one paper that was still financially run by and for the Conservative Party in Yorkshire. The paper did not have the capitalist independence that allowed other editors to pursue a less party-political line. As a consequence, Mann's opposition to the official party policy had to reach a climax one way or the other; Beckett notified him that this climax was to come at the Annual General Meeting of the Yorkshire Conservative Newspaper Association, when the angry Conservative shareholders could vent their collective spleen. The attack was to be made on Mann by Lord Bingley, aided and abetted by Conservative Central Office. Beckett now found himself in an uncomfortable position; he predicted that he would be 'pilloried . . . as responsible for opinions in the paper which people either ascribed to my instigation, or charged to my lack of control'.[40] In the event, having pilloried Mann in private and successfully curbed his editor's more radical instincts, Beckett felt able to defend him publicly at the meeting, thus deflecting the force of Lord Bingley's criticism. Without Beckett's support for Mann's editorial independence, Mann would undoubtedly have had to go, but he had done just enough to placate Beckett, without compromising his principles, to persuade the reluctant proprietor that he had to defend his recalcitrant editor in public. The Conservatives in London were astonished at this outcome of a general meeting that they had fully expected would lead to the long-overdue silencing of Mann, and Hoare wrote to Dawson at *The Times* that he was 'surprised at Rupert Beckett's speech . . .' which looked to him as if it was 'simply a brief provided for him by Mann'. Hoare was however 'glad that the protests were made', as there was no paper that had 'tried to do Chamberlain more harm than the Yorkshire Post in recent months'.[41] Mann was meanwhile congratulated by Eden on an outcome which he hoped would do the 'standard of journalism in this country much good'.[42]

However, as Garvin had admitted in the summer, the result of the self-censorship of the rest of the press was that it was thus cut dangerously adrift from the true feeling in the country – and this cleavage was bound to advance as time went on and the press remained so muted in its criticism or extravagant in its praise. Sir Walter Layton was also aware of the growing public disbelief in both the government and the good faith of the dictators after the *News Chronicle* published a poll at the beginning of November 1938 which, amongst other results, showed that 37 per cent of the population was not satisfied with Chamberlain as Prime Minister and 72 per cent wanted an increase in armaments expenditure. However, there was an even more alarming statistic that Layton refused to publish out of his sense of loyalty to what he perceived to be the national interest – as defined by Chamberlain. This result showed that 86 per cent of the British people did not believe Hitler when he said he had no more territorial ambitions. Instead, Layton sent this particular result to Chamberlain, explaining that he had not 'withheld these figures from publication ... because I have any doubt that they faithfully reflect British opinion ... but because I fear that so blunt an advertisement of the state of British opinion on this matter would exacerbate feelings in Germany'.[43] Chamberlain must have been very grateful for Layton's scrupulousness but it proved more than anything else that the press as a whole was no longer expressing public opinion, or even attempting to express it. The press had become an instrument of foreign policy and on the whole was happy to act as such, whether it be the *News Chronicle* or *The Times*. F. A. Voigt wrote of this phenomenon that 'discontent with the daily Press is intense amongst multitudes of people who are concerned ... over the future of this country'.

Symptomatic of this growing disillusionment with the damped-down organs of the daily press was a sudden growth in private newsletters that occurred in the wake of Munich. These newsletters, styled on Claud Cockburn's *The Week*, were written not by newcomers to journalism, but by journalists who could not find expression for their views in their own newspapers. The diplomatic correspondents were particularly active in this field, since, like the Foreign Office News Department on which they had once fed, they now found themselves out in the cold, excluded from exercising any anti-government influence on the papers for which they worked. Gordon-Lennox of the Daily Telegraph, for instance, founded the most influential of these newsletters, the *Whitehall News Letter*. This became the mouthpiece

101

of the 'Edenites', or the 'glamour boys' as the band of dissident young Tory MPs who gathered around Anthony Eden were called. Voigt of the *Manchester Guardian* and Peter Grieve, an ex-journalist on that paper, started *The Arrow,* which could count amongst its contributors Charles Tower of the *Yorkshire Post*, Iverach McDonald of *The Times*, Lady Milner, Harold Nicolson and 'Bobbety' Cranbourne. In its first issue of 6 January 1939 *The Arrow* spoke of 'unpreparedness for the next crisis', and warned that 'a nation that is prepared has a very different spirit, a different policy, a different resolve from a nation that is unprepared'.

The involvement of so many journalists in these newsletters was indicative of their dissatisfaction with their own newspapers, as it was symptomatic of the wider malaise that afflicted the press as a whole. Those organs that attacked Chamberlain and the dictators now started to do very well and *The Week,* Commander King-Hall's *News Letter, The Arrow* and *Whitehall News Letter* all flourished at a time when the daily press presented a broad front of muted support for Chamberlain. Furthermore, those daily papers that attacked Chamberlain's government, most notably the *Daily Mirror* in its peculiarly strident fashion, also quickly attracted a wide audience. All this pointed to the fact, acknowledged by many journalists at the time, that the press was not reflecting public opinion and that those journals which did set out to articulate the dissatisfaction felt about the contemporary situation were thus bound to do well – as indeed they did. The widespread rumours of self-censorship and collusion with the government filtered down to the readers, who would no longer trust their papers to tell the truth; Voigt noted that dissatisfaction with *The Times* on this account 'is intense'.[44] The News Department of the Foreign Office, which accepted that the government would not look on a publication such as the *Whitehall News Letter* with a friendly eye, came to the same conclusion. Charles Warner wrote that the appearance of such newsletters 'is the reaction of the independent minded journalists to the control of the Press by the Press Lords and other interests and they certainly cater for a real desire on the part of a limited and serious public, who do not get what they want from the ordinary commercially run papers'.[45]

Much as the News Department might have welcomed these developments, it was obvious that such well-informed criticism based on a supposed popular mandate would attract the hostile attention of those at whom the criticism was directed. The *Whitehall News Letter* aroused particular enmity on the part of Sir Joseph Ball. Harold Nicolson, a member of the Eden group, confided to his diary that the Whips were 'terribly rattled by the existence and secrecy of the group itself'[46] and this was confirmed by the activities of Sir Joseph Ball, who utilized his old expertise in the seamy side of life to find out more about them. Ronald Tree, a young and very active member of the group, observed that he was having his telephone tapped and a year later Ball himself told Tree that he had been responsible for this.[47] Victor Gordon-Lennox and Helen Kirkpatrick of the *Chicago Daily News* had their office 'across the street' from Tree in which they published the *Whitehall News Letter*: although it was ostensibly independent of the Eden group, Tree admitted that their 'weekly broadsheet was very much in accordance with our views'.[48] In July 1939, Ball was to start counteracting these newsletters by using his own publication *Truth* to sabotage their campaigns – but apart from this there was little he could do except tap their telephones.

With the European situation apparently stabilizing, Chamberlain was more enthusiastic about the prospects of peace and wrote to his sister in late February that 'all the information I get seems to point in the direction of peace and I repeat ... that I believe we have at last got on top of the dictators'. To harness this, Chamberlain thought that 'we ought to be able to establish excellent relations with Franco who seems well disposed to us, and then, if the Italians are not in too bad a temper we might get Franco-Italian conversations going and if they were reasonably amicable we might advance towards disarmament ... that's how I see things working round'.[49] With this plan laid it remained to prepare the ground for such developments, and so Chamberlain turned to his customary arena for ventilating such optimism, the Lobby.

However, before publicizing his optimism, he preferred to confide in his political colleagues. On 7 March he used the occasion of a dinner of the 1936 Club of senior Conservative politicians to ooze optimism and confidence in the European situation. He was described by Chips Channon as being 'jolly, enjoying himself and amazingly open and confiding'. Channon recorded that Chamberlain 'sees no crisis on the horizon, all seems well: he thinks the Russian danger receding and the dangers of a German war less every day'.[50] Chamberlain was described to Lord Astor as having 'bubbled over with cheerfulness about the European situation' and having 'amazed' his hosts 'by his cheerful optimism'.[51] His next step was to take advantage of a speech that Hoare was due to make to his Chelsea constituents to spread the same message and after consultations between the two, Hoare duly obliged. His notorious speech of 10 March thus heralded the dawn of a 'golden age' of peace and prosperity, in which 'five men in Europe, the three dictators and the Prime Ministers of England and France ... might in an incredibly short time transform the whole history of the world'. But in order to ensure that Hoare's speech appeared in the press in an appealing context of official general optimism, Chamberlain himself addressed the Lobby on 9 March to much the same effect. The result was that on 10 March, the day of Hoare's speech, all the daily papers contained identical and rosy accounts of the contemporary position in foreign affairs. The content of Chamberlain's briefing was identical to what he had told his sister in February, that the Spanish 'affair' would soon be over, that Franco-Italian difficulties could then be tackled and the next step could then be a move towards disarmament. As Oliver Harvey incredulously observed after reading all the separate reports in the press, 'it was felt that if in the course of the present year we could achieve some agreement, it would do much to restore confidence: much depended on Anglo-German relations, but here, too, the position was more promising'.[52]

As one of the Lobby correspondents later wrote of this episode, 'Chamberlain genuinely believed that by inventing and getting published good news he might contrive to relieve sinister threats and receive a morsel of comfort from Berlin and Rome.'[53] Under the rules of non-attribution, the source for this news was variously described as 'from an authoritative source' (in the *Manchester Guardian*) and as 'unofficial and semi-official contacts' (in the *Daily Telegraph*), so the hand of the Prime Minister was successfully concealed by the Lobby system of anonymity for the source. As before, Chamberlain exploited this system to go behind the backs of the rest of Whitehall and spread news of official optimism for the wide-ranging settlement that he had described, knowing full well that this optimism was not shared by anyone in government outside Downing Street and Sir Samuel Hoare.

The Foreign Office, including Halifax, was aghast at the rash and ignorant optimism displayed in the press reports on 10 March and Cadogan was furious at the 'ridiculous rainbow story' which was 'much too optimistic'.[54] Vansittart described the assessment of the international situation as an 'entirely misleading estimate'.[55] In this case, the source for such a rosy and widely reported story could only have come from one place and the Foreign Office soon learned, to its dismay, that Chamberlain had 'received all Lobby correspondents and given them a discourse on foreign affairs. He had never even told Halifax that he intended to do so or discuss what he would say. Number 10 had not even warned the News Department that it was being done. ....'[56] Harvey was flabbergasted by Chamberlain's lack of consultation and was unsure whether to attribute it to 'obtuseness ... jealousy again or determination to do everything himself'.[57]

On this occasion, Halifax confronted Chamberlain with his responsibility for the Lobby briefing. Chamberlain wrote back to Halifax to admit his guilt and professed 'to be horrified at the result of my talk with the Press which was intended only as a general background but was transcribed by them verbatim'. He also promised 'faithfully not to do it again' and apologized for causing Halifax any embarrassment.[58] By this time, the Foreign Office was very wary of such protestations of good faith and Harvey noted that on this occasion Halifax was merely 'amused and half-convinced'.[59] This episode finally brought home to the Foreign Office how Chamberlain had been conducting his own private policy behind its back ever since he had come to Downing Street – using the Lobby correspondents to inspire news stories and editorial comments which ran entirely contrary to what the Foreign Office thought that the government was saying. Cadogan observed that Halifax was 'quite nettled'[60] – a rare condition for the normally placid Foreign Secretary. Halifax had good reason to be particularly annoyed as he himself had been trying to persuade *The Times*, via Dawson, of the dangers of the international situation, to which he was now much more alert than Neville Chamberlain.

What particularly amazed the Foreign Office was that the Lobby correspondents were prepared to transcribe the Prime Minister's words verbatim. The fact that they did so was a testimony to how exceptionally pliant they had become after their years of daily contact with George Steward and Chamberlain. James Margach, a Lobby correspondent, later wrote that 'The Prime Minister deliberately fostered artificial optimism and his views, tenor and spirit were very accurately reported.'[61] At the time the Lobby seemed to have suspended its critical faculties and merely believed everything that Chamberlain said. What incensed Vansittart was the fact that Chamberlain had been able to inculcate such a 'misleading' estimate of the European situation, without a 'proper explanation of the source of the story being put in the papers'. Vansittart told Crozier that 'the Press ought not to do it'; Crozier's lame response was that the *Manchester Guardian* had added that the story came from 'an authoritative source', and that 'Chamberlain had disapproved even of this degree of official attribution.'[62] But this would, of course, mean something only to the Whitehall cognoscenti – to the general public, Chamberlain was able to give the impression that the government was on the brink of the 'golden age' in European politics, whereas in fact he had successfully bypassed the entire government, which now held a view almost diametrically opposed to his own. Through the Lobby, he could with impunity exercise power without responsibility – turning Baldwin's old cliché about the press on its head. To Vansittart, the substance of Chamberlain's message to the Lobby had either shown 'a deliberate intention to deceive the public ... or the grossest ignorance of the international situation'.[63] Whichever explanation was right, and despite Chamberlain's protestations to Halifax, the Prime Minister knew exactly what he was doing in speaking to the Lobby, as it was part of his carefully orchestrated campaign of optimism. He had done it before, and he was soon to do it again.

On this occasion, the government's hopes for the imminent arrival of a 'golden age' of peace in Europe were immediately dashed by Hitler's invasion of Czechoslovakia on 15 March. Chamberlain's policy seemingly lay in ruins. He was fishing with the man who had done so much to support his policy, Sir Joseph Ball, when the news was brought to him. The official optimism of the preceding week was exposed as the wishful thinking that it really was, and those who had long been suspicious of Chamberlain's underhand manipulation of the press started to round on him. Garvin privately denounced 'the cackle of complacency', the 'blindness in the Government' which had been using 'ministerial optimism as a method of rebuking those who had eyes to see'.[64] For Arthur Mann, the episode of 9 March confirmed all his worst fears about the Prime Minister's influence over the press. On 28 March Chamberlain was asked a question in the House of Commons about the statement made to the press on 9 March and, as Mann noted in a leader of the next day, 'the P.M. did not answer the point of the inquiry, which was, in effect ... the source of misinformation upon which the statement was based'. Mann rated this question as one of first-class importance, because the critics of the government knew 'that the optimism expressed with so much ministerial authority was maintaining an extremely dangerous complacency in the nation'. Mann detected 'a growing demand for enlightenment as to the reasons for these dismal judgements by a Government which had allowed the European situation to come to such a pass'.[65]

Quite apart from the revelation about Chamberlain's treatment of the press, the invasion of Prague on 15 March also spelled the apparent end of Chamberlain's foreign policy, and this was universally acknowledged in the press. *The Times*, which only three days earlier had been editorializing on the happy abandonment by Germany of any more claims on her neighbours, declared that the 'invasion, occupation and annexation of Bohemia and Moravia, are notice to the world that German policy no longer seeks the protection of a moral case'. On 19 March, Dawson called at Downing Street for 'some talk'[66] with Horace Wilson; *The Times* now supported the government in stiffening its resolve. For the rest of the press, however, the invasion of Prague marked more of a watershed, and some newspapers, such as the *Daily Mirror*, now began to call for a thorough reconstruction of the government.

As usual, however, Chamberlain was scornful of the mounting tide of constructive criticism. Whilst the rest of the press refrained from demanding any sudden upheaval in the government, Arthur Mann was as usual more direct, and demanded a 'broadening of the basis of the Government and an inclusion of men whose judgement can now be seen by everyone to have been right' – for which demand he was soundly castigated by Beckett.[67] However, a final apparent reversal of the government's policy was signalled on 31 March with the declaration of a guarantee to Poland, a declaration that was precipitated by the startling news of a potentially imminent German invasion of that country brought to Downing Street by Ian Colvin, the *News Chronicle* correspondent in Berlin. However much this might seem to have signalled a complete reversal of the British policy and the acceptance of responsibilities in Central Europe, doubts were immediately raised by *The Times*. Chamberlain announced in the House of Commons on 31 March that 'In the event of any action which clearly threatened Polish independence ... His Majesty's Government would feel themselves bound at once to lend the Polish Government all support in their power.' Leo Kennedy was summoned to the Foreign office the day before by Cadogan to be enlightened on the finer nuances of this pledge. Cadogan recorded that he 'gave him the low-down – hope I can trust him'.[68] Kennedy and Dawson thus composed the leader of 1 April, commenting on the guarantee to Poland, with the government's own low-down at their disposal. They wrote that 'the new obligation which this country issued does not bind Great Britain to defend every inch of the present frontiers of Poland'. *The Times* asserted that the key word in the guarantee was 'independence'; this it distinguished from territorial 'integrity', which might have meant an unconditional guarantee of all the existing Polish frontiers. As it was, *The Times* confidently declared that 'Mr Chamberlain's statement involves no blind acceptance of the status quo.... this country has never been an advocate of the encirclement of Germany, and is not now opposed to the extension of Germany's economic activities and influence'. As Cadogan later noted, this was a perfect representation of the government's thinking, as it meant that the guarantee had not 'effectively given the control of British policy to Poland'.[69]

Chamberlain recorded that these important points about the guarantee were 'perceived alone by "The Times"',[70] which was not surprising as the paper had had the thinking behind the guarantee exactly explained to it. However, a storm of criticism, almost equal to that which had greeted its leader of 7 September of the previous year, now descended on *The Times* – because its leader was seen as an indication of the government trying to water down the commitment to Poland. Churchill spoke in Parliament of the 'sinister passage similar to that which foreshadowed the ruin of Czechoslovakia'.[71] As so often before, Dawson had allowed *The Times* to be used as the sounding-board for the government's efforts to expound its foreign policy to the public. In this case, the attempt to combine a show of strength with the old convictions about the injustices of the status quo in Europe was perfectly put by *The Times*: the complaints that the newspaper was independently watering down the British declaration were quite wrong as the paper was soundly interpreting the mind of the government, which was indeed anxiously searching for room to manoeuvre in its guarantee to Poland. Whether the government was right in propounding such a guarantee at all was another matter but Dawson stood his ground knowing full well that he had done no more than ventilate the government's misgivings about its guarantee, unpalatable as some found it. On 3 April he was cheered by a lunch with Halifax, who told him that 'He and the P.M. thought the article just right', and this steeled him in the face of some 'self-righteous comment from the DT and malignant abuse from the N.C. [*News Chronicle*]'.[72] By now, although Dawson probably did not realize it at the time, the paper that had once been dubbed 'The Thunderer' out of respect for its strong-minded independence no longer advanced any opinion that did not endorse, or which was not directly inspired by, Chamberlain. Dawson's total subservience was consistent, and was to damage fatally his paper's famous reputation.

Evidence that Downing Street had not, indeed, abandoned its appeasement convictions came to the surface again at the end of April. Despite Chamberlain's earlier professions to Halifax that he would not address the Lobby independently, James Margach recalls that on the eve of the Easter recess 'he was at it again ... and he met a group of us for yet another of his sunshine tours. Reassure public opinion, he urged us; the worst was over and there would be no more shocks or surprise coups by the dictators – he was convinced of their good intentions. Have a good holiday, he advised us, free from worry and concern.'[73] Further evidence that Downing Street was 'at it again behind our backs' was provided to Oliver Harvey by *The Times* leader of 3 May, which referred to Danzig, the disputed city in Poland, not being worth a war. To Harvey, this, and the return of Henderson as Ambassador to Berlin, after a brief sojourn in England which many hoped would be more permanent, only helped to cause further 'mistrust in the Government's sincerity in its present policy'.[74] Vansittart was rightly concerned that 'The appeasers are busy again',[75] and blame was this time attached to Horace Wilson – though whether he personally inspired the reference to Danzig in *The Times* is impossible to tell. But by now *The Times* never made any foreign policy utterance on its own initiative, so it was likely that this particular suggestion about Danzig had emanated from Downing Street Vansittart took a very dim view of *The Times*'s recent efforts, which, to his mind, undermined the government's resolve, and he minuted on 16 May that 'it is impossible to exaggerate the harm that is consistently done by "The Times" in its own little way'.[76]

Vansittart had particular cause for concern because, as the tension mounted over the summer, the government once again moved to dampen any provocative comment in the press that might lead to protests from Germany or Italy. It was to repeat the efforts to restrain the press that it had carried out at the same juncture the year before, in an attempt to foster an atmosphere of calm which might be conducive to negotiations. On 9 April, Cadogan saw Barrington-Ward to tell him to 'soft pedal', as he predicted that 'we shall have quite enough abuse of ice creamers'. Cadogan also summed up the difficulty in controlling the press, as the problem was 'to steer between provocation and impression of impotence. If you are too bellicose, you provoke dictators into doing something irrevocable. If you are too passive, you encourage them to think they can do anything.'[77] At the beginning of May, Halifax saw Lord Camrose to urge him not 'to allow such provocative leaders in the "Daily Telegraph" '.[78] Vansittart reported to Voigt that Sir Horace Wilson had been to see R. T. Clark of the BBC to accuse the broadcasters of 'making people believe that war is inevitable and encouraging a war-mentality. . . . then he became rather menacing and hinted that if the BBC did not impose a self censorship one would have to be imposed from outside'. Not surprisingly, Wilson would not 'commit himself to writing',[79] but Vansittart saw this as fresh evidence of the foolhardy attempts that had so obviously failed before to placate Hitler by being more conciliatory towards him. The unfortunate Layton was once again seen by members of the inner Cabinet, and on 12 April Dawson recorded in his diary that Chamberlain had had Layton 'on the mat about spreading false reports in "The News Chronicle" '.[80]

The press formed one part of a greater whole in the government's campaign to give the dictators as little as possible to find offensive during the summer of 1939. As well as tackling the BBC with the same object in mind, the government's watchful eye extended over the performing arts. The Lord Chamberlain had been exercising his ancient legal power over the censorship of plays since October 1938. Cadogan wrote to the Lord Chamberlain in December 1938 reaffirming the Foreign Office's wish that he should ensure that 'All direct references to Germany, to Herr Hitler, or to other prominent personages must be avoided' on the grounds that, as Orme Sargent had minuted, a spate of such plays, which would undoubtedly be 'very popular', would also be 'not only dangerous, but unnecessary'.[81] In May 1939, disturbing news began to filter back to London about the film that Charlie Chaplin was making about the dictators in Hollywood, which, as the British Consul in Los Angeles reported, contained 'bitter and ridiculous ... satire which Mr Chaplin was entering into with fanatical enthusiasm'. As Chaplin himself showed no inclination to curb his satire himself, the Foreign Office turned to the British Board of Film Censors on 16 June to see if they would curb the satire for him, urging the censors 'to give the film the most careful scrutiny should it be presented to you for a licence'.[82] *The Great Dictator* eventually appeared in Britain in 1940 to universal acclaim.

The government also turned its attention to the BBC during this period. Although nominally independent, the very rare radio programmes where the BBC had an opportunity to touch on politically contentious subjects had been under close government scrutiny since the mid-1930s. The BBC Talks Department was the only department which had a responsibility to deal with political subjects outside the news and that department maintained constant and informal links with the Foreign Office in order to prevent the BBC from in any way compromising the government's foreign policy. The BBC's News Department was similarly straitjacketed by its obsessive concern for political neutrality, which merely led, in the historian W. J. West's phrase, to a 'bland neutrality'. Indeed, in a 'highly controversial report' written in the wake of the Munich crisis, a Chief News Editor at the BBC complained, 'I say with a full sense of responsibility, and since I was for over three years Chief News Editor, with a certain authority, that in the past we have not played the part which our duty to the people of this country called upon us to play. We have, in fact, taken part in a conspiracy of silence.' *

* Quoted by W. J. West in *Truth Betrayed* (Duckworth, 1987), pp. 40–1. For a full account of the BBC's relations with the Foreign Office during the 1930s, see Chapter 2 of *Truth Betrayed*;

The 'conspiracy of silence' complained of by the author of the above report, John Coatman, is directly comparable to the 'silent censorship' complained of by F. A. Voigt. Indeed, the suspicion has always remained that even Sir John Reith's evident self-restraint was not good enough for Neville Chamberlain, who personally engineered the removal of the BBC's first Director-General from the organization in 1938. Reith was appointed head of Imperial Airways and replaced by Frederick W. Ogilvie. A classic example of the government's interference with the BBC before Munich is provided by the case of Harold Nicolson's projected radio talk on the looming Czechoslovak crisis on 5 September 1938. As was customary, the script, which was composed by Nicolson and took a very dim view of the government's evident reluctance to commit itself to Czechoslovakia, was passed to the Foreign Office for clearance. Leeper considered the talk excellent, but had to refer it to higher authority; higher authority found it a good deal less than excellent. There thus ensued a long and strenuous afternoon of discussion involving the Foreign Office, Harold Nicolson and his BBC Talks producer, George Barnes, the outcome of which was that Nicolson had to forgo giving his original talk and instead broadcast a script which was, in the opinion of Barnes, 'innocuous'. Even so, arrangements were made for a certain Mr Lidell, the broadcasting engineer who was on duty, 'to be ready to fade out Mr. Nicolson's talk' if he strayed on to controversial ground – such as Czechoslovakia.[83] George Barnes' full account of this episode is reproduced as an Appendix to this book, because it illustrates that the opinion-controlling methods which the government employed with the BBC were very similar to those it employed with the press.

By June, however, many in the press, like Lord Astor, were privately convinced that something would have to be done to strengthen the government, and it was realized that only a declaration in favour of Churchill by the normally loyal supporters of the government in the London national press would put sufficient pressure on Chamberlain. Like Oliver Harvey, Lord Astor was aware that the *Daily Telegraph*, with its record of uncluttered patriotism, was the key paper, and on

the ensuing paragraphs are largely based on West's account. For a rather less damning account of Sir John Reith and his political problems during the late 1930s, see Asa Briggs, *The History of Broadcasting*, vol. 2: *The Golden Age of Wireless* (Oxford University Press, London, 1965), pp. 129–47.

30 June he went to see Camrose together with Eden and Harold Nicolson. After a 'long talk Camrose agreed' in principle that there ought to be a Cabinet reconstruction and that Winston Churchill was the important man to get in. Lord Astor also confided to Camrose that he and Garvin had been for such a reconstruction 'for some time and that Lord Halifax', whom Astor had seen the previous night, was also 'for having Winston in'.[84] The *Daily Telegraph* secured, it was left to Garvin to kick off the campaign in the *Observer* on Sunday, 2 July, and he wrote of Churchill: 'that one who has so firm a grasp of the realities of European politics should not be included in the Government must be as bewildering to foreigners as it is regrettable to most of his countrymen'. The *Daily Telegraph* followed on the Monday, 3 July, with a call for Churchill's inclusion and on the same day the *Manchester Guardian* advised Chamberlain to swallow his prejudices and make use of Churchill's abilities 'in any capacity'. On 4 July, the *Manchester Guardian* and the *Daily Telegraph* repeated the calls of the previous day and were joined by the *Yorkshire Post*, the *Daily Mirror*, the *Evening News*, the *Star* and the *News Chronicle* in expressing similar sentiments. This was an independent campaign on behalf of Churchill, as the man in question was 'careful not to encourage in any way the campaign for his inclusion in the Cabinet'.[85] Arthur Mann was prepared to put the proposition to Chamberlain personally and he wrote to Halifax suggesting this – but Halifax, remembering, perhaps, Mann's previous frosty encounter with the Prime Minister, wisely decided that this would not be very useful if they were 'merely to fall into sharp differences'.[86]

This rising chorus of disapproval was the only serious opposition that Chamberlain had ever had to face from a normally docile press, and his reaction was very typical. Instead of accepting the logic of this united front and the popular sentiment behind it, he tried to stop the campaign in its tracks and then strike back with his own journalistic weapon. There is no doubt that, in Chips Channon's words, the campaign was 'quite threatening, and P.M. is taken aback by it'.[87] Chamberlain's response was not to consider the legitimate claims of Churchill but to send for Lord Camrose and to declare himself 'vexed that Camrose who used to be such a firm supporter should now have committed himself to Churchill'.[88] According to Camrose's account of their interview, Chamberlain explained that his 'own responsibility

113

at the present time was so onerous that he did not feel that he would gain sufficiently from Winston's ideas and advice to counter balance the irritation and disturbance which would necessarily be caused'.[89] Chamberlain could see that he 'did not convince Camrose with this explanation', but was at least 'assured that there was no bitterness in his mind'.[90] However, instead of taking the calls for Churchill's inclusion at face value, the Chamberlainites were only prepared to attribute the motivations of those people who supported Churchill to personal illness or party political malice. Chamberlain was content to attribute Camrose's argument to jaundice, writing to his sister that 'since his illness Camrose is a changed man',[91] much as Beckett was content to attribute Arthur Mann's political views to his nervous condition. Channon, who like the rest of the Chamberlainites was surprised to see the Astors 'take a strong pro-Churchill line', was equally prepared to attribute this conversion to the fact that Lady Astor had been 'frightened by anonymous letters and gossip about the so called Cliveden set'.[92]

In the face of Chamberlain's stubbornness, there was little else to be done, and the newspaper campaign petered out. As Dawson noted, Chamberlain had no 'intention of being bounced into taking back Winston'[93] and it soon became obvious that the press was banging its head against a brick wall. However, apart from resisting this campaign, Chamberlain also sought to go on the offensive and discredit Churchill personally and those who supported him. Chamberlain and his entourage could no longer distinguish personal malice or gratuitous conspiracy from genuine political conviction, and as well as privately discounting the Astors and Lord Camrose on the grounds of personal pique in the case of the former and illness in the case of the latter, Chamberlain turned his hostile gaze on to Churchill. Henceforth, Chamberlain decided to use Sir Joseph Ball to discredit the pro-Churchill campaign in a more public manner.

The chosen instrument for this counter-attack was the journal *Truth* – secretly controlled by Sir Joseph Ball and the business committee of the National Publicity Bureau. As Chamberlain found the natural tide of events running ever more strongly against him, so he increasingly turned to Ball and *Truth* to discredit those opponents who were eventually forced upon him, such as Churchill. On 7 July, while the pro-Churchill press campaign was in full cry, the whole front page of *Truth* was devoted to belittling the idea of Churchill's inclusion in the Cabinet. *Truth* asserted that the 'intrigue was designed to mislead the public' and that there was in fact 'no demand' in the House of Commons 'for Mr Churchill's inclusion in the Cabinet outside his particular courtiers – making up less than half a dozen – who have been christened the glamour boys'. It also took the opportunity to denounce the *Yorkshire Post*, the *Manchester Guardian*, the *News Chronicle* and the *Daily Mirror* as despicable organs, which would 'seize any weapon with which to attack the Prime Minister, and their devices can be dismissed as of no account'. The charges against Churchill were continued in the next issue and on 23 July Chamberlain triumphantly wrote to his sister that Churchill had looked 'very depressed at a dinner at Buckingham Palace', an unlikely event that Chamberlain chose to attribute to the 'couple of witty articles making fun of the suggestion that he would help matters in the Cabinet which appeared in *Truth* (secretly controlled by Sir Joseph Ball)'.[94] *Truth* continued this campaign against Churchill throughout August; the issue of 4 August, for instance, contained sarcastic references to Churchill as an 'indispensable statesman' and compared him to 'Cromwell refusing the crown.' If anything, *Truth* became more eager to lampoon Churchill when he did eventually join the Cabinet at the beginning of the war. On 15 September, *Truth* contained a cynical account of Churchill's handling of the Admiralty and ended with the conclusion that 'In neither small things nor large, do we want any pseudo-Napoleonic stuff at the Admiralty'; and on 29 September *Truth* compared him to Hitler 'in his political fickleness'. It continued in the same vein throughout Chamberlain's premiership.

However, except on *The Times* and in the Beaverbrook and Kemsley press, there was now a common belief that Chamberlain could only be supported, in so far as he was Prime Minister and was thus the essential symbol of unity in the country that might deter Hitler; but any belief in Chamberlain's ability to use that high office to any good effect had now completely evaporated. With the road to Churchill's inclusion in the Cabinet blocked by Chamberlain the press turned its attention to the only other practical move that would deter Hitler, an alliance with Russia. Churchill himself had swallowed years of prejudice to suggest in the *Daily Telegraph* on 8 June the creation of a grand alliance between Britain, France and Russia, and the rest of the press eagerly followed the government's apparent steps to achieve this grand design. For what was realized by everyone across the political spectrum was that the guarantee to Poland was worthless as a practical military possibility unless Russia, a near and powerful neighbour, could be persuaded to join the alliance to guarantee Poland. Those papers which had always advocated the cause of a popular front, or a grand democratic alliance, were particularly enthusiastic about this turn of events and the *News Chronicle*, *Daily Worker*, *Manchester Guardian*, *Daily Mirror* and more reluctantly the *Daily Herald* all threw caution to the wind and championed the cause of Anglo-Soviet solidarity immediately the Polish guarantee was announced on 31 March. The British government's protracted negotiations with Moscow were daily scrutinized and encouraged. The *News Chronicle* was in no doubt that in doing this it was soundly interpreting the united voice of public opinion and in the policy conference of 19 May 1939, it was agreed that 'In view of the almost unanimous feeling of public opinion in favour of an alliance with Russia ... we should continue to press the Government to lose no time in concluding their negotiations with that country.'[95] Ivan Maisky, the Soviet Ambassador to Britain, now became a particularly welcome and ever present figure in journalistic circles and saw most of the editors and proprietors privately to discuss the possibilities of an alliance, and, in particular, to explain the Russian view of such an alliance.

On the other hand, in the face of this rush of enthusiasm, the initial and enduring doubts that Chamberlain had held about Russia's good faith and her military worth as an ally were reflected in *The Times*, which, although it could not be hostile to the negotiations while they were in progress (initiated as those negotiations had been by Chamberlain himself), was at the best lukewarm about them in print. Dawson also sent anything that *The Times* received from its own correspondent in Latvia, R. E. Urch, to Chamberlain which might support the cause of the Baltic states against the Russians who wanted to put soldiers on their soil, thus infringing their sovereignty. The collapse of the Anglo-Soviet negotiations and the signing of the Nazi–Soviet Pact on 24 August 1939 thus came as no surprise to those who had been viewing the negotiations with a realistic eye, but it came as a severe shock to those who had not. For *The Times*, as for Chamberlain, it confirmed all its worst suspicions 'of Russian good faith which some of us had long held'.[96] Leo Kennedy thus took a very sanguine view of the affair, and had written to *The Times*'s special correspondent in Moscow that he would be 'sorry if no pact with Russia is concluded' but would not be unduly perturbed because he was certain that 'we are becoming so strong now that we can get on without her'[97] – a consoling and wayward sentiment shared by Dawson and Chamberlain.

For a paper like the *News Chronicle*, however, which had staked so much on the alliance and believed so much in the practicalities of such an alliance, it was nothing less than a disaster and the policy conference met in some disarray on 24 August to discuss the 'implications of the German–Russian pact'. Gerald Barry, who had been the keenest supporter of the alliance, was panicked into stating that 'Russia and Germany have now obtained complete mastery of Europe' and in the face of this formidable combination he considered that Britain should now advise 'Poland to negotiate its . . . independence with Germany'.[98] Layton, however, revealed his hostility to this course of appeasement and pointed out that 'to advise the Poles to negotiate would be the equivalent to undermining their confidence in our guarantee'.[99] The roles of editor and chairman were now reversed and Layton had his way. Garvin was of the same opinion and refused to consider any 'one-sided signs of concessions', knowing that the Nazis would immediately exploit this to raise 'their terms every time'.[100] Garvin was quite clear that, if the alliance with Russia was not fixed, Britain would 'have to choose between war and humiliation'. However, unlike the previous September, he was quite certain what the proper course to adopt was on this occasion and wrote to Lord Astor that he could not contemplate another 'miserable backdown this time'.[101]

However, there were those who apparently could contemplate such a backdown, and those who were determined to stick by the letter of the Polish guarantee looked on with great suspicion as the remnants of the appeasement press started to orchestrate their own peace moves whilst the tension mounted through August. The entire press was acting in the atmosphere of self-restraint that had governed its actions since the early summer; Garvin, for instance, saw the need to be both 'sober and shrewd whilst the European situation remained so tense'. However, it soon became apparent that elements of the press and the government were anxious to spread the same spirit of optimism and

117

conciliation that had characterized the press in the run-up to the Munich agreement. Garvin noted with anxiety that the 'whole holiday atmosphere during August weakens public feeling. . . . there will be no check on Neville'.[102] He observed also that the press would be no check either, an observation in which there was a great deal of truth.

Lord Kemsley, who since the German invasion of Prague had been very supportive of Chamberlain in his newspapers, was in Germany and saw Hitler on 27 July 1939. Chamberlain had increasingly turned to find his press support in the Kemsley papers and this compliment was returned with ever greater flattery. The Prime Minister recommended the writings of Beverley Baxter in the *Sunday Times* (he wrote the Atticus column) and the *Daily Sketch* as 'a most loyal supporter of the Government' and was quick to draw his sister's attention to a description in the *Sunday Times* of the inwardly harassed Premier looking 'at peace with himself' during a parliamentary debate.[103] To assist Chamberlain in his task of persuading Hitler that Britain did not have aggressive intentions towards Germany and was equally anxious not to offend it, Kemsley spent much of his conversation with Hitler belittling the bellicose Churchill, assuring the Führer that 'far more notice was taken abroad of him than in Britain' and reminding Hitler that 'Mr. Churchill had been unfortunate in his campaigns on at least four occasions in the past, starting with the abdication of King Edward VIII'. Speaking as the 'owner of a large number of newspapers in England' who had used 'all his influence in consistent support of the Prime Minister' he also assured Hitler that Chamberlain still attached 'tremendous importance to the documents signed between him and Hitler at Munich'.[104] If this did not undermine the government's apparent resolution enough, Kemsley also saw Dr Rosenberg, the Nazi theoretician, to tell him to ignore the public and press attacks in Britain on Germany as being unrepresentative of public opinion. He also asked Rosenberg to think of Neville Chamberlain as 'our Führer, as we have to think of the Führer as your Neville Chamberlain'[105] – and therefore, presumably, above criticism. The real purpose of the visit was to exchange a series of articles explaining each side's point of view concerning the European situation, which might be published in the *Daily Sketch*, with the intention of diffusing the tense atmosphere. These were prepared for publication by 17 August, but by the time Dr Dietrich, the German Press Attaché, had

Neville Chamberlain leaving 10 Downing Street for his first meeting with Hitler at Berchtesgaden, 15 September 1938

Sir Horace Wilson (left) and Neville Chamberlain walking through St James's Park

Chamberlain at Heston airport before flying to Munich for his third meeting with Hitler, surrounded by (from left to right) Sir Kingsley Wood (Air Minister), Lord Hailsham (Lord Chancellor), Chamberlain, Leslie Hore-Belisha (War Minister), and Lord Halifax (Foreign Secretary)

The visit to Rome, January 1939. From left to right: Count Ciano, Lord Halifax, Chamberlain and Mussolini

The War Cabinet, November 1939. Left to right, standing – Sir Kingsley Wood (Air Minister), Winston Churchill (First Lord of the Admiralty), Leslie Hore-Belisha (War Minister), Lord Hankey (Minister without Portfolio). Left to right, seated – Lord Halifax (Foreign Secretary), Sir John Simon (Chancellor of the Exchequer), Neville Chamberlain, Sir Samuel Hoare (Lord Privy Seal) and Lord Chatfield (Minister for the co-ordination of Defence)

(*Above left*) Sir Robert Vansittart leaving his home in Mayfair, 1934. (*Above right*) Sir Reginald ('Rex') Leeper

(*Above left*) Sir Nevile Henderson (left) and Sir Alexander Cadogan crossing Downing Street for a meeting with the Prime Minister in August 1939. (*Above right*) Anthony Eden with his loyal Private Secretary Oliver Harvey at 10 Downing Street in January 1938

Geoffrey Dawson, Editor of *The Times* 1912–19 and 1922–41

Robin Barrington-Ward, deputy Editor of *The Times* 1927–41, Editor 1941–48

1st Viscount Rothermere

Lord Beaverbrook

Lord and Lady Camrose at Cowes in 1936

1st Viscount Kemsley

(*Above left*) Rupert Beckett, Chairman of the Yorkshire Conservative Newspaper Association.
(*Above right*) Arthur Mann, Editor of the *Yorkshire Post*

(*Above left*) J. L. Garvin, Editor of the *Observer*, in 1941. (*Above right*) Lord Astor, proprietor of
the *Observer*, with his wife Lady Astor at Epsom racecourse in 1925

(*Above left*) Gerald Barry, Editor of the *News Chronicle* 1936–47. (*Above right*) Sir Walter Layton, Editor-in-Chief of the *News Chronicle*

(*Above left*) W. P. Crozier, Editor of the *Manchester Guardian*, 1932–44. (*Above right*) F. A. Voigt, Diplomatic Correspondent of the *Manchester Guardian*

arranged for publication in Germany of the British view, the idea had been overtaken by events and Sir Horace Wilson asked Kemsley to stay his hand on 28 August.

While Lord Kemsley was trying to arrange this exchange of views with Germany, Lord Beaverbrook was trying to draw the press closer to the government's views in much the same way as he had done the previous September. In July, he 'casually' suggested to Lord Perth that it would be useful to institute 'certain Press conferences to be held by the Prime Minister, so that the newspaper proprietors could obtain some guidance on affairs generally, particularly with regard to the international aspect'. This suggestion was regarded as unfeasible due to the pressure of work on the Prime Minister, but Chamberlain did take advantage of this approach to offer a 'homily on leakages and over critical articles' at a lunch for the newspaper proprietors hosted by Sir Roderick Jones, the Chairman of Reuters.[106] However, returning to his theme of the previous September, Beaverbrook embarked on his policy of unbounded optimism in the face of the gathering storm and on 7 August the *Daily Express* published notes on the European situation from its European correspondents, ten out of twelve of whom reported that 'there will be no war this year'. On 11 August, the *Daily Express* asserted in its headline that 'Britain will not be involved in a European war' – again attempting to placate Germany with soothing words. As the situation deteriorated, Beaverbrook's scheme of interviews with the press proprietors was resurrected and on 28 August Sir Samuel Hoare recorded that 'P.M., Halifax and Henderson asked me to see the Press.' This was to be a rerun of the previous year's meetings and Hoare was entrusted with the task of making sure that the press would 'go quietly'. He was anxious to ensure that the press did not exasperate Hitler or offend him into doing something rash; his advice was exactly commensurate with the psychology of appeasement that the government was still practising towards Germany. Hoare's notes contained the advice not to 'emphasize H's contradictions' in his 'communications', which were admittedly 'very vague', as the object of keeping the tension down was to 'get Poles and Germans together' to negotiate. Hoare saw the press on the 28th, 29th, 30th and 31st – when he saw Beaverbrook twice. He was anxious to impress upon the newspaper proprietors the necessity of not 'forcing the pace', and of not 'jumping at the first good point'. He himself was confident that Polish negotiations would start and he also recorded that Horace Wilson was 'very optimistic'.[107]

This time, however, he found the press in a less pliant and more bellicose mood. He particularly recorded that Layton was 'rather restive' – 'will it be another Munich?' – and that talking with Geoffrey Dawson was now 'futile'.[108] As *The Times* now transformed itself into the most resolute and bellicose paper of all, its military correspondent, Basil Liddell Hart, noted that Kennedy had 'blossomed into a fire-eating last ditcher'. On 2 September Liddell Hart remarked that it was now interesting 'to observe how most people are itching to be at them – indignant that we have not already declared war'.[109] Hoare's efforts were thus wasted and the press endured his lectures on this occasion with sullen resentment, as it seemed that the government was preparing for another Munich. By 1 September Hoare was left to see only Beaverbrook, who later recorded that his newspapers had been 'invited by the Government itself to make the declarations of "there will be no war" – the purpose being to influence opinion favourably so that there might be delay and time for consideration'.[110] Beaverbrook was, however, now alone and the declaration of war on 3 September, after the Germans refused to withdraw their invading troops from Poland, was greeted with almost unanimous approval.

Like the Lobby correspondents earlier, the editors and proprietors were now less receptive to the pleadings of the government, which had made them look so foolish on so many previous occasions. The close contact between the Chamberlain government and the press had, in the eyes of the editors and proprietors, discredited such a liaison as it had also discredited the press in the eyes of the reading public. In the words of James Margach, who as a Lobby correspondent had placed his faith in Chamberlain and had then been assiduously misled and manipulated by the Prime Minister in his search for appeasement, 'Chamberlain's dictatorial personal influence on newspaper proprietors, editors and writers made his Premiership, in my experience, the most inglorious period in the history of the British Press.'[111]

4

Chamberlain and the Ministry of Information: The Pay-Off

On the outbreak of war, the morale and reputation of the press were both at a very low ebb. By so closely associating itself with the fortunes of Chamberlain's government, it was now tarred with the same brush of failure and naivety that was to bedevil Chamberlain himself until his ultimate fall from grace in May 1940. Furthermore, in actively working for the now discredited policy of appeasement, the press had forfeited the trust and confidence of the reading public – a trust that it had definitely had and which it was never to regain. Most of the press had clearly abandoned any shred of the independent critical stance that many people looked for in a newspaper and so had forsaken such vestiges of 'objectivity' or 'independence' as they may have been able to claim for themselves before Chamberlain had come to power. Most journalists and editors were conscious of this feeling and the more senior members of the profession expressed their disaffection by founding their own newsletters as an independent alternative to the discredited newspapers. The press had allowed itself to be manipulated blatantly by Chamberlain's government, but it was only the failure of that government's policies which impressed this fact upon it. There were many in the press who felt angry and resentful at the way they had been so disdainfully maltreated and many editors began to react against their former pusillanimity by displaying an unusual degree of resentment and suspicion towards the government. Sir Samuel Hoare found this out for himself in his last futile attempts to intimidate the press in the final days of peace in August 1939; the Lobby had finally expressed their resentment to Chamberlain himself in April of the same year. Chamberlain, for his part, remained entirely unrepentant. Nor was this surprising as he had reaped an admirable harvest from the time he had invested in cultivating his government's contacts with the press. He had successfully demonstrated how a government in a democracy could influence and control the press to a remarkable degree. The danger in this for Chamberlain was that he preferred to forget that he exercised such influence, and so increasingly mistook his pliant press for real public opinion. Whatever the true nature of that amorphous entity, public opinion, may have been in the years 1937 to 1939, many journalists of all political persuasions were convinced, as we have seen, that the press was no longer reflecting it. Chamberlain's mistake was in believing that by controlling the press he was capturing public opinion – of course, the truth of the matter was that by controlling the press he was merely ensuring that the press was unable to reflect public opinion. By dint of his government's unprecedented ability to influence the press, by 1939 he was already living in a dream world that was largely of his own creation – and which was to make his own downfall in the summer of 1940 virtually beyond his comprehension.

Public disaffection with the press was demonstrated both by the growth in circulation of anti-government newspapers and by the findings of Mass-Observation, the market research organization set up by Tom Harrison. In March 1940, after what was for that era extensive research, Mass-Observation concluded that 'the power of the National Press as an opinion-forming influence is waning. People now place it third among the factors which form their opinions. At the outbreak of war they put it second. A year before that ... it had come first.' In August 1940, Mass-Observation noted that 'people feel they have been deceived over Chamberlain ... and that when the press emphasize matters ... both bewilderment and suspicion result among many ordinary people'. The report pointed to the fact that 'there is a majority of more than three to one who feel at present that the BBC is a more reliable source of information of news than the press'; this reflected a situation which was in 1940 largely a novelty, but was in fact never to change.[1] In a longer study on the subject, Mass-Observation drew a profounder conclusion on the relationship between the contemporary politician and the press which exactly describes the attitude of Chamberlain and his inner Cabinet. This study observed that 'politicians easily and constantly ... tend to mistake the press and their friends for public opinion. They convince themselves ... that the whole Nation is absolutely in favour of them and their actions, and when the press does criticize them ... they tend to think that the press is making a fuss or Rothermere being tiresome.'[2] Even given Mass-Observation's natural self-interest in its claim to be the more accurate interpreter of public mores, these reports contained a large measure of truth. By accepting Chamberlain's invitation to help him pursue the government's policy of appeasement rather than sticking to the more mundane task of accurately reporting both news and the state of public opinion, the press had forfeited the public's faith in the efficacy of its news and views.

This sentiment was also reflected in the burgeoning success of any publication that did not support Chamberlain or appeasement and which did not entwine itself in the political infighting of the government and its system of disseminating news. Such a newspaper was the *Daily Mirror*, accompanied by its Sunday stablemate, the *Sunday Pictorial*. These two publications thrived on the anti-Chamberlain, anti-appeasement policies which they advocated and which seemed to attract a lot of public sympathy, if their circulation figures are anything to go by. By the beginning of the war, the circulation of the *Daily Mirror* had risen by one million over its 1933 figure to over one million seven hundred and fifty thousand. The *Sunday Pictorial* had shown a similar growth in its circulation and by 1939 was selling over two million copies. The *Picture Post* magazine had also done spectacularly well on an aggressive anti-Fascist, anti-appeasement policy and had seen its circulation rise in four months in 1939 from thirty thousand to one million three hundred and fifty thousand and by the beginning of the war was read by 15.87 per cent of the population, second only to the *Radio Times* in its popularity as a weekly magazine. Both of these publications owed their success as much to their revolution in style and mood as they did to their politics, but it was nonetheless a good indication of the market that existed for the politics of bellicose anti-Hitlerism.

The *Daily Mirror* also represented a feeling of popular iconoclasm against the ageing and spineless Establishment that seemed to want to collude with the dictators; it was a mood that the *Daily Mirror* was vigorously expressing in its columns before the outbreak of war and was to continue to do so, with unexpected results, during the war itself. This disillusion with the government and a press that seemed to be so completely dominated by the government was also illustrated by the popularity of newsletters. Claud Cockburn's *The Week* had always been popular and in the late 1930s his formula was copied with great success by a number of others who were disenchanted with Chamberlain and could not see a platform for expressing this disenchantment in the existing press. Commander King-Hall's newsletter, which was started in 1936 with an initial list of 600 subscribers, was a spectacular success, for by November 1937 the *King-Hall Newsletter* had 10,000 members (as the subscribers were grandly called); by November 1938 it had 37,500 and by May 1939 it had 53,017. In King-Hall's own words, this newsletter 'maintained, with what now reads like monotonous regularity, that unless measures were taken to deal with the Nazi menace it was as certain as anything can be in this world that there would be a war. The newsletter emphasized the need of rearmament based on a National Government'.[3] Amidst considerable controversy, King-Hall circulated his newsletter to Germany in July 1939 in order to reassure those Germans who opposed Hitler that Britain did mean business and would fight for Poland. The Foreign Office looked upon this enterprise with some misgivings, especially Sir Nevile Henderson, who predictably complained from Berlin that far from impressing upon Hitler Britain's sense of determination over this issue, it would merely defeat 'it's own purpose, and might even definitely drive Hitler to listen to his own extremists'.[4] Henderson might have objected to King-Hall's politics, but there were many who felt that he represented their views and were glad that he commanded an adequate medium through which he could express them. Oliver Harvey, in the wake of Munich, looked on in despair at the slow pace of rearmament and the lack of urgency in the government and the press on this issue but consoled himself with the thought that 'meanwhile King-Hall's newsletter hammers away week after week on exactly the right lines, bringing home the real nature of the totalitarian challenge. Is the country beginning to stir?'[5]

As well as expressing anti-appeasement and anti-Chamberlain views, the newsletters also served a secondary function in expressing dissatisfaction with the press. Both *The Week* and the *King-Hall Newsletter* delighted in exposing the subservience of the press to the government and frequently regaled their readers with caustic stories of the Lobby briefings that Chamberlain or George Steward conducted. *The Week*, which largely relied upon the indiscretion of the diplomatic correspondents for its stories, gleefully related the twists and turns of the government's contacts with the press proprietors and editors. These accounts, like those of the Cliveden set, were usually wrong in detail but right in general substance and tone; thus, for instance, *The Week* reported the government's meetings with the press before Munich but attributed the liaison to Halifax instead of Hoare – yet it drew the correct moral that 'the episode provided a somewhat grim demonstration of the degree to which in fact the Government is able to orchestrate the supposedly free and independent British daily Press'.[6] The *King-Hall Newsletter* became equally scathing about the acquiescence of the press in the face of government influence and was particularly sarcastic about Chamberlain's ill-timed Lobby briefing of 9 March 1939, remarking that 'the political correspondents were so startled by all this, that they forgot to doll it up in their own words to give the impression of diversity, and on Friday one had the curious impression as one studied the papers that they were all employing the same writer'.[7]

Just as *The Week* and the *King-Hall Newsletter* were mainly supplied with this sort of story by discontented journalists so the same journalists were also prepared to start their own newsletters in order to get their views read and appreciated. As editorial and proprietorial control tightened in 1938 in response to the government's pressure, so the journalists who opposed the government's policy found themselves unable to influence their papers in the way that they would have wished. It was the diplomatic correspondents, reared by the anti-appeasers Leeper and Vansittart in the Foreign Office, who particularly suffered and so were especially active in setting up such organs as the *Whitehall Newsletter* and *The Arrow*. These newsletters were expressions of discontent at the state of the press by the journalists themselves; if the journalists no longer felt that they were free to express their views in their existing newspapers, it was only logical that the public would gradually sense this disquiet with the existing press and turn to other channels of communication. Not only did established journalists turn to founding their own newsletters to air their views, but amateurs also turned to this method of expression during the Phoney War to register their own discontent at the lack of realism with which many thought the press was confronting the situation. Mass-Observation recorded that these minor newsletters had a combined circulation of about 100,000 by March 1940 and counted, amongst others, *Independent Newsletter* and *Fair Hearing* founded in September 1939; *Europe Tomorrow* and *Inside Nazi Germany* which first appeared in October 1939; *Documentary Newsletter* and *Central Europe Observer* which came out during the first months of 1940. The disillusionment with the British press was thus clearly evident, both in the journalists who worked on the papers and the public who bought them. Although it is hard to discern accurately the reason for the rise or fall of a newspaper's circulation, it is perhaps not surprising that in view of this a paper like the *Daily Mail*, which most complacently supported Chamberlain and openly praised Hitler, saw its circulation drop quite sharply in the last two years before the war whilst the *Daily Mirror* went from strength to strength.

If both the journalists and the public were united in their sense of disaffection with the press, they were strangely divided on why the press had been so eager in its support for appeasement and so loath to take a firmer stance against the dictators. Without the evidence of the close political contacts between the government and the press during the years of Chamberlain's premiership to chew on, most observers were thus convinced that all the evils of the press could be attributed to the insidious demands of the advertisers. So widespread was the antagonism felt against the advertisers that both an ex-editor of *The Times* and the less venerable Mass-Observation could be categorical in their denunciation of the evil influence of the advertiser. Wickham Steed wrote that 'only a high minded' newspaper owner would be willing to risk 'loss of circulation and therefore of advertising revenue by supporting what may be unpopular causes or by insisting upon distasteful truths'.[8] Mass-Observation hinted meaningfully that these advertisers 'represent the large business interests, and ... these interests may come into serious conflict with the interest of the State as a whole'.[9] King-Hall likewise agreed that the over-optimistic reporting of papers like the *Daily Express* and the *Daily Mail* was due to their 'appetite for increased advertising revenue', which was apparently 'capable of making them see rainbows in Hades if they think it would help them sell space to a retailer'.[10]

This conviction had to compete with a more intangible feeling that the government did have ways of manipulating the press that were both more subtle and dangerous; but the lack of evidence for this latter feeling meant that when the Royal Commission on the press came to study this subject, most of the attention was focused on the alternative and more workable theory of advertising influence – with the result that the Royal Commission asked the wrong questions and thus ended up with very little. This was, in retrospect, not surprising, because it was the journalists who asked for the Royal Commission and who provided most of the motivation and evidence for it, and they were not likely to reveal how they themselves had been so assiduously manipulated by Downing Street or the Foreign Office over so many years. The Royal Commission on the press was set up partly to investigate the supposed abuse of the press up to and after Munich, but its obsession with advertising meant that it could offer little by way of explanation for why the press had behaved in the way that it did. Advertising was an easy scapegoat for which one did not have to blame journalists; the real avenues of control open to the government were both effective and antithetical to the freedom of the press and they remained firmly obscured by the irrelevant flounderings of the 1947 to 1949 Royal Commission and, for that matter, of subsequent Royal Commissions as well.

It was thus sadly ironic that the first journalistic casualty of the war was Arthur Mann, Editor of the *Yorkshire Post* and the only journalist or editor who had used his position not only to oppose Chamberlain and appeasement consistently since 1936, but to write about what he called the 'effective censorship' that operated 'through subtler channels'. As we have seen, Mann himself had been involved in an often bitter dispute with his chairman and directors at the *Yorkshire Post* over his opposition to appeasement, so it might have seemed reasonable to expect that with the beginning of the war, which seemed to justify all he had been saying for the previous three years, his editorial position would have been enhanced. However, at the same time as fighting Beckett over the policy of the paper, Mann had also engaged in an argument with him over the general character and financial viability of the paper. It is evident that Beckett and some of the directors consciously linked the two issues in their own minds, attributing the sluggish financial performance of the paper to the supposed unpopularity of Mann's anti-government views and editorials – a view which Beckett directly communicated to Mann in October 1939. As a result of this, Beckett concluded that 'some attempt, drastic possibly, must be made to attempt to remedy the financial state of affairs' of the Yorkshire Conservative Newspaper Association. Beckett could point to the fact that the flagship of this company, the *Yorkshire Post*, was losing between £40,000 and £50,000 per annum with a net sale of 29,000, so his obvious conclusion was that 'it is futile to go on vainly attempting the sale of a newspaper in a form and style that the public have shown consistently that they do not want'. Beckett's drastic remedy was to merge the *Yorkshire Post* with its stablemate, the *Leeds Mercury*, and to make the new morning paper 'much lighter to the touch' in matter – in other words to take it down-market. Beckett also pointed to the necessity of having 'shorter and fewer leaders', as one of his criticisms of Mann's editorship was that his pursuance of anti-appeasement had meant an undue preponderance of long, earnest leaders and articles on foreign policy.[11] The inference to be drawn from his linking of the financial performance of the paper to its politics was that, if those heavy and long leaders had been in support of Chamberlain, he would not have objected to them. Mann vigorously protested against such an amalgamation of the two papers on the ground that the new paper would be compelled to 'lower its quality' to attract the more substantial sales that Beckett was looking for and thus it would lose the unique position of influence and importance that it had gained in the previous twenty years, when it was 'often quoted in the capitals of Europe'. However, Mann also looked to the paper's financial and thus political attachment to the Conservative Party as the very reason for its downfall. In a reference to the previous February when the shareholders' meeting had tried to unseat him he offered the alternative thesis that 'this pronounced and avowed attachment to the party has not helped our circulation ... I have no hesitation ... in saying that this blatant attempt to muzzle the newspaper in the supposed interest of the Conservative Party was harmful to that reputation for honest independence of judgement that any great journal must preserve, if it is to live.'[12]

However, in this particular battle of wills Mann was to lose, because Beckett, reinforced in his judgement by the looming prospect of diminishing sales and advertising due to the advent of war, forced through his desired change and amalgamated the *Yorkshire Post* and the *Leeds Mercury* into a single paper on 25 November 1939, reducing its price to 1d. Mann refused to edit the new paper and resigned; the *Yorkshire Post and Leeds Mercury* quickly ceased being quoted in the 'capitals of Europe' and soon struggled to raise an echo outside the capital of Yorkshire.

Mann was understandably incensed by Beckett's treatment of him in particular and by the state of the press in general. In 1941 he was to leap at the chance of defending another editor who apparently faced problems similar to his own, namely J. L. Garvin. In a letter to Brendan Bracken, who had recommended him to Garvin to represent the latter's interests on the Tribunal set up by Lord Astor to review the terms of Garvin's editorship, Mann gave his reasons for helping Garvin in his difficulties:

> It is because the journalistic principles of editorial responsibility and integrity have been so largely departed from in the London Press and also in some provincial offices that the newspapers have lost so much influence with the public in recent years. It has, to my mind, been a very short sighted sort of commercialism in some cases and in others the wire-pulling politicians who have been responsible. But in any case it has been bad for democracy which depends on the clash of honest opinion based on an objective study of the facts which is the editor's job.[13]

If the press thought that it had enough problems to deal with on the outbreak of war, its miseries were soon compounded by the new Ministry of Information (MOI). The genesis of the MOI and the conflicting ideals which governed its character and operations have been adequately described elsewhere,* but what mostly concerned the press was the Press and Censorship Bureau set up in the MOI's headquarters at the Senate House of the University of London in Bloomsbury. This bureau was supposed to control not only the censorship of the press,

---

* See Ian Mclaine, *The Ministry of Morale* (George Allen & Unwin, 1979).

but also the dissemination of news from the government. The initial planners of the MOI had seen the Ministry as a centralized, comprehensive organization for the processing of all the government's news and propaganda. This was a revolutionary concept which would at one stroke have dismantled the autonomous quasi-official system of press departments at the various Whitehall ministries and replaced them with a centralized system of official, attributable briefings given by clearly identifiable government spokesmen. This bold plan was whittled down by a combination of official prejudice and lack of interest. By September 1939, as one historian has remarked, 'An all-embracing organization had failed to evolve. Enemy propaganda was lost altogether, departments were to keep their own Press officers, the B.B.C. retained its independent status.'[14]

However, despite the comparative emasculation of the Ministry compared to its original bold conception, the setting up of the Press and Censorship Bureau did, for the first time in British history, envisage the centralizing of the various government press officers under one roof to give collective briefings on the record to all journalists. 'Specialist departments' from the various Whitehall Ministries were set up to which all journalists were allowed equal access, and the relevant officers gave attributable briefings to all. This was a novel concept, and was acted upon only because the government ministers who had the job of overseeing the setting up of the Ministry did not pay enough attention to the details of the new arrangements to realize the implications of these profound changes in Whitehall's method of news dissemination.

However, the Ministry's performance of its duties at the beginning of the war brought the whole organization quickly into disrepute and it became prey to attacks from Parliament and, most vociferously, from the press. Initially, the censorship proved to be very inadequate and inconsistent, and infuriated the press with its apparent pettiness and stupidity. As Admiral Thomson, who was to become the Chief Press Censor, wrote of the early days of the war, the initial confusions arose because of the lack of practical training before the war which meant that the working of the Censorship Department of the Press and Censorship Bureau was 'very much a case of the blind leading the blind'. He admitted that neither the trainee censors nor their instructors had 'any ideas of the workings of the press' and the papers were

to make great play of the revelation that out of the staff of 999 the
MOI could boast only forty-three professional journalists.[15]

The censorship, which was voluntary and was restricted to factual
information that might have been of use to the enemy, quickly became
the nightmare of the London and provincial editors. On the third day
of the war, Geoffrey Dawson was noting in his diary that the 'censorship were committing incredible follies', after which his diary was
almost solely concerned for a fortnight with 'the ineptitude of the
Ministry of Information'. The situation was not relieved by the
appointment of Lord Macmillan as the new minister and by 16 September Dawson had concluded that the only way that his friend,
Sir Edward Grigg, could deal with the situation in his capacity as
prospective Permanent Secretary to the Ministry was to 'devote
himself to a ruthless purge and reduce an enormous staff of highly
paid essay-writing young men to a tenth of its size'. Nine days later,
Dawson saw Grigg again, who, having tried to tackle the problem
was in a 'state of despair about it'.[16] The minister responsible for the
pre-war planning of the MOI, Sir Samuel Hoare, looked on with a
mixture of horror and amusement at the amount of vitriol poured on
to the new Ministry by the press. He confided to his diary that the
papers were 'very bitter'[17] about it and so characteristically divested
himself of any responsibility for what had swiftly turned out to be
a political liability. Everyone had their favourite story about the
incompetence of the Ministry of Information: Harold Nicolson was
told by a journalist that on enquiring about the text of a leaflet which
had been dropped in millions over Germany, he was told by a censor
that 'we are not allowed to disclose information which might be of
value to the enemy'.[18]

The main complaint of the press was that, as Edward Cadbury
wrote to Sir Walter Layton, there was a 'total inadequacy of the news
which had been sent out for publication with regard to the war'. The
author of this observation, like the rest of the press, attributed this
phenomenon to the 'heavy-handed' censor.[19] The press was unanimous
in its view that, now that the nation had embarked on this supposedly
terrible and devastating war, there was comparatively little news of
any kind coming in. However, it became apparent after a few weeks
that the real culprits in bringing about this state of affairs were not
the censors, incompetent as they may have been, but the service

131

ministries and the Foreign Office, which were refusing to release any information. The Press Committee of the MOI made this clear in a letter to the Prime Minister of 28 September 1939, in which the journalists pointed out that 'the trouble here is not with the Ministry of Information News Department, but with Government Departments from whom the Ministry has to obtain news for distribution by us'.[20] The ensuing battle against what became known as the 'Sealed-Lip School' was to last the length of the war itself, but the controversy of September 1939 had an immediate consequence which was to ensure that the 'Sealed-Lip School' was always to triumph. Faced by a press that was united in its condemnation of the MOI and in particular of its handling of the news and censorship, it was obvious to the government that something had to be done. Sir Samuel Hoare, perhaps prompted by Beaverbrook, tried to push the energetic newspaper proprietor, Brendan Bracken, on to the Prime Minister as a possible saviour of the Ministry, but Hoare recorded on 14 September that Chamberlain was 'dead against Bracken', just as he was to be against anyone who had crossed swords with him over appeasement.[21]

However, the eventual solution that was to cripple the Ministry for the rest of the war emanated from the press itself. On 21 September, the Lobby Journalists Committee addressed a letter to Chamberlain to propose a reversion to the old system of decentralized, confidential briefings that had existed before the war. The existence of a centralized system of open news dissemination which the Ministry had hesitantly initiated had bypassed the wholy Lobby system. To preserve the privileged institutional position of the Lobby as the premier journalistic forum for collecting news and guidance from ministers, the Lobby took advantage of the early traumas of the Ministry to strangle the new system at birth. In their letter to the Prime Minister the Lobby Committee pointed out that the system at the MOI, which dealt with 'the Press of the world' was 'inappropriate to confidential relations between the Government and dominions press'. The Committee pointed out the obvious advantage of the Lobby system to the government: 'there must be many occasions when the Government will wish to communicate information to the British and dominion newspapers only, and, in the national interest, to ensure that the dissemination of such information is rightly restricted to these channels. This will particularly apply to the confidential and background guidance.' The Lobby thus urged the government to resume 'those conferences which had proved so mutually valuable in the past', a suggestion which merited a pencilled 'yes' in the margin from Chamberlain as he, above all others, was bound to remember how 'mutually valuable' the Lobby had become. The Lobby also suggested that these conferences 'should *not* take place at the Ministry of Information, when publicity about them would be inescapable, but privately at the House of Commons or in the appropriate department.... the normal channels of communication between the Government and the Lobby should be kept open.' The letter ended by pointing out the disadvantages to the government of using the MOI centralized system as well as the advantages to the government of the Lobby system:

> The Lobby would point out that failure to use their organization is likely to involve very serious political and diplomatic disadvantages. Under the new system many Ministerial conferences are held which are attended by journalists with no experience in the political field. They may be first class crime reporters, for example, but it is not expected that they can interpret or present matters of political importance in the manner to which Lobby journalists, by their experience and training, are accustomed.[22]

The Lobby was thus appealing to its proved usefulness to Chamberlain as a way of preserving its privileged institutional independence; and it was not surprising that the Prime Minister jumped at these suggestions as his solution to the problem of the MOI. The Lobby's preservation as a secret, privileged institution was the pay-off for years of uncritical subservience to the Downing Street Press Office.

However, the rest of the press soon learned of the Lobby's proposals to monopolize once again the channels of government–press communication to the exclusion of everybody else, and on 28 September the Press Committee of the MOI, representing over 200 journalists using the Ministry, addressed their own complaints about the course of action proposed by the Lobby to Chamberlain. They expressed their fears that 'The Government News Departments now at the Ministry of Information are to be decentralized,' but objected to this on the grounds that the proper solution was 'to secure a greater flow of news from these departments to the Ministry, and to appoint more trained journalists to assist in their work'. This was their remedy for 'the stranglehold on the news exercised by some of the Government Departments'.[23] The Press Committee and the Lobby were putting forward different solutions to the same problem – but in order to preserve the institutional privileges and mystique of the Lobby, and thus their own standing (both professional and financial) on their papers, the journalists of the Lobby were driven to appeal to their usefulness to Chamberlain as their trump card.

From a meeting of Lobby representatives with Sir Horace Wilson on 29 September, it became obvious that there was indeed a deep cleavage within the ranks of the press on this issue. Referring to the solution proposed by the Press Committee, the Lobby correspondents told Wilson that they were 'not impressed by a sudden conversion of men who up to 24 hours previously, had been the foremost of the Ministry's critics'. The Lobby, standing on its dignity, had 'flatly refused to attend any meetings' with the humble Press Committee. In conversation with Wilson the Lobby argued that ministers could hardly be expected 'to talk for confidential guidance to a motley collection of all sorts of reporters who were not experts in dealing with the matters under discussion'. The Lobby journalists expressed their collective annoyance at the creation of the MOI in the first place, for it seemed wholly unnecessary 'to create an entirely new machine which was merely interposing itself between Ministers ... and those journalists who were expert in their particular jobs, and whom for years Ministers had been in the habit of talking to confidentially for guidance'.[24] Indeed, the whole structure of Whitehall's system of unattributable briefings was threatened by the mere existence of the new MOI, and the other specialist correspondents in the press were equally incensed at the creation of a ministry which threatened their customary privileged positions as the only journalists with access to the inner recesses of Whitehall. It was that access which made them valuable to their papers; if such access was open to everyone their professional status and privileges would correspondingly decline. In industrial terms, the Lobby correspondents were fighting for the perpetuation of a closed shop that would protect their status and income.

Lord Macmillan, the Minister of Information, on receiving the Lobby's complaints from Chamberlain, was quick to reassure the

Prime Minister that his proposals for reforming the Ministry would remove the Lobby's 'grounds for complaint'.[25] His plan to divest the Ministry of all its news and censorship functions meant that the decentralization of news dissemination was achieved and the various government departments were now able to exercise absolute discretion over what news they released and to whom it was given. It was a famous victory for the incestuous relationship between the Whitehall departments and the specialist correspondents – and a sad and irreversible defeat for the freedom of information.

These proposals were announced by Lord MacMillan on 3 October 1939. As Ian Mclaine has observed, 'It was a famous victory for the service departments.'[26] However, it was just as much a victory for the Lobby, which had managed to preserve its premier position in the journalistic hierarchy only by pointing out how advantageous its system of news gathering was to the government. It was a triumph of selfish self-preservation over the wider interests of the press – and one that was to be permanent. It is all the more surprising that the Lobby journalists were prepared to do this after their admitted malleability in the hands of Chamberlain and Steward, of which they themselves had protested to the Prime Minister in April 1939; but when it came to the actual preservation of the Lobby itself, these considerations obviously faded into the background. If all the journalists had backed the proposals of the Press Committee, the government would eventually have had to yield and force the government departments to be more forthcoming; as it was, the Lobby allowed the government to be as selective and unattributable in its treatment of the press as it had always been. Thus, ironically, the opening of the war brought a chance to develop a more open system of government which was torpedoed by the selfish considerations of a few journalists. The control of news, which now lay in the exclusive hands of the separate Whitehall departments, was, as it had been, in fact a subtler and much more effective form of censorship.

Under the rulings announced on 3 October, the Press and Censorship Bureau was thus removed from the MOI altogether and the Whitehall ministries once again retained ultimate control over the issuing of news – and over the way in which that news was to be issued. To those who had had any experience in dealing with the relationship between the government and the press, such an outcome of the unhappy birth pangs of the Ministry of Information was not really surprising. George Steward, for one, had warned A.P. Waterfield, the civil servant seconded to examine the prospective functioning of the MOI in July 1939, that those responsible for planning the Ministry would face a hopeless task if they tried to centralize all news conferences under one roof. Steward told Waterfield that such a system would come up against the impenetrable barrier of the 'human element' – as indeed it did. Not only did he warn Waterfield that the Lobby would be unlikely to acquiesce in such a centralized creation, but he also suggested that other Whitehall press officers would be unlikely to be happy working under the aegis of another ministry. With admirable foresight, Steward said that the specialist correspondents would never stoop to receiving information from the planned centralized press sections at the MOI which were available to any journalist, but would 'always claim recourse to the parent departments for their background information'. Likewise, the specialist correspondents would never condescend 'to merely receive Government hand-outs, as this was a job that was seen as the exclusive preserve of the third class, the humble reporter!'.

Having dissected the psychological hierarchy of the newspapers, Steward then turned his attention to the Whitehall departments and pointed out to Waterfield that it would be highly unusual if any press officer of a historic and prestigious Whitehall department, normally of a senior rank, would be willing to place himself under the control of a temporary civil servant at a newly created ministry such as the one that Waterfield had the task of setting up. Steward correctly questioned whether any officer in such august institutions as the Admiralty or the Foreign Office would allow himself to be happily integrated into such an arriviste amateur ministry as the MOI: 'it would be too much to expect of human nature that those senior officers would ever willingly transfer to the Ministry and work under the control of other press relations officers after having been in their own departments'.[27]

Despite Waterfield's scepticism of Steward's remarks, Chamberlain's Press Officer was proved absolutely right and within a month of the start of war the much vaunted MOI was comprehensively dismantled, attacked by those very specialist correspondents that Steward had warned the MOI planners about and by the Whitehall departments who jealously defended the threatened encroachment by the new MOI on their own traditional methods and prerogatives of news dissemination. The overall result of this two-pronged, and successful, attack on the MOI was that the system of news-gathering from the point of view of the press continued much as it had done before the war, and from the point of view of the various government departments it meant that they were free to cultivate their customary coteries of sympathetic specialist correspondents and to decide their own policies on news and information, just as 10 Downing Street and the Foreign Office had, for instance, done before the war. So, despite the fact that the war period saw the operating of Britain's first Ministry of Information, it also, and more importantly, saw the rapid growth of the Whitehall departments' network of separate press officers – a network which expanded and operated quite independently of the Ministry of Information, which had originally been conceived to do their job for them. By 1944, the civil ministries employed 661 civil servants as press officers, whilst the War Office employed 530 officers in this capacity and the Air Ministry 115. The Foreign Office retained its own News Department, which acted solely at its behest. Indeed, if anything the control by the Foreign Office News Department of the diplomatic correspondents increased during the war as access to other sources of information abroad was rapidly curtailed by the Nazi occupation of Europe.

The Whitehall departments thus looked upon their absolute control of their own news dissemination as essential in view of what they saw as the notoriously slack censorship rules. Once it became clear that the freedom of the press was to be, as far as circumstances would permit, preserved during the war, so the service ministries and the Foreign Office just circumvented the formal censorship system by refusing to issue any news to the Ministry of Information to give to the press – thus rendering the formal process of 'press censorship' carried out at the MOI virtually superfluous. The fact that there were only four prosecutions against newspapers during the war under the various censorship regulations is often taken as a token of the responsibility of the press and the eminent sagacity of the British government; but it owed just as much to the fact that, due to what Voigt had earlier described as the 'silent censorship' exercised by the various ministries, the press was seldom able to acquire any information of enough military or diplomatic importance to offend under Defence Regulation 3 or 2(c). An Air Ministry memo of 1941 expressed this view of the press and the MOI perfectly, explaining that the Air Ministry was 'absolutely convinced ... that the Ministry of Information cannot possibly be permitted to perform the function of controlling the issue of operational news without grave dangers to security. The Ministry is notoriously dominated by the press and it would be impossible to guarantee that secret information would not leak out if it was supplied to the M of I. ... The trouble is much too deep seated to be curable.'[28] The Admiralty was the most notoriously secretive department and, for reasons that were very similar to those stated above, the MOI was told by an Admiralty representative in February 1940 that 'the fundamental principle was that the effective censorship on Admiralty questions should be done by and at the Admiralty'.[29]

Despite continuous efforts by successive Ministers of Information throughout the war, the MOI was never able to recover from the blow inflicted upon it by Chamberlain's decision of October 1939, and so as far as news dissemination was concerned the Whitehall departments were able to continue throughout the war, and indeed after the war, in much the same vein as they had before. Nowhere was this continuity more evident than in the Foreign Office, which sought, on the whole successfully, to continue throughout the war its own well-tried system of informal censorship and news control. Indeed, the News Department of the Foreign Office deployed the very success of its 'informal' methods of news control as an argument against tighter 'formal' statutory censorship whenever such a step was considered by the government (as it frequently was) during the war. The News Department rightly recognized that it was essential for Britain to maintain a 'formal' liberty of the press despite the occasional embarrassment for the government that might ensue from such liberty. At one Foreign Office meeting to discuss the matter of censorship, a senior official, Sir Orme Sargent, echoed the view of the News Department when he pointed out that 'the maintenance of the liberty of the press in wartime was valuable as definite evidence that we were really fighting for the liberty of the individual in speech and thought'. He also argued, quite correctly, that despite the volumes of complaint about the press from British ambassadors abroad, 'although temporary embarrassment has been caused from time to time to our relations with several foreign powers owing to press indiscretion, there was no justification for saying that during the war anything which had been said in the press had seriously affected the course of our relationship with any foreign power'.[30]

The News Department argued along similar lines. Charles Peake was constantly warning against the evils of being too high-handed with the press as he frequently had to endure a torrent of abuse from other Foreign Office officials about what was regarded as the absurdly lax wartime censorship. He minuted against a complaint about an article in the British press from the Embassy in Rome that the Foreign Office 'should be on guard against thinking that we can regiment the entire press in Britain at the bidding of the Italian Government or because we think it polite. We are not in a position to do so, nor do I think it desirable to do so.'[31] On the other hand, the News Department could point out that on the whole it was remarkably successful at regimenting the press along the lines required by the Foreign Office, and that the odd lapse in this record of success was infinitely preferable to a more obviously oppressive censorship system. William Ridsdale of the News Department argued that any more draconian 'formal' censorship was unnecessary as 'there was already a very large measure of cooperation between the press and the F.O. News Department', and there was only a 'small minority' of newspapers which refused to take their advice. Risdale consequently argued that any further statutory legislation would only rebound on the Foreign Office by antagonizing the press: 'the press might take umbrage and the amount of cooperation . . . would be diminished rather than increased'.[32]

The Foreign Office News Department could only argue for the continuation of its own system of guidance and news control if its own methods of tacit censorship were successful, as they undoubtedly were. Peake defended his own techniques, which rested entirely upon 'persuasion': he pointed to the excellent results obtained from his guidance policy, but added that for it to be effective 'persuasion . . . must be reasonable and in the case of the opposition press, it is wise sometimes to let them exercise their judgement even if that judgement is not the same as ours'.[33] As another official from the department minuted, for instance, the solution to the problem of a recalcitrant journalist who was threatening to publish something that might not be welcomed by the Foreign Office was not to threaten the journalist with legislation but to take him 'into our confidence rather more'.[34] This was exactly the Leeper method; the more the individual journalist could be made to feel that he was sharing responsibility for foreign policy, the more likely he would be to bow to the demands of that foreign policy. As soon as the News Department had managed to disentangle itself from the MOI in October 1939, it was free to exercise its careful campaign of persuasion and the Foreign Office could indeed, as Sir Orme Sargent had noted, have little cause for complaint about the extent of the influence it could exert on the press despite what many of its officials regarded as its deplorable lack of legal or punitive powers during the war. Not everyone, however, could be satisfied. Commenting on the action that could be taken against the *Daily Mirror* after the paper had once again annoyed the Ambassador in Madrid with a provocative article attacking General Franco one frustrated official was driven to comment that 'it seems to me that one solution would be for the proprietor of the *Daily Mirror* to become involved in a nasty accident. This would certainly be his fate in any other country.'[35]

Just as the Foreign Office relied on the News Department's contact with the specialist correspondents throughout the war, so it also relied to an equally great extent on those personal contacts with the proprietors which had worked so well before the war and which now proved just as effective. The Foreign Office was particularly keen to keep anything out of the press which would antagonize Mussolini whilst Italy was still neutral (in the period up to June 1940), or which would antagonize the Franco regime throughout the war. The most effective way to do this was to cultivate those informal, personal contacts that had served so well during the appeasement period. Lord Perth, the former Ambassador to Rome, was particularly quick to point out how 'sensitive Mussolini was to criticism'.[36] On 15 December 1939, Perth went to see Lord Beaverbrook about various articles deprecating the Italian armed forces, which it was known had 'caused great indignation' to Mussolini. According to Perth Beaverbrook confessed his complete ignorance of these articles; 'anything that could offend Italy was completely contrary to the policy of the newspaper. This was evident by the leading article in the *Evening Standard* two or three days ago which had been written under his direction – he

140

promised to go into the matter and to haul over the coals those responsible. He even talked of writing to Mussolini on the matter.' Perth asked the Foreign Office to keep this conversation 'highly confidential' as he 'had seen Lord Beaverbrook entirely on his own initiative'.[37] This was still the most effective way of curbing the press; having been assured of Beaverbrook's willingness to help the Foreign Office, Perth was writing to the Editor of the *Evening Standard*, Frank Owen, asking him to 'earnestly . . . control very closely any reference to Italy in the important paper for which you are responsible'.[38] The appeal to the Editor's vanity and the appeal to his sense of responsibility was the old concoction, and in this case Perth could also remind Owen of Beaverbrook's own views on the matter, which he had ascertained only two weeks before.

Exactly the same contacts were maintained to try and curb the natural tendency of the press to attack Fascist Spain, which again militated against the Foreign Office policy of trying to keep Franco out of the war. Franco was another dictator who swiftly let his sensitivity become known. During 1940, when it was most essential to keep Spain pacific, Sir Samuel Hoare, the new Ambassador in Madrid, bombarded his old political ally Beaverbrook with a string of requests not only to prevent the *Evening Standard* and the *Daily* and *Sunday Express* from printing anything that might drive Franco into the arms of Hitler and Mussolini, but also to suggest publication of leaders 'saying that things were greatly improving in Spain and suggesting that we are not in the least engaged or interested in stirring up a revolution against the Franco Government'.[39] Beaverbrook was most anxious to give all his 'assistance . . . to make smooth' his friend's path, and after one adverse article in July the proprietor took action to ensure that 'the trouble is not likely to occur again.'[40] Nothing of this exchange was even shown to the Foreign Office, which likewise had to rely on personal contacts at the behest of Hoare to dampen other organs on the subject of Spain. The *News Chronicle* had always been markedly opposed to Franco's regime, which is why William Ridsdale of the News Department took special care to see Vernon Bartlett, the paper's diplomatic correspondent, virtually every day. An article by William Forrest in the paper on 18 July 1940, exhibiting a strongly anti-Franco prejudice, finally forced the Foreign Secretary to write to Sir Archibald Sinclair, the Liberal leader, Air Minister and political mentor of Sir Walter Layton, Chairman of the *News Chronicle*, to urge him to see Layton to 'moderate the expression of hostility to the Spanish Government' in the *News Chronicle*. Layton was in entire agreement and 'undertook to speak to the *News Chronicle* about it'.[41] In October, Halifax met the newspaper proprietors himself to lecture them on the same subject, warning them that the attitude of the press 'on Spanish affairs is a factor of major importance in making or marring our policy to Spain which is dictated exclusively by the exigencies of the strategical position and is not influenced and cannot be influenced by any political or ideological sympathies'.[42] These various informal and personal efforts constituted the most effective form of guidance that the Foreign Office could proffer – the same process was to be repeated with similar consequences over the vital issue of Anglo-Soviet relations later in the war.

Thus, just as the service ministries operated their own private censorship by rigidly controlling the flow of news, so the Foreign Office did likewise but it also exercised those effective methods of personal contact both at the level of the News Department with the specialist correspondents and at ambassadorial or national level with newspaper proprietors and editors. Those ambassadors and officials operating this form of 'silent censorship' could point to its success in order to appease the more repressive instincts of most of their colleagues. The creation of the MOI at the beginning of the war represents the only formal attempt by the government to break the magic circle of personal, unattributable contact between the press and the government to this day. As it is, with Chamberlain's reforms of October 1939, the system of news dissemination favoured by institutions such as the Lobby remains intact even now. Indeed, the reason that it does remain intact is solely because it works so much in favour of those disseminating the information; it must always be regretted that one section of the press connived in dismantling a novel and, in the long run, potentially more open structure of news dissemination in the first month of a war fought as much as anything else for the liberty of thought and expression. As it is, the striking pattern of continuity in the government–press relationship between the pre-war pattern and that of wartime in departments like the Foreign Office can be seen either as a tribute to the freedom of expression retained in wartime, or as a condemnation of the extent of suppression in peacetime. Either way it was Steward's 'personal touch' that predominated.

5

The Final Act:
September 1939 to May 1940

With the start of the war the press immediately adopted an appropriately defiant and bellicose tone in expectation of the imminent clash
of arms. Nowhere was this new attitude better demonstrated than
in the offices of *The Times*, as Dawson and Barrington-Ward were
determined to shake off the stigma of appeasement and approach the
war, now that it had come, in a positive and energetic fashion. Having
been so misled by the government in the past, Dawson and Barrington-
Ward would now treat it with a good deal of scepticism, a sentiment
widely shared by the rest of the press and one which was to manifest
itself in various ways throughout the rest of Chamberlain's premiership. Chamberlain was immediately made aware of Dawson's new-
found sense of conviction when he summoned the Editor of *The Times*
to Downing Street on 2 September in time-honoured fashion to tell
him of the plan 'for War Cabinet ... Labour on the whole preferring
to stand out, Winston and Hankey to come in'.[1] However, if Chamberlain was expecting to draw the usual panegyric from Dawson's pen,
he was very much mistaken. Dawson's subsequent editorial of 4
September argued the advantages of having a small, non-departmental
War Cabinet, similar to that system devised by Lloyd George from
1916 to 1918 – by inference suggesting that Chamberlain's largely
peacetime Cabinet would prove too large and unwieldy to be effective.

Dawson compared his preferred scheme for a War Cabinet to the qualities that Churchill brought to the government: 'Mr Churchill comes in now, as a matter of course, because he is a man of energy, most fertile imagination and warlike temperament. These are qualities essential in a War Cabinet.'

Dawson's clarion call for a small, non-departmental War Cabinet was to be echoed in most of the press in the following months and reflected a steadily mounting suspicion that Chamberlain and his Cabinet were not possessed of energy, fertile imagination and least of all a warlike temperament. But Dawson's critique startled many, simply because he had differed from Chamberlain – drawing, for instance, the unaccustomed plaudits of the erstwhile anti-appeaser Leo Amery, who wrote to Dawson to declare himself 'most encouraged' by Dawson's criticisms of Chamberlain's 'hybrid type of War Cabinet'.[2] Dawson, however, although critical, was still prepared to give Chamberlain the benefit of the doubt, replying to Amery that 'I am sure it was not what the PM originally intended.'[3] The Prime Minister, doubtless taken aback by Dawson's rare words of criticism, deployed his usual tactic on such occasions of merely sending someone to see the recalcitrant editor to allay his fears; in this instance, Maurice Hankey, an ex-Cabinet Secretary and newly promoted Cabinet Minister, was despatched to assure Dawson that the 'War Cabinet ... was working very well'.[4]

The new militancy of *The Times* was also illustrated by the enforced departure of the ubiquitous Basil Liddell Hart as the paper's military correspondent. Just as Dawson and Barrington-Ward became more aggressive and eager in their approach to the war, so Liddell Hart allowed himself to be overwhelmed by the apparent impossibility of winning the war and the futility of even trying. He thus favoured 'a definite declaration that we were renouncing military action, in the offensive sense ... that we were not planning to punish the aggression that had taken place ... and this would allow Germany and Russia, now contiguous, to rub against each other'.[5] Such pessimistic prognostications were no longer welcome in *The Times* office, and both Dawson and Barrington-Ward grew rapidly disenchanted with their military correspondent, whom Barrington-Ward now described as 'a monolith of egotism and vanity'.[6] With such an obvious cleavage in opinion, Liddell Hart was to leave the paper in October, but he was soon to spread his pessimism in other quarters.

As Chamberlain showed no inclination either to refresh his War Cabinet with some anti-Municheers (with the inevitable exception of Churchill) or to prosecute the war effort with the vigour that was obviously required, disenchantment with him grew. Ironically, this disenchantment manifested itself most seriously amongst the Cliveden set, and *The Times* slowly transformed itself into one of Chamberlain's most constructive critics. However, it was the owner of the *Observer*, Lord Astor, who became the most vehement critic of Chamberlain. Whilst Dawson's doubts about the Prime Minister's capabilities only surfaced after the outbreak of war, Lord Astor's doubts and suspicions went right back to Munich. His faith in Chamberlain's appeasement policies had evaporated in the face of Hitler's 'negotiating' techniques in the weeks before the Munich agreement, and whilst he might have supported the Munich agreement itself as the only available solution to an almost impossible situation, he was under no illusions about what it meant for the future. As he rightly explained to an American friend a year later, the difference between his own view of Munich and Chamberlain's was that whereas he had seen it 'as a right get out of a situation in which we had been caught unarmed', the Prime Minister had 'looked on it as, in itself, a triumph'.[7] Lord Astor swiftly rid himself of any hopes that he might have entertained that Hitler was amenable to reasoning and diplomacy, and realized that Britain was simply dealing with 'a more heavily armed gangster'.[8] On 21 September 1938, as Chamberlain was flying out for his second talk with Hitler, Astor was writing to Garvin of the advice that he had given to 'a junior Cabinet Minister' that 'Britain was bound to lose face whatever happened now – that the best chance of restoring some kind of world position for ourselves and of regaining our self-respect was to set up a new and national Government for defence with a striking programme of increased output of aero engines ... to negotiate from strength.'[9]

From October 1938, the *Observer* began to campaign for an increased air rearmament programme, but after Hitler's invasion of Prague in March 1939 Lord Astor was determined to effect more radical changes in order to make 'Hitler and the Germans feel that we will be firm'.[10] This was the motivation behind his campaign to bring Churchill into the Cabinet in July 1939, a move that demanded the personal exorcism of decades of mistrust of Churchill's powers of

146

judgement on Astor's part. As late as April 1939 he was reminding Garvin, who had always been a keen supporter of Churchill in any capacity, that 'Winston's constant brandy drinking and big cigars have at last appreciably diminished his physical efficiency,'[11] an opinion perhaps coloured by Astor's total abstinence. Given the failure of the campaign to get Churchill into the Cabinet and Chamberlain's steadfast refusal to listen to criticism, even if it came from such respectable quarters as the Astor family, it was hardly surprising that with the onset of war and Chamberlain's apparent refusal to countenance any drastic change in policy or personnel Astor should begin to turn his mind to the removal of Chamberlain altogether.

Lord Astor, like the rest of the Cliveden set, was a survivor of the heroic age of Lloyd George – 1916–18 vintage – and, like Lord Lothian, had served on Lloyd George's Secretariat during the last two years of the First World War. Like Dawson, Astor saw all too clearly the vital differences between Chamberlain in 1939 and Lloyd George at the height of his powers in 1917, and he shared with the Editor of *The Times* a sense of frustration at Chamberlain's continuance with what they saw as peacetime administrative practices and policies during a period of war. Astor wrote to remind Dawson on 4 October 1939 of their cherished distinction between the present 'so called War Cabinet and the real War Cabinet of 1917'.[12] This criticism was now to become a continual refrain amongst the remnants of the Cliveden set. As the autumn turned to winter and Lord Astor's frustrations with Chamberlain grew, so he fell into constant and, given his allegiances, rather surprising contact with the Eden group of Conservative backbenchers. On 3 October, Harold Nicolson recorded that Astor had 'recommended that the P.M. should be removed and that Winston Churchill should take his place. The question is how and when.'[13] Astor recorded that the group had been 'very pessimistic about their prospects of improving matters', and he told them that 'the Press could support but not initiate a revolt or criticism'.[14] Lord Astor also indulged in some surreptitious fraternizing with the Labour front bench in the House of Commons; on 3 January 1940 he was writing to Garvin that one of his 'Labour Front Bench friends' had told him that they wanted 'to overthrow the present Gang – but they say they can only do so if they get some support both in the House of Commons, from the Conservative Back Benchers and also from our

Press – otherwise they feel that their fight is hopeless'.[15]

However, between Lord Astor's private hopes of uniting Parliament against Chamberlain and of using the *Observer* to this end, lay J. L. Garvin. Garvin shared much of his proprietor's feelings about Chamberlain and his lacklustre government, agreeing, for instance, that 'the more one looks at it the more one sees that we have no real War Cabinet at all such as he has created; and that the present promiscuous Council of ten whose minds mostly are clouded with departmental detail is as ordinary as any "peace Committee" of ministers in normal times'.[16] Like Lord Astor, he had privately entertained severe doubts about Munich and was bitterly disappointed at what he called in a letter to Astor on 3 November 1938 'Neville's mediocre sequel to the crisis', adding that 'this peace with humiliating weakness, and apparent incapacity for any kind of great organization, is something worse than I ever saw in my time'.[17] However, Garvin's approach to this problem was radically different from Astor's, as he believed that the duty of an editor faced by such a national crisis was to support the Prime Minister, come what may. He consistently refused to allow any criticism of Chamberlain in the paper, and thus began an increasingly bitter and acrimonious correspondence with Astor. Garvin might have shared Astor's private misgivings over, for instance, the British guarantees to Poland and Roumania in April and May 1939, but he warned Astor that it was not possible to say so in the paper, as it was 'not possible for us to enable the Germans to say or think that the P.M. has lost the confidence of the country and that the nation is already split or splitting'.[18] Garvin was thus quite consciously suppressing what he felt to be the truth – a maxim that had governed his writing in the immediate aftermath of Munich too.

To Lord Astor, this was a dishonest policy. When a tribunal was convened in August 1941 to consider Garvin's new contract as editor, his attitude towards Chamberlain in 1939 and 1940 was the subject of Astor's main complaint against him. Astor wrote in a memorandum for the Tribunal that 'there were many grave deficiencies and serious inadequacies in Mr Chamberlain's administration.... on more than one occasion I pointed out to Mr Garvin certain weaknesses.... helpful criticism based on knowledge might have helped to accelerate changes in that Government – changes which would now be recognized as having been desirable'. Astor concluded that 'Appeals to people's loyal support for the Government of the day which convey the impression that matters are much better than they are is not the most helpful tune a great paper can play in a crisis.'[19] Garvin, for his part, refused to let the *Observer* criticize the government or Chamberlain, pleading the cause of unity in front of the enemy – to which his proprietor later replied in a rage of frustration that the country would thus go to its doom 'united in silence.... Public opinion can't make itself felt unless it is instructed by someone.'[20] Blocked by Garvin, Astor turned his mind to fomenting parliamentary opposition; Garvin vowed to 'hold' himself in 'until the shot is sure', however 'mad' this made him in the process.[21] He preferred to focus his anger on 'Liddell Hart and the little cold feet club'.[22]

Garvin and Astor were confronting the classic dilemma for a journalist during wartime. A later editor of the *Observer*, Ivor Brown, confronted by exactly similar circumstances in 1942, was to write: 'If there is criticism of the wartime Government, the enemy, especially in these times of radio-warfare, can always exploit it, as we exploit any signs of unrest in Germany. But, if there is no criticism then the nation suffers and the claim to be a liberal democracy looks idle.'[23]

No paper felt its responsibilities more in this matter than *The Times* and it continued to give reserved support to the government in terms of its general policy. However, in detail *The Times* now embarked on a campaign of judicious and authoritative criticism that did as much to undermine confidence in Chamberlain as anything else. Dawson found his criticisms of Chamberlain's government shared by many of his contemporaries – be they appeasers or anti-appeasers. One of the latter was the senior Conservative backbencher, Leo Amery, who became a powerful critic of the war effort in the pages of *The Times*. Amery wrote to Dawson in November 1939 about the concern felt by 'everybody' at the economic conduct of the war; 'the trouble lies in the absence of any one person whose wholetime business it is to direct the economic aspect of the war and of any organization which would enable such direction to be effective'.[24] Dawson was impressed by these arguments and published an article by Amery on this theme a few weeks later, which the admiring Editor described as 'one of the best and most important contributions that "The Times" has had since the war ... and is ... producing an admirable correspondence'.[25] Like other veterans of Lloyd George's administration, Amery also

149

kept up his demands for a small War Cabinet, strengthening Dawson's own convictions on the subject. In April 1940 Dawson received a memorandum from Amery in which he put the argument for a 'Cabinet which will think ahead in terms of policy and not of routine day to day administration . . . like a general staff, free of departmental work'.[26] Perhaps prompted by these thoughts, two days later Dawson renewed the demands for a smaller and more effective War Cabinet in a leader entitled 'Relief for Ministers' on 16 April. Given the considerable political gulf separating Amery and Dawson before the war, for Chamberlain it was an ominous meeting of minds.

Another survivor of the First World War who was now under-employed and dissatisfied with the government was Sir William Beveridge, who found the pages of *The Times* a fertile ground on which to scatter his seeds of doubt. Beveridge was particularly important in this respect as he was working on his criticisms with a distinguished group of ex-mandarins who found themselves out of favour under Chamberlain's government but were later to run most of the war effort under Churchill. This group consisted of J. M. Keynes, Sir Arthur Salter, Sir Walter Layton and Beveridge himself – Keynes was to dub them the 'old dogs group', who would meet regularly at his house in Gordon Square to put forward alternative policy ideas and initiate criticism of the government's administrative machinery. Like Astor, Garvin, Lothian and Dawson (the Cliveden set) and the likes of Leo Amery, the 'old dogs group' very much drew their inspiration from unfavourable comparisons with the halcyon days of Lloyd George's administration – which most of them had served. Beveridge found his greatest supporter in Barrington-Ward, who had reached very much the same conclusion as Beveridge that 'sooner or later, and probably very soon, the whole British economy . . . must become a planned economy'.[27] Barrington-Ward was thus finding himself in agreement with Beveridge at a very early stage of the war and it was to be the beginning of a profitable partnership that was to help take *The Times* leftwards and give Beveridge one of his firmest supporters. At the beginning of October 1939, *The Times* published a long article on the economic direction of the war, or rather the lack of it. Beveridge argued for an economic general staff and a central staff of statisticians, to remedy what he described in private as the 'hopelessly weak' central organization of government. In his own opinion Beveridge, like

Barrington-Ward, was convinced that 'the present crew ... have no conception at all of how to plan a war or how to conduct it'.[28] Although he could not go as far as this in the pages of *The Times*, he did use the paper to argue in more temperate language for economic planning and a small War Cabinet.

Likewise, Keynes' scheme for post-war credits was published in *The Times* in November, when it was called 'Compulsory savings'; but he later changed what he called 'that obnoxious title'[29] to make it more palatable to the trade unions, as Labour felt that the original scheme was merely 'a veiled attack on wages of the working class'.[30] Sir Walter Layton used the *News Chronicle* policy conference to impress upon his colleagues the sense of urgency that the 'old dogs group' felt was needed in the conduct of the war effort, and he published several articles on this theme. In a memo that was published in the *News Chronicle* at the beginning of December, Layton argued that 'the existing programme of 55 divisions should be capable of fulfilment in 1941 not as at present contemplated late in 1942 ... '.[31]

In gathering opinion about the war effort, W. P. Crozier was also alerted to the complacency and inefficiency in government circles by a variety of sources, and the *Manchester Guardian* took up a similar critical position to *The Times*. Vansittart, as always, was prominent amongst the government's critics and he told Crozier in January 1940 that 'we need a much greater national effort in this country. We must have more men called up ... people simply did not understand the urgency or need for a greater effort'.[32] However, Crozier also got much the same message from Churchill, except that the First Lord of the Admiralty could not be as vocal as the compulsively indiscreet Chief Diplomatic Adviser. In January, Churchill warned Crozier that 'the war effort *must* be intensified'; he referred to 'munitions and said that we were now where we were in 1916, but we must get as rapidly as possible to 1918'. He urged Crozier as he was leaving to 'take a firm line, tell them what sacrifices the Government expects of the country, and set the appeal high'.[33] In March, Churchill was still complaining of the slow rearmament programme and told Crozier that 'a much greater effort was needed and that a million of women must come boldly forward'.[34] Brendan Bracken, Churchill's loyal disciple and pps, reinforced his strictures and confided to Crozier that 'Chamberlain hates criticism', so 'if you want anything done by the Government

151

you have got to push and push and push!'.[35]

Whilst the 'old dogs group', the remnants of the Cliveden set and assorted anti-appeasers turned to the press to ventilate their disappointment with Chamberlain as a war leader in comparison with Lloyd George, there was another section of the press which began to look to the future for its inspiration. Just as Lord Astor could find Chamberlain wanting in the context of his own experience in government, there was a younger generation who came to feel that Chamberlain provided no inspiration or vision for the future either. Now that Britain had embarked on the war, many more radical minds began to try and define her 'war aims' or 'peace aims' – what Britain was fighting *for*. In the political and military vacuum of the Phoney War, it soon became obvious that the government's professed war aim to 'smash Hitler' was not going to be enough for a great many people who wanted something more constructive than this stolidly negative mission. Sir Stafford Cripps, the renegade Labour politician who was to challenge Churchill for the premiership in 1942, was one MP who spoke of the need for war aims in the House of Commons on 13 October 1939, and he received a crop of letters in support, one of which can be used to illustrate the feeling that was abroad in the country at this time. A Mr Nelsey from London wrote: 'there is a rapidly rising tide of resentment against a policy of "Smash Hitler and leave the rest to us". There are several million men in this country who have heard that before and who won't be caught a second time.'[36]

To articulate this sentiment in the press and amongst the government's policy-makers, an organization called the Post-War Bureau was founded on 15 November 1939 which was 'to provide contacts and publicity for all those groups and individuals who were interested and working on the correlated subjects of war aims, peace terms, general European construction and world order'. The moving spirit behind this new organization was Sir Edward Hulton, owner of the Hulton Press and the proprietor of the *Picture Post*, which now became, under the energetic editorship of Tom Hopkinson, one of the main campaigners for an inspiring vision of a post-war world. The first meeting of the new organization was held at Sir Edward Hulton's London home at 11 Hill Street in Mayfair, and from the start the Bureau counted a large number of journalists and press proprietors amongst its members, including Hulton himself, Tom Hopkinson,

David Astor (the second son of Lord Astor, who was soon to be very influential in the affairs of the *Observer*), Gerald Barry and Sir Walter Layton from the *News Chronicle* and Francis Williams, Editor of the *Daily Herald*. The activities of the Bureau were limited to the arranging of meetings, the holding of press conferences and 'the preparation of articles and material for circulation to the Press'.[37] As an organization in its own right, the Post-War Bureau was a singularly ineffective body and it soon petered out; but it was important as a precursor for the much more influential and popular 1941 Committee which would take shape during the course of 1940. These unofficial ginger-groups were important to the press as it put them in contact with some of the main advocates of post-war reform and reconstruction at a very early date and provided the attendant journalists and editors with the material they needed to articulate the yearning for positive war aims in their papers. Francis Williams in the *Daily Herald* was a prominent supporter of the Post-War Bureau, and from an early stage of the war he began a campaign for an ideological vision of the war that was eventually to cost him his editorial chair.

The concern with post-war aims and the deficiencies of the government's war effort were expressions not only of hope for a better future, but also of profound disappointment with the existing government. The first steps in what was to become known as the search for the 'New Jerusalem', which ended in the litany of wartime government proposals that were to form the basis of Attlee's post-war political consensus, were thus inspired by a desire to improve the war effort as a whole. The government, for its part, refused to discuss any prospects for 'war aims' along the lines of what the likes of Edward Hulton were proposing and deftly skirted round the subject altogether – as, indeed, Churchill was to try to do when he was Prime Minister. However, not only did the enthusiasts for a New Jerusalem in the press meet with stolid resistance from the government, they were also confronted by considerable resentment on their own papers as well – to say nothing of some other sections of the press.

Typical of this situation was the plight of Francis Williams, Editor of the *Daily Herald*, who from the beginning of the war met resistance to his post-war aims and his critical attitude towards the government both from his 'A' directors at the TUC and his 'B' directors at Odhams. Williams first clashed with Sir Walter Citrine, the most senior of the

'A' directors and General Secretary of the TUC, over the paper's 'Mr Muddles' column, which attempted to expose the muddle and waste surrounding the government's war effort. Citrine's complaint was that such a column would be a gift to the Conservatives, who would want to highlight such defects in a programme of state control, and labelled it 'stunt journalism'.[38] Williams replied that the *Daily Herald* was obliged to point out 'muddle and inefficiency' as part of its duty to its readers.[39] At the same time as fighting the 'A' directors over politics, Williams was also clashing with Odhams over the commercial implications of those politics. He later claimed of Southwood that 'with the period of the phoney war all his determination to put unpleasant things out of sight came back. The phoney war restored his faith in the commercial ethos.'[40] He explained to the Royal Commission on the press that he himself was 'extremely critical of much of the policy of the Chamberlain Government' in various leading articles which were then 'sub-edited' as there was 'a substantial body of commercial opinion which would be critical of that sort of comment . . .; it was a culmination of that kind which in fact led to my own resignation'.[41] This is very hard to verify and was later denied by Odhams: but it would be consistent with Southwood's general policy and his actions before Munich. Matters came to a head over Williams' plans for a 'new declaration of the rights of man' to be drawn up by H. G. Wells, which would be published and then debated in the columns of the *Daily Herald*. According to Williams, 'Men and women all over the world are deeply concerned that out of this war should develop a new conception of international society that will enable them to live peaceably and in freedom.'[42] This was apparently too much for Southwood, who refused to contemplate such an unsettling series of articles and Williams resigned, to be replaced by the non-socialist Percy Cudlipp. Williams later published his own ideas on the war in the appropriately named *War by Revolution* pamphlet and got H. G. Wells' ideas published as the Sankey Declaration.

Williams contended that he left the paper because Southwood 'didn't want to make the war any worse', and it is certainly true that just as much of the press campaigned against Chamberlain for not prosecuting the war vigorously enough or for failing to give a satisfactory account of the country's war aims, so there was also an important number of press proprietors, such as Southwood, who were distinctly lukewarm about the fact that the war had to be fought at all and who desired the 'business as usual' approach that Lord Astor had earlier identified as Chamberlain's crippling vice.

On the *News Chronicle* a similar situation prevailed, as the Cadbury brothers used the now weekly policy conferences to smother any novel proposal on war aims or war methods proposed by Gerald Barry and Vernon Bartlett, or even by Sir Walter Layton. The Cadburys thus fought anything that would hot up the war, or any expression of a plan that would antagonize an apparently docile Germany. They thus took particular exception to the plans for war aims which they feared might define a settlement that would be irrevocably unacceptable to Germany. On reading the first such statement of war aims in a leader in the *News Chronicle* on 7 October, Laurence Cadbury expressed himself doubtful about 'whether we want to be manoeuvred into stating too precisely our peace aims' and quoted Harold Nicolson's observation that the soldiers just wanted 'to fight Hitler, not *for* anything'.[43] The policy conferences soon came to be dominated by this clash over war aims and on 12 October Laurence Cadbury questioned 'how far the public was interested in the discussions of our war aims. He felt that the man in the street envisaged it as a war to smash Hitler and was more concerned in achieving that aim than with discussing peace terms.'[44] The journalists and Layton, however, sensed that as everyone seemed to be 'bewildered by the course of the war ... it was all the more necessary to make clear now what the allied aims were'.[45] Henry Cadbury and Edward Cadbury were united in their suspicion of Layton's memoranda on war aims, and Gerald Barry, to get just one Layton contribution published, had to agree at the next policy conference that it was 'unnecessary to give undue space to the discussion of war aims'.[46]

The Cadburys also argued against a campaign for war aims on the ground that, since in their opinion there was little interest in the subject, such articles and editorials would not do anything for the paper's circulation. The circulation figures of the *News Chronicle* were causing the Cadburys some anxiety at this time as they had been on a downward trend for some years, and by the spring of 1939 Laurence Cadbury was impressing upon Layton the fact that he was 'very disturbed about the drop in circulation'.[47] With the early collapse of advertising rates due to the war conditions, Laurence Cadbury was in fact more interested in casting around for ideas as 'possible antidotes to falling sales in these days of no canvassers' rather than worthy articles on war aims and the need for economic planning. One idea proposed was a monthly feature, to be heavily advertised, such as 'a character sketch by Trotsky on Stalin',[48] but, sadly, Stalin had murdered his potential scribe before he could be contacted. The Cadburys, given their commercial and political considerations, were thus keen supporters of the government's apparent policy of 'business as usual', and argued against any intensification of the war effort or attacks on Chamberlain.

If the *News Chronicle* was thus divided on the subject of war aims and the government's war effort, the Cadburys' objections to both these matters were unequivocally echoed in the *Daily Express*, as Lord Beaverbrook went further than Southwood or the Cadburys in his search for a policy of 'business as usual'. As Beaverbrook had been foremost amongst the press proprietors in supporting appeasement, it was only logical that he should be unenthusiastic about a war which he viewed as totally unnecessary. So although the paper generally supported Chamberlain, as it had done all through appeasement, the *Daily Express* campaigned against any intensification of the war effort that it could find. In this context, as A. J. P. Taylor has written, the 'Daily Express became the channel for any sort of grumble and grievance. It campaigned against rationing, against the blackout, against increasing the army, even against buying aeroplanes from America.'[49] Beaverbrook was willing to give support in his newspapers to opponents of the war and the *Sunday Express* thus printed a notorious interview with Lloyd George at the beginning of October, in which the ex-Prime Minister expressed the opinion, shared by Beaverbrook, that Poland had not been worth fighting for and had had an undemocratic and tyrannical government which had not been worth preserving. Lloyd George offered his pessimism and defeatism to anyone who would listen.

Beaverbrook took a view similar to Lloyd George's and as well as campaigning against the war effort in the *Daily Express* he indulged in some more dubious enterprises of his own. Whilst Sir Samuel Hoare loyally pressed the proprietor's services upon a reluctant Prime Minister, Beaverbrook looked elsewhere to conspire against the unnecessary war. Chamberlain reported to his sister in January 1940 that he had heard from a 'first hand authority' that Beaverbrook was 'very anxious to enter the Government . . . as Minister of Agriculture!'. However, Chamberlain could not act on this suggestion as he had 'since learned on *unimpeachable* authority that when the Duke of Windsor was here this week Beaverbrook tried to induce him to head a peace campaign in the country promising him the full support of his papers'.[50] Whether this was true or not, others, previously unacquainted with his views, could be greatly surprised by his cynicism. Harry Boardman, who was asked to lunch at Stornaway House, Beaverbrook's London residence, where he was invited to leave the *Manchester Guardian* and join the Beaverbrook press, was 'shocked to see how half hearted he is about the war'.[51]

Even Chamberlain and Hoare began to worry about their erstwhile supporter, and Hoare wrote to the Prime Minister advising that it 'would be very good tactics if he were able to have a talk with Max' as he was in an 'uncertain mood as to which side he should come down on'.[52] Their concern was fully justified for, unknown to them, Beaverbrook was attempting to finance the anti-war Independent Labour Party politicians Jimmy Maxton, John McGovern and Campbell Steven, with whom he had dinner on 5 March 1940. He was also helping the MP Richard Stokes, who was arguing for a 'negotiated peace *now*' before the situation got any worse for the allies.[53] Beaverbrook encouraged Stokes to speak out, and promised him that if he spoke at the Labour Party Conference in Bournemouth he would 'arrange for the Express to report you'.[54] Later in March, he promised Stokes coverage of a proposed public meeting, in order to state the case for a 'negotiated peace now', an enterprise that Beaverbrook considered 'most suitable'.[55] He could also refer Stokes to an article by the Red Dean of Canterbury in the *Evening Standard* of 28 March 1940 which advocated such a move. These attempts at a negotiated peace were the other side of Beaverbrook's public campaign against the war effort which he ran in the *Daily Express*. Fortunately for Beaverbrook, Hitler struck in Norway before he could go any further down this path and he swiftly repudiated these contacts once he was Minister of Aircraft Production under Churchill.

Whatever else Beaverbrook, Lloyd George and Liddell Hart might have achieved, they did provide a tempting target on which the rest of the press could practise its patriotism. Garvin and Lord Astor were united in their condemnation of 'Max and the shocking stuff in his journal'; Garvin was equally scornful of Lloyd George, who was 'certain to be a wrecker in any war conducted by others: his hatred of Neville is a mania'.[56] However, the most compulsively bellicose of all the press was the Mirror Group of newspapers, who now earned a reputation for uncomplicated patriotism and anti-Hitlerism that was to last for the rest of the war. On 15 October 1939, the *Sunday Pictorial* displayed on its front page a banner headline: 'We Accuse Lloyd George', which went on to charge him with preferring to bargain 'with the man who has broken every promise he has made – Adolf Hitler'. Indeed, the *Sunday Pictorial* and the *Daily Mirror*, which had earlier given a great deal of support to Churchill, openly supported the First Lord of the Admiralty for the premiership. There is some truth in Hugh Cudlipp's later assertion that the Mirror Group 'recorded more swiftly and encouraged more surely than any other newspaper the surge of public opinion which demanded Churchill's entry into the War Cabinet and subsequent premiership in 1940'.[57] As early as 1 October 1939, the *Sunday Pictorial* was declaring that 'Churchill will be our next Premier' – Cudlipp, the Editor, ominously adding that 'there are many enfeebled trees to fell before we plant sturdy saplings'.

The government thus seemed to be trapped between the majority of the press who expressed the need for a more efficient prosecution of the war effort and a vocal minority which expressed exasperation with the war as a whole and argued for a relaxation of the emergency war measures. Each sentiment, as has been seen, masked deeper misgivings which could not be expressed in print but which were nonetheless sincerely held. Either way, the government found itself confronted with a chorus of understated disapproval. Its response was to do nothing – which proved very effective in disheartening its critics. By December, most of the critics who were writing in the papers had the impression that they were wasting their breath. Beveridge was in despair, and wrote to those who encouraged him to keep on at the government about the poor management of economic affairs: 'being outside it is far better to avoid public discouraging criticism for the present and hope that somehow or other changes will be brought about in the Government or the attitude of the Government, which will make things better'.[58] Layton gained the same impression and lamented on 14 December that 'there had been very little reaction to his article on speeding up the war',[59] whilst Geoffrey Dawson sensed that people were 'getting a little bored' with the constantly unfavourable comparisons with the heroic endeavours of 1916 to 1918.[60]

The government combined a policy of ignoring criticism with one of fostering Chamberlain's customary sense of absurdly inflated optimism about the possible course of events, which was used to deflect much of the criticism about their apparent inactivity. Chamberlain, as usual, relied on the 'personal touch' of his inner Cabinet and entourage to stifle criticism, without doing anything about it. Thus, after Beveridge's article on economic affairs had appeared in *The Times*, he was immediately contacted by Sir Horace Wilson, who assured him that his proposals were actually operating; but Wilson's description of the economic machinery of Whitehall was, to Beveridge, '*not* very close to what I had in mind'.[61] Sir John Simon wrote to Garvin to soothe his concern over the *Observer*'s call for a special economic minister, pointing out that there were 'great practical difficulties in such a plan'; he had also attacked the paper's demands for a small War Cabinet.[62] Lord Astor went to a private meeting between Hore-Belisha, the Minister for War, and the press in the House of Commons which Lord Camrose, proprietor of *The Daily Telegraph*, agreed was 'a most thin and disappointing performance', whilst Astor found Samuel Hoare 'far too complacent and apt to ridicule L. G. and his regime'.[63]

But whilst the government thus blocked any suggestions for improvement, it also blunted the cutting edge of any criticism by holding out the possibility that Germany would soon collapse due to her own internal political and economic contradictions. Chamberlain himself had outlined this frame of mind in a letter to his sister in the first week of war, when he advanced a scenario in which the time for 'discussing peace terms' might not be a long way off, for he had observed:

> such a widespread desire to avoid war and it is so deeply rooted that it surely must find expressions somehow. Of course the difficulty is with Hitler himself. Until he disappears and his system collapses there can be no peace. But what I hope for is not a military victory. I very much doubt the feasibility of that – but a collapse

159

of the German home front. For that it is necessary to convince the Germans that they cannot win.[64]

This was to be the scenario that Chamberlain and his entourage were to present to the press for most of the Phoney War, and it raised the possibility of an easy victory by merely sitting tight which few could resist.

On 24 September, Halifax was putting the same point to Dawson, who recorded that the Foreign Secretary 'still reckons on a short war, that this Germany may crack'.[65] At the beginning of November, Vernon Bartlett reported to the *News Chronicle* policy conference that David Margesson, the government Chief Whip, 'had seemed to accept Nevile Henderson's thesis that the generals and Göring were genuinely in favour of peace, and that we should come to terms with them'. Vernon Bartlett even reported that Horace Wilson had suggested to him that 'it was important that there should be some kind of internal revolution in Germany, since amongst other things, it would have the effect of anticipating possible trends of French ideas for the direction of a vindictive peace'.[66] Thus, even before battle was joined, Chamberlain's chief adviser was contemplating how to avoid the pitfalls of the Versailles Treaty! Whilst encouraging the unlikely thesis of the possible moderate German revolution, the Chamberlainites also pointed to Germany's apparent economic weaknesses, which would forestall her attempts to make war. Hoare outlined the salient points of this thesis to Crozier of the *Manchester Guardian*, who was sufficiently convinced to ask his Central European correspondent to 'keep an eye on the economic state of things in Germany ... as the smaller businesses are said to be getting into serious difficulty'.[67]

The Chamberlainites were also eager to ascribe any adverse criticism that they read in the press to a range of irrelevant or extraneous factors. Hoare, for one, was willing to attribute the press criticism to 'the lack of advertising and betting news', which meant that the journalists found 'anti-Government stunts the best way to sell their papers'.[68] Whilst Chamberlain's personal popularity declined as the Phoney War progressed, so the Prime Minister became more and more disdainful of any criticism, reflecting in January 1940 that 'papers must live and ... they sell better if they abuse the Government than if they praise them'. Chamberlain was no longer capable of seeing anything behind criticism except evidence of a mean and petty spirit, and he responded in kind, admitting to his sister that the way in which 'anonymous journalists who only know a smattering of the facts' prescribed to him how he should change his Cabinet *et al.* now filled him with 'a sick resentment'.[69]

Further evidence of this 'sick resentment' that now consumed him surfaced in the columns of *Truth*, the weekly newspaper run by Sir Joseph Ball for the benefit of the Chamberlainites. Ever since Chamberlain had had publicly to reverse his appeasement policies after Hitler's invasion of Prague in March 1939, *Truth* had increasingly become a receptacle for that 'sick resentment' which Chamberlain felt at the combination of circumstances which had forced him to adopt policies which he found thoroughly uncongenial – policies which, as we have seen, he probably hoped could still be reversed through a compromise peace with Germany. Since Ball's takeover of the paper in 1936, *Truth* had leaned over to give Hitler and the Germans the benefit of the doubt whenever the Germans looked set to make their next move – thus, like Beaverbrook in the *Daily Express*, hoping to calm Hitler with soothing words. As the German army massed on the Czechoslovak border in August 1938, the author of the anonymous notes entitled 'Entre Nous' (probably written by the Editor Henry Newham) opined:

> I must confess myself unable to think the worst of the army manoeuvres now beginning. . . . It seems natural to me that the German military authorities should wish to test the quality of the first class of the reservists. . . . I do not feel that this action is more provocative in itself than the recent conduct of the French manoeuvres near the Italian frontier.

In the same issue, there was also a bizarre appraisal of 'Hitler as Artist' by a certain Anthony Gibbs. This is probably the most unfortunate article ever to appear in a British newspaper. Gibbs reviewed a selection of the Führer's watercolours helpfully provided in book form by the Nazi Party, and proceeded to praise the 'sensitiveness' of Hitler as a watercolourist (his pastel shades being particularly admired). In conclusion, Gibbs posed the delicate question of whether it might be 'possible that the real Hitler, the genuine little

Adolph, is a sensitive child, intensely occupied with his own shy moods...'.

Six weeks later Nazi troops entered Czechoslovakia.

After Munich, *Truth* became increasingly damning of Chamberlain's opponents, who were collectively branded as Jewish/Communist traitors to the true English cause, which was friendship with Germany. Its racialist and xenophobic undertones became more prevalent, as the insinuation was made that anyone who disagreed with Chamberlain was being unpatriotic and 'unEnglish'. Writing of a demonstration in Whitehall against the impending Munich agreement, *Truth* noted that of the 4,000-strong crowd:

> The people who were most vociferous on this occasion are the sort who are unsurpassed in lulling their ideological opponents with their mouths, but very backward when the work has to be done with weapons in the field. Very few of them are British, almost none of them are typically British, thank heaven.

Such prominent Jewish figures as George Strauss MP were accused of cowardice in failing to enlist during the First World War: a libel for which *Truth* had to pay Strauss substantial damages. The *Daily Mirror*, a most vociferous critic of Chamberlain, came in for particular abuse from *Truth* which attempted to make much of the *Mirror*'s widely distributed and unidentified shareholdings by alleging that it was thus secretly manipulated by subversive Jewish interests. 'The Jew-infested sink of Fleet Street' was thus invited to come clean about its ownership so that the British people could be made aware of whether 'it acts in reference, not to the welfare of the community as a whole, but only to a small section of the community'.[70]

With Chamberlain's apparent reversal of policy in April 1939, *Truth* merely increased the number and intensity of its attacks on those politicians who had apparently been proved right by the course of events and upon those policies which Chamberlain was now forced to adopt. On 7 July 1939, when European attention had come to be focused on the British government's guarantee to Poland, *Truth* did all it could to persuade its readers that Poland and Danzig were not worth fighting a war with Germany for (as many of the appeasers privately believed): 'If we set aside the ideological passions of Mr.

Gollancz* and his tribe in the tents of Bloomsbury, the truth is that no appreciable section of British opinion desires to reconquer Berlin for the Jews or to see the Vistula run red with British blood. . . .'

The paper's anti-Semitism was again in evidence in November 1938, when it remained strangely silent about the mass Nazi pogroms of that month which were otherwise widely reported in the British press and which did much to alienate British sympathy for Hitler in the wake of Munich. From the summer of 1939, as one of Vansittart's researchers surmised, the paper 'was run not to express the real official views either of the national government as such or even of the Conservative party as such, but the views of the extreme "appeasement" group that still remained'.[71]

Further evidence of this was provided by the paper's incessant snipings at Eden and Churchill – even after they had both been reluctantly taken into the government in September 1939. The attacks on Churchill have already been remarked upon; but on 8 March 1940, the paper also turned its acidic gaze on Eden. It praised Chamberlain for having shifted Eden from the Foreign Office 'where his head had swelled to the size of a balloon', and finished its polemic by lamenting that 'his sojourn in the wilderness did not diminish his opinion of himself, and he inflicts on us ultra-chauvinistic speeches about the war which ... he was largely instrumental in bringing about'. Thus the Prime Minister, through the agency of Ball and *Truth,* apparently sanctioned the bitter denigration of two of his most senior ministers (Eden was at the Colonial Office) throughout the Phoney War.

However, as well as vilifying the anti-Municheers, *Truth* also supported any peace feelers and played down the 'hate' against Germany – even employing the well-known Fascist, Major-General Fuller, to write a piece repudiating British government claims about the existence of German concentration camps.[72] Fuller had been Oswald Mosley's military adviser during the 1930s. *Truth* also praised several books and pamphlets by a variety of right-wing pacifist organizations, such as the British People's Party and the Link – on 9 February 1940, for instance, publishing a letter from the Marquess of Tavistock which advocated a peace with Germany which could be 'concluded on terms which would satisfy any reasonable person'. The campaign in *Truth*

* The left-wing Jewish publisher.

against the more prominent anti-appeasers thus went hand in hand with a discreet peace campaign which derided any action or sentiment that might have unduly antagonized Germany or intensified the war effort. This bears a striking resemblance to other evidence that has come to light indicating that Chamberlain was trying to pursue a quite different policy behind the required noises of belligerency that official policy and national sentiment demanded of him; as such, *Truth* exactly reflected his views and was to reach its nadir with its extraordinary anti-Semitic attack on the ex-War Minister, Hore-Belisha, in January 1940.

If Chamberlain and his inner Cabinet were beginning to find that there was too much criticism for their liking, they could still bask in the refreshing praise of the Kemsley press – the *Sunday Times* and the *Daily Sketch*. On 19 November 1939, John Colville (then working in Downing Street and an ardent admirer of Chamberlain) recorded in his diary that 'Kemsley and Baxter are carrying on a journalistic war against the Sunday Pictorial which has lately contained scurrilous attacks on the P.M. (and which George Steward thinks is run by Winston's supporters).'[73] While the Chamberlainites were still running personal press vendettas against Churchill, the rest of the press were seething in frustration. The exception was *The Daily Telegraph*, which remained quietly supportive of Chamberlain after its critical stance over Munich, as Lord Camrose decided, for better or for worse, that patriotic duty demanded that the paper support the Prime Minister.

As the Chamberlainites attributed the attacks on them in the press to mean, petty or personal motives, thus dismissing such criticisms out of hand, they equally failed to realize that what *did* appear in print was but the tip of a rapidly growing iceberg of discontent. Lord Astor swiftly despaired of Chamberlain and his government and, despite his longstanding personal antipathy towards Churchill, now recognized that 'the feeling for Winston as P.M. is growing'.[74] Garvin, however, was overawed by Chamberlain's seemingly impregnable position and confessed that 'it is impossible to see ... how the political situation is to be altered...'. He admitted to envisaging a private scenario of Chamberlain becoming 'stronger and stronger up to the end of the war', as the Prime Minister was, in his view, 'more confident than ever'. Garvin concluded with the pessimistic thought that 'Neville is no Asquith.'[75] Astor, however, was not so ready to face up to such a future and devoted an increasing amount of time to conspiring for a more revolutionary overhaul of the government. But he recognized that in order for such a coalition to materialize, there had to be a 'disaster' of sufficient magnitude to merit such a drastic move; and Astor expressed his fear to Garvin that 'the tragedy is that there may be no open scandal during the next few months to stir things up and so when March arrives we won't have our complement of guns, tanks, planes etc'.[76] The disillusionment with the government amongst the Conservative backbenchers, especially amongst the younger MPs serving in the forces who were acquainted at first hand with the lack of armaments, also helped to reinforce Astor's judgement: a feeling shared by Sir Edward Grigg, who was able to discern a restlessness with Chamberlain's tight party discipline, 'A babble of voices ... getting critical of the whips'.[77]

Astor was to get his 'open scandal' sooner than he expected, but unfortunately the man who precipitated it was ill suited to the occasion. On 5 January, Leslie Hore-Belisha, the Minister for War, resigned and for a few days he represented a real threat to the survival of Chamberlain. His resignation caused a great furore in the press, which, Harold Nicolson shrewdly observed, was less a 'pro-Belisha than an anti-Chamberlain outburst'.[78] The press used Hore-Belisha's sudden resignation to attack the government, and the months of frustrated criticism suddenly boiled over into a chorus of unrestrained abuse. The exact reasons for Hore-Belisha's resignation remain a mystery, but Chamberlain's admission to his War Minister that 'there is prejudice against you' summed up a host of intangible hostilities that seemed to necessitate his removal. Hore-Belisha's own analysis of this prejudice rested on the hostility he had aroused among the 'Military and high social caste' on account of his being 'a Jew and an ordinary person not of their own caste'.[79] More particularly, the generals also resented the democratic reforms of the army that he had instituted in the late 1930s. The anti-Semitic undertones behind his resignation were to be cruelly confirmed by *Truth* a few days later.

Hore-Belisha had always been notorious for courting the press, and immediately he resigned he was doing the rounds of Fleet Street to present his resignation in this rather flattering light. Papers like the *Daily Mirror* were quick to take his side and Hore-Belisha's thesis of a conspiracy between the Palace and the reactionary generals against him appealed exactly to the paper's sense of anti-Establishment iconoclasm. The *Daily Mirror* and the *Sunday Pictorial* took up his case with great gusto, as did the *Evening Standard*, the *News Chronicle* and to a lesser extent the *Daily Express* and the *Daily Mail*. Chamberlain was later informed by a journalist on one of these newspapers that on the afternoon of his resignation 'H-B made the rounds of the proprietors or editors of all the principal London papers and presumably gave them the same distorted story.'[80] Hore-Belisha, probably unknowingly, had stumbled across a groundswell of resentment of which he was quick to take advantage. Chamberlain, under his unflappable exterior, was, according to Halifax, 'very worried'.[81]

However, Hore-Belisha was too mindful of his own career to become a martyr to any cause; as the experienced politicians of all political persuasions had known for a long time and as Hugh Cudlipp of the Mirror Group was soon to find out. Even on *The Times*, Hore-Belisha found some support for his position, coming from those who had previously opposed appeasement and Chamberlain. Dawson was summoned to Downing Street on 5 January to hear Sir Horace Wilson's version of the War Minister's resignation and he loyally rallied to Chamberlain's side, but returned to *The Times* to have a 'hard evening' trying 'to give a brief to Mason and Coote (who were very pro-Hore-B) almost re-writing some of their stuff'. Consistently with his general analysis of events, Dawson was not prepared to support Hore-Belisha, but on the other hand he found 'nothing to enthuse' about in the government reshuffle which occurred as a result of Hore-Belisha's resignation.[82] As expected of him by Downing Street, Dawson put this point of view very succinctly in his leader on the subject on 7 January. His reaction was echoed by those in Parliament who might have been expected to make the most of Hore-Belisha's resignation to discomfort the government. Harold Nicolson looked upon the press campaign for the ex-Minister with cynical amusement, and recorded in his diary that 'we in the House would assume that it is due to the fact that having told so many lies he had sacrificed the confidence of the country...', but he was equally aware that 'The Press are really anti-Chamberlain and are exaggerating this in order to attack him.'[83] Even such critics of Chamberlain as Lord Astor could not bring themselves to work up any enthusiasm for Hore-Belisha. Astor had always advised Garvin against giving him any support in the columns of the *Observer*. On 9 January 1940, Astor was reiterating his suspicions of Hore-Belisha to Garvin and instructed his editor to warn Howard Gray, the *Observer*'s political correspondent, 'not to make a martyr of him.... it will be very hard for the army if the stunt papers succeed in making the public believe that the Generals and aristocrats sacrificed the democrats – this is the line which H.B. himself is trying to spread.... I know his shortcomings.'[84] Thus, when the 'open scandal' that Astor and the anti-Chamberlainites had wanted did arrive, they were unable to exploit it. Hore-Belisha's qualities of self-advertisement and political cowardice could not hope to endear him even to those who were increasingly desperate about the calibre of the government that he had resigned from, and they were personal qualities which Hore-Belisha was soon to demonstrate to what Dawson dismissively referred to as the 'stunt Press',[85] which had made his resignation a cause célèbre in the first place.

Fortified by his apparent popularity, Hore-Belisha went out of his way to consult the Mirror Group, the Beaverbrook press and the *News Chronicle* in the week after his resignation. He presented himself as the alternative to Chamberlain as Premier and predicted that his resignation speech would ignite the movement that would bring Chamberlain's government down. On 13 January, he was discussing his speech with Hugh Cudlipp and confided that he now considered 'himself in a wonderful position heading straight for the Premiership'. Asked whether he might join the Labour Party to achieve this, he replied that 'The material in the Labour Party was of such poor quality that it would be impossible with it to form a Government which would stand up in war time.'[86] Michael Foot later related to Lord Astor how 'H.B. had informed Max [Beaverbrook], Cummings [of the *News Chronicle*], Swaffer* and others that he meant to fight and he had accordingly prepared the ground for him.'[87] However, having built up his support, Hore-Belisha's courage failed as the day neared on which he was to make his fighting resignation speech. Cecil King, executive director of the *Daily Mirror*, in close contact with Hugh Cudlipp throughout this episode, recorded in his diary on Wednesday, 17 January that 'up to Saturday night he [Hore-Belisha] was determined to fight. On Monday night he rang up Cudlipp and was less sure about

* Hannen Swaffer worked for the Beaverbrook press.

the wisdom of fighting; and when the moment came he climbed meekly down.' Of the speech Cudlipp had prepared for him, and which he had repeatedly expressed his determination to use, the only phrase preserved was about making the army 'too democratic to fight for democracy'.[88] Hore-Belisha did indeed make a timid and ineffective resignation speech that was clearly designed to enhance his prospects of an early return to government. On 20 January, Chamberlain was able to write to his sister that 'The Belisha affair was a flop much to the disappointment of the M.P.'s who had crowded the House in hopes of a sensation, and still more to the disgust of the popular Press.'[89] However, Chamberlain had certainly left nothing to chance and between Hore-Belisha's resignation and his speech the Chamberlainites had moved quickly to slander and besmirch the reputation of their ex-colleague in a manner that suggested an extreme nervousness about the level of support that he was able to command in the press. After Sir Horace Wilson had called in Dawson to use *The Times* to publish Chamberlain's version of Hore-Belisha's resignation, 'the whips and Chamberlain himself spread a whispering campaign about Belisha and commissions on army contracts . . . about his quarrels with Gort; about his interference in strategy'.[90]

However, if this was to be expected, politicians on all sides were taken aback by the racialist, vitriolic abuse poured on Hore-Belisha that now appeared in Sir Joseph Ball's *Truth* in its issue of 12 January, an issue that was printed in unusually large quantities and sent to every member of the House of Commons and the House of Lords as well as a host of others in public life. The paper contained a long article consisting of allegations about Hore-Belisha's past financial ventures and business failures, tinged with a liberal sprinkling of anti-Semitism. The allegations against him were repeated in the issue of 19 January. In Chamberlain's own triumphant words to his sister, the articles in *Truth* were about 'a number of companies with which he was connected before he became Financial Secretary, all of which speedily came to grief with the loss of shareholders' money'. The allegations not only of incompetence but also of financial impropriety had, in Chamberlain's view, 'created a good deal of feeling among M.P.'s that they don't want him back'.[91] According to Vansittart's later investigations of *Truth* in 1941, these articles had become a 'matter of notoriety', and represented:

a deliberate effort to kill Belisha once and for all as a political force. It is well known that Belisha had been a very particular target of German and pro-German propaganda, and if the view is well founded that his support of Munich had been luke-warm rather than zealous, and that as from the beginning of the war he belonged to the more aggressively anti-German section of the Cabinet, the vindictive hostility of 'Truth' to Hore-Belisha was clearly evidence of the continuing Chamberlainite hostility to what it termed the 'War Mongers'.[92]

After the disappointment of Hore-Belisha's resignation, the press relapsed into a mood of resentful acquiescence. Privately, editors and proprietors, except on the Kemsley press, were convinced that, in Lord Astor's phrase, the War Cabinet was 'a farce', and that everyone was 'waiting for a disaster to force the P.M. to reconstruct the Government'. Even Lord Camrose admitted that he was 'now critical of every Minister', but still felt restrained about attacking the government on the grounds of national unity and patriotism and did 'not want to say anything against the P.M.'. Lord Astor had been privately convinced for some months that Chamberlain had to go, and now considered the 'only way of bringing about drastic change which alone can save us would seem to be to insist upon a coalition. . . . it is *more* important to have a coalition than to keep Neville as P.M.'.[93] What support the government might still have enjoyed was finally dismissed by the Cabinet reshuffle of 3 April, which displayed a disdainful disregard for all those who had been arguing for widespread change. The government lost its chance to inject any fresh blood or energy into the Cabinet and the press was unanimous in its condemnation of the ineffectual and timid reshuffle. Camrose now confided to Harvey that he was 'outraged at the British Cabinet changes, especially Sam Hoare' – who, at this vital juncture, became Secretary of State for Air.[94] Astor wrote to Garvin to confess that he was 'terribly disappointed'.[95] *The Times*, as Colville observed, was 'very disagreeable', as were the *News Chronicle*, the *Daily Mirror* and the *Manchester Guardian*.[96] However, the old dilemma now returned in its starkest form – the press was prepared to attack the government in detail, but hung back from criticizing Chamberlain himself or the individuals in the government because that would split the nation and help the Germans. Editors and proprietors were thus still prepared to support Chamberlain on these grounds, even though such loyal supporters as Camrose were now privately convinced that the Prime Minister would at least have 'to jettison his unpopular colleagues'.[97] Dawson penned a leader to the same effect which appeared in *The Times* on 16 April, entitled 'Some Relief for Tired Ministers' – in this case, it was prompted by Halifax! The message of this was obvious, but Dawson heard the next day that Chamberlain had been 'peeved about my leader ... which was meant to be helpful'.[98] In the face of such criticism, Chamberlain merely admitted to Chips Channon that he was indeed 'surrounded by old men who get easily fatigued'.[99] But his self-belief was such that even at this late stage, and with such criticism from such well-meaning quarters as *The Times*, the Prime Minister was still incapable of noticing that one of those 'old men who get easily fatigued' might have been himself.

A tortuous paralysis now gripped the press, and nowhere was this more apparent than on the *Observer*. To the last, Garvin refrained from outright criticism of Chamberlain – much to the mounting fury of Lord Astor. Garvin stressed the 'need for unity' to a proprietor who had by now run out of patience and argued a case 'for a radical reconstruction – unless these disasters are to continue and unless we are to find ourselves in 1941 also inadequately prepared'. By the spring of 1940, the succession of 'disasters' that Astor was referring to included the Russian subjugation of Finland (which left Britain and France impotently and idly looking on) and, more importantly, the disastrous British expedition to Norway, which had to withdraw from that country at the end of April leaving it in German hands. Given such obvious examples of failure and incompetence, Astor warned Garvin that the public façade provided by the press of continuing faith in Chamberlain was seriously misplaced: 'Neville's stock in the country is not as high or even in Parliament as Margesson* believes.' To Garvin's point that 'a real exposure' of the government's incompetence 'by the "Observer" alone would be ineffective', Astor argued that given the state of seething but unarticulated discontent 'a strong line by the "Observer" might well do the trick'.[100]

The increasingly fraught correspondence between Editor and pro-

---

*David Margesson MP was the Conservative Chief Whip and a loyal supporter of Chamberlain.

prietor continued through March and April. Astor tried to sweeten the pill for Garvin by advocating that Chamberlain should serve in a new administration headed by Churchill, but even this failed to yield any practical results in the columns of the *Observer*. On 3 May, Astor made his last appeal to Garvin before the coming Sunday issue (on 5 May) that would precede the parliamentary debate on the Norwegian fiasco. Lord Astor wrote:

> someone must start a move for reconstruction – or else if there is united silence the country will merely become disheartened – if the Press wait on M.P.s and M.P.s wait for a word in the Press nothing will happen.... there is obviously no need to be personal but I do feel that the situation is so bad that it justifies you in making a move – public opinion can't make itself felt unless it is instructed by someone – no one could object to a demand for a strong coalition with real ministerial reconstruction.[101]

Garvin, however, could still restrain himself, and Astor's attempts to co-ordinate a rebellion in Parliament with his own newspaper were stillborn. As it was, he had to confine himself to membership of Lord Salisbury's 'Watching Committee', a group of critical but discreet senior Conservative politicians to voice his discontent within the inner sanctums of government. The breach between Astor and Garvin was never to be healed, and the Editor's stubbornness on this occasion proved to be his undoing in 1942 when Editor and proprietor fell into sharp differences over the terms of Garvin's new contract – a dispute culminating in his dismissal from the paper. On that occasion, the issue in dispute was exactly the same, Garvin stolidly defending Churchill when the latter's fortunes were at a low ebb while the Astors were manoeuvring for his removal. But the seeds for the breach between Astor and Garvin were sown in the spring of 1940.

The dissident voices within the government shared Lord Astor's view of the situation and Brendan Bracken, for instance, was quite open in telling W. P. Crozier that 'things were rotten, and they were getting worse. We were not winning this war, we were on the way to lose it.' Bracken, like many others, expressed disgust with David Margesson and his use of the Whips to prevent opposition on the government back benches from making itself heard. Bracken praised the *Manchester Guardian* for printing a leader descriptively entitled 'Margesson and the Gag', which was 'first rate and all true'. On the same day, 29 March, that Bracken was seeing Crozier, *The Daily Telegraph* carried a leader expressing Camrose's views about the need for unity and how this meant that MPs could not express opinions that might endanger the survival of the government. Bracken exhorted Crozier to 'give them Hell'.[102]

Those in the government who did not have a vested interest in bringing it down, such as Hoare, completely failed to appreciate the true state of feeling in the press and preferred to attribute mild hostility to boredom and irritability rather than face reality. There was no awareness that what little criticism there was in the press was but the tip of an iceberg of real discontent. In considering the chorus of exasperation that greeted his shuffle to the Air Ministry on 4 April, Sir Samuel Hoare could merely record that the *Daily Telegraph* was 'sniffy about me'.[103] Even after the Hore-Belisha affair, Hoare could still write to Lord Lothian to assure him that 'Chamberlain's position is still very strong.'[104] Chamberlain himself remained equally serene and, as his letters to his sisters demonstrate, increasingly looked to the *Sunday Times* for support and encouragement as it alone faithfully extolled his virtues.

As criticism did mount, however, the personal touch was again looked to in order to quell criticism. As the Finns prepared to capitulate to the Russians on 10 March, Chamberlain gave 'the lead' to the Lobby on 9 March that 'responsibility for what happened to Finland this week is with Norway and Sweden and not with France and Britain'.[105] The government assiduously played on the better nature of the press to still its criticism in the promise of better things to come. Sir Samuel Hoare was once again very active and spread his largesse around the editors and proprietors, promising them confidential talks in return for pledges of support. Rothermere was thanked for his 'splendid support' as he had been a 'friend upon whom the Government can really depend'. Hoare asked him if they could 'see each other from time to time as I shall much value talks with you'.[106] Garvin was summoned on 3 April to hear Hoare talk about the 'wonderful opportunity that he had been given to increase aircraft production' and was assured that as the conflict intensified so Chamberlain was relying on this 'to bring Labour in, on the argument, also, that the fewest changes now will facilitate fuller changes later'.[107] Hoare wrote in similar terms to W. P. Crozier. But, as the situation in Norway deteriorated, previously unexplored channels of communication were now exploited. Thus J. R. S. Scott, Director of the *Manchester Guardian*, was approached by Sir Kenneth Lee, the Director-General of the MOI, to be told that 'complaints had been made from certain quarters (the PM) about attacks in the M.G.'. Sir Kenneth suggested that the paper was being 'small minded' in its attacks on the government, to which Scott replied, with obvious irritation, that 'holding the views that we [the *Manchester Guardian*] did, our restraint, out of regard for the national position, has been remarkable'.[108] Indeed it had, and yet by playing so relentlessly on the symbolic nature of 'national unity' to still criticism, Chamberlain was also constantly undermining the value of that symbol by himself continuing to behave in a strictly partisan and petty manner.

On 30 April, Lord Salisbury's Watching Committee met to discuss the Norwegian disaster and Harold Nicolson reported a 'glum crowd. The general impression is that we may lose the war.'[109] However, the government's survival was now the immediate issue and the political controversy now turned on the question of who had been responsible for the fiasco. Churchill now found himself in a potentially embarrassing situation as he had been, as First Lord of the Admiralty, politically responsible for the Norwegian operation. The Chamberlainites sought to exploit this to deflect criticism from Chamberlain himself and Nicolson recorded that 'the Whips are putting it about that it is all the fault of Winston who has made another forlorn failure'.[110] The press was, in fact, understandably suspicious about Churchill's position, especially as he was now given increased powers over the military direction of the war as he became Chairman of the Military Co-ordination Committee. W. P. Crozier saw him on 1 May, and accused him, in short, of being too old and too tired for the increased burden of responsibility. Crozier recorded the typically Churchillian response: ' "Look here, do I look tired?" He came right up to me and pushed his face almost into mine....'[111] Churchill's supporters were understandably nervous that his previous press support would now ebb away if too much responsibility was pinned

173

on him for the Norwegian fiasco. Vansittart, who saw Hugh Cudlipp of the Mirror Group (one of Churchill's staunchest supporters) on 1 May, gave the distinct impression that the Churchill faction was 'nervous that our papers will throw Churchill over on this Norwegian issue, and that he wished to dissuade us from doing so' – which Vansittart did by blaming the withdrawal from Norway on Horace Wilson and Chamberlain.[112]

With the announcement of the emergency debate on Norway to be held on 7 May, those papers that had been arguing for change since the beginning of the war now reiterated their arguments – but still refrained from criticism of Chamberlain and the other personnel of the government. On Sunday, 5 May, Chips Channon noted in his diary that there was a 'storm of abuse' of Chamberlain, which still, though, did not extend to demanding his removal.[113] However, to the very last, the most avid pro-Chamberlain press proprietors stuck by the Prime Minister – deluding the latter with their unfounded words of support into misjudging the situation. The *Daily Telegraph* still stayed only mildly critical, while the *Daily Express* and the Kemsley press stayed very supportive. Indeed, Chamberlain was so impressed by the enthusiasm of the *Daily Express* on 6 May for his dying cause that he sent Beaverbrook a letter to thank him for the 'splendid article' in his support, adding, 'when so many are sounding the defeatist note over a minor setback, it is a relief to read such a courageous and inspiring summons to a saner view'.[114] He was given further relief by the loyalty of Lords Rothermere, Camrose and Kemsley. While Rothermere was convalescing with his fatal illness, his son, who was now in charge of the *Daily Mail*, took a very critical line of the government: but the force of this was diluted by telegrams from Rothermere himself to the effect that he entirely disapproved of the *Daily Mail*'s attitude which was beyond his control and exhorted Chamberlain to 'hold on and you will win'. He later telegraphed that Chamberlain's speech during the debate on 8 May 'convinces everyone in Paris as it must have done throughout the world'.[115] Lord Kemsley was even more outspoken in his abuse of Chamberlain's critics and wrote to the Premier on 9 May to express his 'disgust' at the result of the debate in Parliament and at the 'scenes which disgraced the house' when it was learned that the long awaited Conservative backbench revolt had finally taken place. Kemsley wrote hysterically that he 'would have liked to have had the power to subject the unruly elements for a couple of days to German discipline, which is at least efficient and patriotic', and concluded by giving Chamberlain absurd assurances that 'the overwhelming mass of the people regard the hysteria of your critics with contempt'.[116]

Garvin refused to accept Astor's demands to call for a reconstruction and Camrose was equally obdurate. With this cushion of support, Chamberlain was genuinely surprised by the revolt in the House of Commons on 8 May which saw the majority that he had gained at the time of Munich of 222 reduced to 81. It was left to the MPs to unseat Chamberlain, as the Premier was able to spin his magic over the press barons to the end; but amongst those who voted against Chamberlain was Lady Astor, thus publicly expressing the disenchantment with Chamberlain felt by the hosts of the Cliveden set which Lord Astor had found himself unable to make public in the columns of the *Observer*. Perhaps it was the deceptive support for Chamberlain dished up by the press barons to the end that persuaded the Prime Minister to cling to office for another two days after his adverse vote in the House of Commons. Only on 10 May did Churchill become Prime Minister after a last attempt by Chamberlain to use the pretext of the German invasion of the Low Countries of that day to continue as Premier. As it was, Chamberlain had virtually to be prised from office in a manner as undignified as his efforts to muffle opposition to himself during the preceding years.

There is no doubt that in his dealings with the press Chamberlain succeeded in deceiving himself as much as anybody else. That even after the Battle of Britain Chamberlain could still write in his diary that he had been privately entertaining the 'possibilities of further political activity and even the possibility of another premiership after the war' demonstrates how devoid of reality his perception of public affairs had become.[117] Not surprisingly, *Truth* waxed eloquent about the vicious and unseemly conspiracy that had brought about Chamberlain's downfall. For *Truth*, the 'vast impersonal forces' of history were decidedly not working against Chamberlain and the appeasers – the Prime Minister had merely been stabbed in the back by those who 'had private grudges to work off against him'. For *Truth*, such people took the opportunity to deprive him of the premiership 'so heartily as to sicken some M.P.s who, though by no means followers of Mr Chamberlain, derive little pleasure from the spectacle of personal spite dressing itself up as high minded patriotism'. The last phrase is as good as any to describe the last eighteen months of Chamberlain's premiership.

Epilogue

Although it is now often assumed that the elevation of Churchill to the premiership was inevitable, in fact the press reflected the deep divisions on the subject of Chamberlain's successor that existed in Westminster and Whitehall. As it became clear in the aftermath of the House of Commons debate on the Norwegian fiasco that Chamberlain's position as Prime Minister was no longer tenable, all the old doubts about Churchill's judgement, age and impetuousness began to resurface. The widely canvassed alternatives to Churchill as Prime Minister were Lord Halifax and Lloyd George. In fact, only the Mirror Group of newspapers wholeheartedly enthused over the prospect of a Churchill government – the rest of the press were, to say the least, distinctly lukewarm. Such reservations about Churchill were not merely of academic interest, considering how swiftly and triumphantly he did eventually consolidate his tenancy of 10 Downing Street, but were pregnant with consequences for British politics during the war and after it.

It is evident, for instance, that the favoured candidate of the Cliveden set was Lord Halifax. Although Lord Astor might have encouraged Garvin to believe that he would support Churchill as the new Prime Minister, when it came to the crunch the candidate whom Astor consistently backed was Lord Halifax, a preference that was shared by Salisbury's influential band of Conservatives on the Watching Committee. On 9 May, Astor was happily writing to Garvin that 'the feeling for Halifax grows ...' and that Lord Salisbury himself had been deputed to inform Halifax that in the opinion of the Watching Committee Chamberlain could no longer be PM 'as he could not unite the Nation'.[1] It was thus much to Astor's dismay that Churchill actually did become the new Prime Minister on 10 May and on 11

177

May he was writing despondently to Garvin that he and the Watching Committee 'had hoped that the King would call on Baldwin and L.G. [Lloyd George] to advise him and that they would recommend Halifax'.[2] On *The Times*, Dawson and Barrington-Ward were likewise dubious about the wisdom of taking on Churchill as the new Prime Minister. On the *News Chronicle* similar doubts were raised about the accession of the illiberal Conservative maverick. On 9 May, Sir Walter Layton urged those present to support Lloyd George, as 'an announcement that Lloyd George had taken over the Premiership would have a terrifically healing effect here, and a correspondingly depressing effect in Germany', whilst doubting whether 'Churchill was up to his former standards of efficiency'. Only A. J. Cummings argued in favour of Churchill.[3] The *Daily Herald*, mindful of Churchill's blemished record in the field of industrial relations and his penchant for firing on strikers, also preferred Halifax. Given that most of the rest of the press had been vociferously supportive of Chamberlain and the government up to the last minute, it was hardly surprising that after the dust had settled Chips Channon should have had cause to record on 11 May that 'the Press is lukewarm about the new Prime Minister'.[4]

Indeed, for those who privately held such doubts about Churchill's abilities and potential as the nation's war leader, the personnel and methods of Churchill's new government tended to bear out all their worst fears. On 11 May, Lord Astor wrote to Garvin that the Salisbury Watching Committee was to 'remain in being', as he was convinced that Churchill's new government could not be 'the final solution'.[5] By the autumn, all of Astor's doubts seem to have been justified when he wrote to Garvin that 'the Civil Service felt that the administration was the weakest in living memory.... in political and Civil Service circles there is considerable disquiet – about Winston's personal staff (Lindemann and Co.) – about his assumption in fact of the role of generalissimo as well as P.M. . . .'.[6] Furthermore, Churchill seemed just as reluctant as Chamberlain had been to adopt the well-tried and seemingly victorious Cabinet system of Lloyd George, instead surrounding himself with cronies such as Beaverbrook – 'too many people of potential influence mistrust him and his motives'.[7] Geoffrey Dawson echoed such concerns, recording in his diary that Churchill's new appointments were '*not* too well chosen' and that the government

178

contained 'too many friends'.[8] Dawson's contact within Whitehall, Sir Arthur Salter, confessed that he too was 'worried by the present structure of the Government – a dictatorship of Winston and some unofficial cronies'.[9] With the departure of Lord Halifax to the Washington Embassy in December 1940, the administration was, for Dawson, thus 'reduced entirely to thugs and under-secretaries'.[10]

Given this initial lack of enthusiasm for Churchill amongst the press in 1940, it was therefore hardly surprising that the press was to become very important during a war in which the normal adversarial politics of the Houses of Parliament were suspended, as several newspapers became the focus of opposition to the government. In contrast to *The Times* and the *Observer*, the Mirror Group believed that, although the *right* Prime Minister had been chosen, Churchill was then too lenient towards the old Conservative 'Municheers' whom he retained in his government (such as Chamberlain, Halifax and Sir John Simon) and so became shrill in their denunciation of a government which they perceived to be little different from Chamberlain's in terms of personnel and political content. On 12 May, Cecil King of the Mirror Group was confiding to his diary that he could not see how Churchill's new appointments 'were any improvement' on the previous government.[11] The subsequent and frequent tussles between the *Daily Mirror*, the *Sunday Pictorial* and Churchill during the war have been frequently documented (not least by the Mirror Group journalists themselves), and the new mood of popular iconoclasm and radicalism that was abroad during the war and which was perfectly reflected by the Mirror Group newspapers undoubtedly helped to bring about Churchill's defeat in the 1945 general election.

However, of just as much importance in the development of wartime politics was the transition of *The Times*, and the *Observer*, those two bastions of appeasement, into the most sophisticated and articulate propagandists for the New Jerusalem, that compromise between private enterprise and socialism that would become known as the welfare state. Indeed it was the same motivation to find a just and fair solution to the problems of Europe in the 1930s that drove those same appeasers on *The Times* and the *Observer* to search for an equally fair solution to Britain's social problems during the war years. Although for some curious reason Corelli Barnett cannot bring himself to use the word 'appeasement' (preferring the phrase 'moralizing internationalism'), that author has recently described this continuity between the work of the ' "enlightened" Establishment' between the wars in Europe and at home during the 1939–45 war. As Barnett unsympathetically points out, the wartime vision of a New Jerusalem:

> emanated from the same kind of people, indeed in some cases the very same people, whose earlier utopian vision of a world saved from conflict through disarmament and the League of Nations had done so much to bring about Britain's desperate plight in 1940–1, by persuading British governments in the 1920s unilaterally to disarm, so rendering Britain helpless in the face of aggression in the 1930s, and by even then delaying her eventual rearmament by their passionate opposition. For New Jerusalemers and pre-war 'moralizing internationalism' alike were drawn from the Labour and Liberal parties, from the small 'l' liberal intelligentsia and, garlic in the salad flavouring the whole, from the religious with a social mission – what may be collectively termed the 'enlightened' Establishment. And New Jerusalem and moralizing internationalism were alternative expressions of the same belief that the evils besetting man could be banished by the creation of an ideal society founded on justice, virtue and good feelings. Whereas the 'enlightened' Establishment had evangelized this belief in the form of moralizing internationalism so successfully before the war as to determine the broad aims, and cramp the choices, of British total strategy, it now proceeded no less successfully to render a similar service, in the form of New Jerusalemism, with regard to the purposes and priorities of British domestic policy after the war.[12]

The Times and the *Observer* were perfect reflections of this often neglected aspect of British history. After the retirement of Dawson in September 1941, Barrington-Ward, a radical Tory motivated principally by Christian ideals, transformed *The Times* into the main vehicle for social reform, while applying the same principle of appeasement that it had applied to Nazi Germany during the late 1930s to Soviet Russia in the period 1943–8 when that country too was consuming vast tracts of European territory under a camouflage of peaceful protestations. E. H. Carr, the Assistant Editor of *The Times* from

1941 to 1946, was mainly responsible for directing the reformist policies of *The Times* during this period, and just as he became the
most powerful and articulate exponent of the 'New Jerusalem' in the
columns of the newspaper, so he also became the most outspoken and
forceful exponent of accepting the Russian occupation of Eastern
Europe at the end of the war – in a manner that led many outraged
Times readers to recall the unfortunate days of appeasement in the
1930s which they thought the paper had put behind it. But Carr
had been recruited from Aberystwyth University in 1938 by Dawson
precisely because he was the most lucid academic exponent of appeasement writing on international affairs – his book *The Twenty Year
Crisis* (Macmillan, 1939) remains the most eloquent defence of the
principles of appeasement in the English language. Carr's attitude
towards Russia was thus absolutely consistent with his support for
Dawson's attitude towards Germany in the late 1930s; the principles
underlying his writing were exactly the same. It was Carr who penned
the most famous definition of what Barrington-Ward described as the
'peaceful revolution' that would lead to the welfare state in his leader
entitled 'The Two Scourges' that appeared in *The Times* on 5
December 1940. For Carr,

> The great twin scourges which have most deeply touched the
> imagination and seared the conscience of the present generation
> are the scourge of war and the scourge of unemployment. For
> those who feel the need to look beyond the end of the present
> struggle, the abolition of war and the abolition of unemployment
> are the most urgent and imperative tasks of our civilization.

Churchill might have agreed with these aims, but it was the means
to achieve them – the welfare state and accommodation with Soviet
Russia – that swept him from power. Churchill might have been the
wartime Prime Minister, but it was the spirit of *The Times* that more
exactly reflected the spirit of the age – a spirit that was to wreak a
terrible revenge on him at the general election of 1945.

The influence of the press on the voting public during the war
cannot be accurately measured, but there can be little doubt that *The
Times* and the *Observer*, both enthusiasts for Chamberlain, did much
to convert Conservative opinion during the war years against Chur-

chill. On the other hand, those stalwarts of unbending Conservatism, Lords Kemsley, Camrose and Beaverbrook, were to stick by Churchill just as they had stuck by Chamberlain. Lord Astor's *Observer* followed a similar course to *The Times*, and after Garvin's enforced resignation in 1942 the *Observer* developed on a steadily leftward trend under the supervision of David Astor, Lord Astor's son. By the end of the war it was barely recognizable as the organ that Garvin had presided over in the 1930s.[13]

Of the other 'press barons', few survived the politics of appeasement with their reputations intact. Neither did their papers prosper. The *Daily Mail* and *Daily Herald*, once the two great rivals of the *Daily Express*, soon lost their way and saw their circulation figures drop to new lows every year. However, although all the press barons, especially Lord Kemsley and Lord Rothermere, were subsequently to be denounced for their roles in the politics of appeasement, there was only one who emerged virtually unscathed from his association with Chamberlain's government – Lord Beaverbrook. Although this was partly because few realized at the time quite to what extent he was involved in the government's appeasement policies, it was also due to his heroic and essential endeavours as Churchill's first Minister of Aircraft Production. It was fortunate for Beaverbrook that his old friend Churchill was so magnanimous in insisting that Beaverbrook take office under him in May 1940, for it served to obscure Beaverbrook's involvement in policies that had rendered Britain virtually defenceless in 1940 – a state of affairs that Beaverbrook now found himself charged with remedying! Beaverbrook was also fortunate in that *Guilty Men*, which was to fix the popular demonology of appeasement in the public mind for a generation does not censure him. The authors were, incidentally, Michael Foot and Frank Owen (writing under the pseudonym of 'Cato'), who were both to be editors of the *Evening Standard* during the war. As few suspected at the time, Beaverbrook thus owed the salvation of his political career to the magnanimity of Churchill, and the salvation of his reputation to his journalists.[14]

Chamberlain himself died in November 1940, ushered to his death by the crush of failure and disappointment. On the day that his official resignation from Churchill's Cabinet was announced in the press, he noted in his diary:

All the papers have short, cold, and for the most part deprecatory notices of my part in the international politics of the last few years. Not one shows the slightest sign of sympathy for the man or any comprehension that there may be a human tragedy somewhere in the background. However, that is just what I expected.[15]

The last comment was perhaps more of a reflection of his own bitterness than any mendaciousness on behalf of the press. Indeed, Chamberlain himself was equalled in his bitterness at the turn of events in the Chamberlainite cause by Sir Joseph Ball, who vowed to carry on and use *Truth* to propagate the struggle against their enemies – which meant anyone or anything that had crossed Chamberlain's path, be it Churchill, Eden, the Russians or the Jews. Ball's obsessional devotion to Chamberlain now bordered on hysterical fanaticism. With Chamberlain on his deathbed, Ball wrote to the ex-Premier to thank him for his 'retiring allowance', for which Ball apparently found his 'vocabulary totally inadequate for [the] purpose' of expressing his true gratitude. Nonetheless, mustering his prose, Ball went on to add:

> ... I am very proud to have been so closely associated with you in your great work during the past 10 years or more. The Work of the C.R.D. [Conservative Research Department], the establishment of ... the National Publicity Bureau, and finally, the greatest privilege of having played a definite part of my own in helping you in your great search for peace. But in the course of this long association we have both made many powerful and unscrupulous enemies, some of whom are in high places today! But I have no intention of 'giving them best', and I am fully determined that, come what may, the full great truth about your great and sustained effort to save the peace of the world ... shall be told.... I am determined that whatever abilities I may possess in matters of political controversy and propaganda should be devoted to placing before our country ... the true facts of your single-handed search for peace.[16]

Remarkably, Ball was as good as his word and continued to use *Truth* to propagate the 'Chamberlainite' view of political affairs. The paper became very anti-American and bitterly anti-Soviet (even after the Soviet Union had been invaded by Germany), and continued to sneer at Churchill and Eden, even during the Battle of Britain. More insidiously, from Ball's point of view, the paper also championed the cause of the 18BS – those detained in 1940 as likely to be subversive to the state during the period of extreme peril that Britain then faced. These were mainly British Fascists and foreigners of any description. The most interesting point about this particular campaign of *Truth*'s is that Sir Joseph Ball and a director of Truth Publishing Company (the solicitor Charles Crocker, who had succeeded Henry Brooke on the board of directors) were both drafted on to the secret Home Defence Executive which was formed in May 1940 specifically to detain these supposed subversives under Defence Regulation 18B. Ball was Vice-Chairman; the Chairman was Lord Swinton, from whom the organization derived its better known *nom de plume* of the 'Swinton Committee'. Thus one had the curious instance of two members of the Swinton Committee, which had been set up to imprison subversive elements, running a paper that was championing the cause of those right-wing British elements whom they were supposed to be imprisoning. *Truth* was, for example, particularly outspoken in supporting Admiral Sir Barry Domville, an ex-Director of Naval Intelligence and an ex-Chairman of the pro-Fascist organization Link. The inescapable conclusion is that Ball, drafted on to the Swinton Committee because of his background in MI5, was contemporaneously running *Truth* to plead the cause of those whom he was forced, by the prevailing national sentiment, to imprison.

Charles Crocker was forced to resign his directorship of *Truth* in the autumn of 1940 when his connection with the Swinton Committee was published, whilst Ball resigned from the Swinton Committee at the beginning of 1942 to be replaced by a former Permanent Secretary at the War Office, Sir Herbert Creedy. The reasons for Ball's departure from the Committee have not been disclosed, but it is probable that it had something to do with the fact that *Truth* had been attracting a lot of unwelcome attention in the autumn of 1941 owing to its persistent anti-American and anti-Russian attitudes. This had led to a debate in the House of Commons on 15 October during which several MPs demanded its suppression on the ground that it was causing disunity amongst the allies and therefore undermining the war effort. Unfortunately, the Home Office could find no legal grounds on which this could be done, but speakers during the debate such as Aneurin

Bevan and Joseph Wedgwood did raise the question of rumours that 'Truth was connected in some way to Conservative Central Office and that Ball and Crocker had been, or still were, members of the Swinton Committee.'[17] After these connections had been publicly and embarrassingly ventilated on the floor of the House of Commons, Ball rapidly began to cover his tracks. On 30 October, only a fortnight after the debate, the Lloyds Bank City Office Nominees shareholding (the block of 1,800 shares bought by Ball with NPB funds) were discreetly transferred to the new Editor of *Truth,* Colin Brooks. As Vansittart's researchers concluded, 'it seems reasonable to infer that the object was to divest the National Publicity Bureau of an asset which had certain scandalous implications'.[18] After this *Truth* minded its ways without entirely mending them; three months later Ball left the Swinton Committee.

The extent to which Ball was still obsessed by the memory of Chamberlain was also demonstrated by his tenacious hold over the Conservative Research Department; he successfully blocked the appointment of Duncan Sandys, Churchill's son-in-law, to be his successor as Director, and the appointment of R. A. Butler to that post in 1946 seems to have been acceptable to Ball only because Butler had been a loyal Chamberlainite during the years of appeasement. When Butler did finally prise Ball out of the department, he found that there were no 'funds or even records'.[19] Ball had destroyed all documentary evidence of the Conservative Research Department and the NPB during his years with those bodies to conceal his handiwork and could thus enjoy a retirement which was as inconspicuous as he had managed to make his career for the Conservative Party.

Truth is, of course, the English translation of *Pravda*. The least that can be said for *Pravda* is that the Soviet government is quite open about its ownership of the paper even if one might complain that the press is thus 'state-controlled'. *Truth* represented an attempt by a caucus within a British government to influence events anonymously via the control of a newspaper in a most mendacious fashion without accepting any responsibility for doing so. There lay 'power without responsibility – the prerogative of the harlot throughout the ages'. The best that can be said for *Truth* is that it ceased publication in 1955.

Conclusion

'Bobbety' Cranbourne was surely right when he wrote to Arthur Mann in August 1940 of Chamberlain's premiership:

> In a parliamentary democracy, there should rightly be two checks on the actions of Government: Parliament itself, and the Press. During the last few years neither has in fact functioned properly. The House of Commons has been gagged by a far too rigid use of the powers of the Whips. The Press has been gagged by the determination of certain owners to subordinate accuracy to their own personal interests and ambitions. If the truth seems likely to hamper those ambitions, I am afraid that only too often it is the truth that goes by the board. . . . I do feel that the Press Lords must bear a heavy burden of responsibility for the situation in which we find ourselves today.[1]

There is no doubt that the Chamberlain government did consciously set out to control and manipulate the press during those years – it was, after all, an apparent prerequisite of a settlement with Hitler. Furthermore, whilst constantly trying to curb the freedom of the press, the government consistently denied that any attempts were being made to do so – thus, for domestic consumption, maintaining the fiction of a liberal democracy with a 'free and independent press'. The fact that the government tried to control the press should not, perhaps, surprise us. After all, every government prefers a flattering press which will help its policies to an unflattering press which will hinder them. What is surprising, however, is that Chamberlain's attempts to fashion the press to his liking proved to be so successful, and the blame for this has to be laid at the door of the press, which was prepared to forfeit its traditional role of passive observer (as the public would have understood it) for the more seductive and superficially glamorous prospects of political power. This seems to have applied to all levels of the press, from the humblest of the Lobby through to the most mighty of the press barons. What happened during the 1930s was that having derided the press for exercising 'power without responsibility', the government gave the press sufficient responsibilities to ensure that it could exert very little independent power. The press freely surrendered the cherished and supposedly important role that Macaulay had famously assigned to it in his definition of the fourth estate. By September 1939, the press had become not so much the watchdogs of democracy as the harlots of democracy – at every level forfeiting their independence for power and fortune (and frequently a peerage).

Indeed, the system of news dissemination developed by Whitehall in the 1930s allowed the politicians and officials in Westminster and Whitehall to exercise all the power without responsibility. The clandestine system of non-attributable briefings was developed by every department once it was seen how advantageous it could be. The Whitehall departments, be they the Foreign Office or 10 Downing Street, succeeded in making their particular coteries of specialist correspondents valuable extensions of their own power; during the years of appeasement, the press became little more than a battleground for the rival departments – although due to the rules of non-attribution very few people realized this at the time. The Lobby system at Downing Street, with its secretive and anonymous 'sources', could also combine government briefings with party briefings through Ball or Sir Robert Topping (of Conservative Central Office), thus ensuring that the essential boundaries between government and party became blurred. The Lobby was merely an important and sophisticated part of contemporary Conservatism.

The episode of appeasement also stands as a warning to those journalists and editors who choose to turn political activist in the service of a political cause. By acting as the self-appointed conduit for the inner Cabinet in the press, Dawson allowed himself to surrender totally his independence – whilst probably not realizing that he was doing so. At the same time, *The Times* acted, according to its own traditions, anonymously and so no one could be quite sure who the 'certain quarters' of its leader columns might be. The only people who could be sure were the Germans, via the obliging George Steward. But as it is certain that Dawson knew nothing of Steward's activities at the German Embassy, it is also evident that Dawson was used by Chamberlain to an extent that Dawson himself was unaware of. A sad fate for 'The Thunderer', and after the paper's involvement in the politics of appeasement, *The Times* was never to regain the prestige that it had once held.

Yet by the same token it must be borne in mind that those officials who did attempt to use the press to alert the country to the dangers of the dictators were mostly civil servants going beyond the boundaries of their official duty – in much the same way as George Steward undoubtedly exceeded his official duties. Vansittart and Leeper were autonomously trying to subvert the policies of the elected government of the United Kingdom. Their methods of alerting Britain to the Nazi menace were, in many ways, just as deplorable as those which Chamberlain used to implement his own policies. Steward's comments to Dr Hesse in the aftermath of Munich would seem to imply that Chamberlain was positively proud of acting unconstitutionally and of subverting the Cabinet system, but there can be no doubt that Vansittart acted equally unscrupulously in using the press in the way that he did – to sabotage government policy which he was supposed to be executing. Vansittart and Leeper have, perhaps, been justified by events: but this should not obscure the fact that they were doing much the same things in using the press to oppose appeasement as Chamberlain was doing in Downing Street to pursue appeasement. Nonetheless, the fact that Vansittart and Leeper were forced to act outside the accepted parameters of civil service conduct and yet seem to have been justified in doing so by the consequent course of events is perhaps more of a comment on those very codes of conduct that they were forced to contravene than it is on Leeper and Vansittart personally.

What were the consequences of Chamberlain's tight control of the press during the late 1930s? The most obvious consequence was that no alternative policy to appeasement as pursued by Chamberlain could ever be consistently articulated in the British press, nor were the facts and figures that might have supported such an alternative policy ever put in front of the majority of the British public. It is a striking fact that only those papers which had absolutely no contact with the government, such as the *Daily Mirror*, were able to oppose appeasement; and the *Daily Mirror* could only articulate a mood of fear and resentment rather than consistently advance a sophisticated and practical policy alternative. As we have seen, there was no lack of journalists willing and able to argue alternatives or put awkward facts before the public – Anthony Winn, Colin Coote, F. A. Voigt, Charles Tower, Victor Gordon-Lennox, Alexander Werth, Robert Dell, Gerald Barry, Vernon Bartlett, Arthur Mann and even J. L. Garvin and Lord Astor – but they were constantly prevented by their editors or proprietors from doing so. If a democracy can be defined as a healthy, continuing clash of opinion, then the Chamberlain government, through its close control of the press, certainly succeeded in subverting democracy during the years 1937 to 1940.

Sir Samuel Hoare (by then Viscount Templewood) interviewed Sir Horace Wilson for his autobiographical defence of appeasement, *Nine Troubled Years*, in 1947. During the course of this interview, Chamberlain's former chief adviser alluded to the argument that appeasement *had* to be adopted because there had been 'No education of the country ... to support a more robust stand against the dictators'.[2] This is a myth that still endures. Chamberlain, helped by the press barons and certain editors, did his utmost to ensure that there *was* no 'education' of the country, thus allowing him to pursue his policy of appeasement as the only available policy option. The only editor who did manage to sustain an argument in his leader columns against appeasement was Arthur Mann, who suffered tremendous personal and political pressure as a result. Indeed, his courageous stand was rewarded by the disembowelment of his paper in 1939.

The second important consequence of Chamberlain's handling of the press was that he thus managed artfully and successfully to obscure the divisions over his policy that existed not only in Whitehall and Westminster but throughout the country. As this book has shown, editors and proprietors quite consciously suppressed and censored any news or reports that might show such signs of divisions; even 'editorial' writers like Garvin were quite aware of the fact that they were consciously holding back comment and facts for the greater good of pursuing the appeasement of Germany. After Chamberlain's and the press's protestations of optimism and hope were found to be bankrupt, the reputation of the press for honesty and truth correspondingly fell, with the result that most people soon came to rely on the radio news for a more balanced and authoritative version of world events. The rhetorical question 'You don't believe what you read in the papers?' was seldom heard before 1939.

Although public opinion polls were in their infancy in the late 1930s, and were few and far between by today's standards, even a most cursory glance of the polls that were taken show that the press, in its support for Chamberlain and appeasement, was dangerously out of step with public opinion. In February 1938, the British Institute of Public Opinion asked the question 'Do you favour Mr. Chamberlain's foreign policy?' This solicited the following answers:

Yes – 26%
No – 58%
No opinion – 16%

On 22 September 1938, as Chamberlain flew to Godesberg for his second meeting with Hitler, a Mass-Observation poll showed that only 22 per cent supported Chamberlain and 40 per cent opposed his policy. One of the most telling polls was the one that Layton refused to publish in the *News Chronicle* in the wake of Munich – revealing that 86 per cent of the population did not believe Hitler's protestations that he did not have any more territorial ambitions. If this figure is a reliable guide, it is evident that the people as a whole had a much shrewder idea of Hitler's intentions than the press. Or maybe it was not so much a case of being shrewd or otherwise, but simply that the press all too frequently allowed Chamberlain to do its thinking for it.

But perhaps the most important consequence of Chamberlain's assiduous manipulation of the press was the effect that it had on Chamberlain himself. The study of the press and appeasement demonstrates the pitfalls for those politicians who choose to exercise such a close control of the press. Chamberlain, and to a certain extent the rest of the inner Cabinet, were so mesmerized by the game of news control as exercised in the conspiratorial corridors of Whitehall that they became almost totally incapable of detecting real 'public opinion', as distinct from what they had persuaded their hirelings in the press to say (or more often what not to say). Chamberlain, in particular, operated in a political vacuum for the last eighteen months of his premiership, unable to accept any criticism at face value, constantly attributing such unwelcome intrusions to personal spite or the inspired machinations of another part of Whitehall. It was a similar vacuum to the one that Stalin was already occupying in Soviet Russia, and which rendered the Soviet dictator incapable of believing that the Germans had invaded Russia for a full week after the invasion had actually taken place. Such close control of the press not only subverts democracy, but eventually corrodes the minds, and particularly the judgement, of those who care to exercise such control.

Appendix

An account by George Barnes, BBC Talks producer, of the censorship of Harold Nicolson's broadcast, 5 September 1938:

12.00 noon: Received script from Nicolson. Rang up Foreign Office. Saw Mr. Leaper [*sic* – Leeper] who read the script and said that so far as his personal opinion went, he thought it excellent, and could be broadcast as it was. In view, however, of Sir Horace Wilson's message to the BBC, and of the gravity of the situation, he would take it himself to Sir Alexander Cadogan. As the latter was then with the Secretary of State, the Foreign Office's decision could not be given until three o'clock.

I went immediately to the Travellers' Club to tell Nicolson that we could not give him any information until after 3.00 pm. He agreed to remain at his chambers until he heard from me. He expressed his approval of the BBC's attitude in this matter and agreed that if the Foreign Office took objection to the script they would probably object to the script in toto and in that case he would be prepared to re-write it.

3.30 pm: Mr. Leaper telephoned to say that the Foreign Office cannot take any responsibility for Mr. Nicolson's script as submitted, and that in view of the gravity of the situation, and of the pace at which it is changing, the Foreign Office would prefer that no talk at all on the subject was broadcast tonight.

I asked if this was an instruction. He replied that the Foreign Office could not instruct the BBC on a matter like this, but that the recommendation was very strong.

Saw C(P) [Controller Programmes] who said cancel but that if Harold Nicolson would talk on some other subject that would be a better solution than an alternative programme, e.g. records. If he refused, we must cancel the talk, but the gravity of the situation must not be given as our reason for so doing.

Telephoned to Harold Nicolson and communicated Foreign Office's message and BBC wish that he would talk on another subject, giving as his reason the delicacy and the rapidly changing character of the situation. He suggested cancellation and asked for half-an-hour to think it over.

4.15 pm: Nicolson telephoned to say that he would give the talk and would not refer to the international situation. He told me in confidence that he had been in communication with the Foreign Office and had been told that his script had been seen by the Secretary of State in person.

He asked that no change should be made in the announcement.

Informed *The Listener* that script would not contain mention of international situation and agreed to post script to printers.

7.00 pm: Saw Mr. Nicolson at King's Bench Walk. He showed me his new script. The first two pages were the same (A). The next two were an expansion of them and a careful working up to the phrase 'I am going to talk this evening about other things' (B). Then followed one-and-a-half pages describing the beating up at the altar of the Bishop of Rothenburg by Nazis (C). Then two paragraphs criticizing German diplomatic methods (D). The last half page of talk was about milk at 7d a quart, with the German babies of 1914 as the chief example (E).

I made some verbal changes in (B) which can be seen on the broadcast script. I asked that (D) should be deleted. Mr. Nicolson agreed provided that he did not have to think of anything else to put in its place. I then said that in my opinion (C) should also be deleted because we had been asked by the Foreign Office not to mention the crisis, and it seemed to me that a story in which the listeners' sympathy was enlisted against Nazi methods was not keeping to the letter of the promise. Mr. Nicolson did not agree and said that he understood that the Foreign Office meant that he was not to talk about the actual Czech crisis. He could see no reason for deleting (C) and as he had spent the whole afternoon re-writing he preferred to cancel the talk rather than alter it. I argued with him until 8 o'clock. In view of the importance which the Foreign Office would seem to have attached to this talk, it seemed to me that cancellation was as bad as allowing Mr. Nicolson to go a little further than we wanted, since cancellation could only be interpreted by listeners as meaning that the international situation was very grave. Mr. Nicolson was very angry and asked me to suggest alternative subjects if (C) was deleted. I suggested the Persian Railway and Lord Halifax's speech about the international accommodation for foreign students. He rejected both but eventually agreed to re-write his script if he had time, but still threatened to cancel if I objected to anything more, or if he could not find anything else to talk about.

I then returned to Broadcasting House and arranged with the announcer and Mr. Lidell, who was on duty, to be ready to fade out Mr. Nicolson's talk if, in my opinion, he departed too far from his script. I also arranged for the talk to be recorded and copies to be made from this recording. I met Mr. Nicolson at 9.30 and he produced a third script which was, in my opinion, innocuous. He apologized for the difficulties he had made and expressed himself as much more angry with the Foreign Office than with the BBC. As he did not wish me to remain I left him at 9.55 pm.

My impression on leaving Mr. Nicolson was that he had been made angry
(a) by the waste of time in having to re-write twice;
(b) by the Foreign Office's veto on his talk after the nice things which they had said to him personally about his previous talks.

He felt that the Foreign Office were only able to take such a strong line because they could rely upon him not making public their veto. He said that he would have to think over very seriously about how to reply to letters from listeners who were disappointed because he had not talked about the Czech crisis. I have spoken to Talks Ex. about an extra fee, and recommended that he should be offered an extra fee of twelve guineas.

Bibliography

I The Literature on the Government and the Press: A Review

(All books cited below were published in London unless otherwise stated.)

The literature on the press offices of the Whitehall departments is small and inadequate. The only study by a historian is by Philip Taylor, who looks at the origins and development of the Foreign Office News Department in chapter 1 of *The Projection of Britain: British Overseas Publicity and Propaganda* (Cambridge University Press, Cambridge, 1981). This chapter also includes an excellent portrait of Rex Leeper and his work for the Foreign Office. No study has ever been attempted of the Downing Street Press Office, but we do have the first-hand testimony of the long-serving Lobby correspondent James Margach to give an insider's view of the workings of the Press Office under successive Prime Ministers. His book on the subject, *The Abuse of Power: The War Between Downing Street and the Media from Lloyd George to Callaghan* (W. H. Allen, 1978) is a candid and instructive examination of the Lobby system, whilst his second book, *The Anatomy of Power: An Enquiry into the Personality of Leadership* (W. H. Allen, 1979) is a more general look at politics from a Lobby correspondent's perspective. A contemporary account of the state of play between the government and the press as seen by journalists is the very useful work by Michael Cockerell, Peter Hennessy and David Walker, *Sources Close to the Prime Minister: Inside the Hidden World of the News Manipulators* (Macmillan, 1985). Colin Seymour-Ure has a brief consideration of the role of the Lobby in the government–press relationship in his book *The Press, Politics and the Public: An Essay on the Role of the National Press in the British Political System* (Methuen, 1968), although this work tries to take a more general look at the impact of the press on politics in general, without reaching any very precise conclusions.

Stephen Koss's monumental *The Rise and Fall of the Political Press in Britain*, vols 1 and 2 (Hamish Hamilton, 1984) looks at the press in its relationship to the political parties, thereby perceiving the subject through a deceptively small prism. Numerous biographies of press proprietors give a detailed view of the political activities of the press barons, the most substantial studies being A. J. P. Taylor's biography of *Beaverbrook* (Hamish Hamilton, 1972) and David Hubback's biography of Sir Walter

Layton, *No Ordinary Press Baron* (Weidenfeld & Nicolson, 1985). There is only a very inadequate biography by R. J. Minney of Viscount Southwood (Cassell, 1954) and none at all of Kemsley, Camrose or Rothermere, leaving a major gap in newspaper history.

There is a plethora of autobiographical works by journalists and editors. The best book on the press and the government is still *The Press, Parliament and People* (William Heinemann, 1946) by Francis Williams who was writing from the advantageous position of having been both a journalist and a government press officer, first in the Ministry of Information and then as Attlee's Press Officer. His autobiography, *Nothing So Strange: An Autobiography* (Cassell, 1970), is a good account of his work for the Beaverbrook press, the *Daily Herald* and for Attlee and the MOI. The best account of working for Beaverbrook is by the celebrated editor of the *Daily Express*, Arthur Christiansen, in his *Headlines All My Life* (William Heinemann, 1961). Tom Driberg, a Beaverbrook journalist and much else besides, gives a waspish account of the proprietor in his *Beaverbrook: A Study in Power and Frustration* (Weidenfeld & Nicolson, 1946). Sir David Low's *Autobiography* (Michael Joseph, 1956) is also useful in this respect. Mirror Group journalists and editors have been particularly effusive in recalling the glory days of the *Daily Mirror* and the *Sunday Pictorial* in the 1940s and 1950s. Hugh Cudlipp's *Walking on the Water* (Bodley Head, 1976) and *Publish and Be Damned* (Andrew Davers, 1953) are both lucid accounts of his own journalistic career and that of the Mirror Group, whilst rather different perspectives are offered by Cecil King in his autobiographical *Strictly Personal* (Weidenfeld & Nicolson 1969) and his published diaries *With Malice Toward None* (Sidgwick & Jackson, 1970). Tom Hopkinson, editor of *Picture Post* has also written an instructive autobiography, *Of This Our Time* (Hutchinson, 1982).

Journalists have also been very ready to write biographies and histories of their own newspapers. On the whole, since almost none of the papers has kept in-house historical archives these works tend to be sketchy and uninformative. The exception to the rule is *The Times*, which has always kept extensive archives and so has managed to produce a flow of excellent and impressive histories of the paper written by its own staff. The volumes most relevant to this study are the *History of The Times*, vol. 4, part 2: *1921 to 1948*, written by Stanley Morrison (published by the Office of *The Times*, 1952) and the *History of The Times, 1939 to 1966* by Iverach McDonald (Times Books, 1984). No comparable histories exist for any other British newspaper, except David Ayerst's rather more brief study of *The Guardian: Biography of a Newspaper* (Collins, 1971), which is also based on some archival material and is especially good on the *Manchester Guardian* during the 1930s. A similar work is in the process of being written on the *Observer* by Dr J. Stubbs. Two excellent biographies have also been written of the two editors of *The Times* during the period under study, *In the Chair: Barrington-Ward of The Times, 1927–1948* (Weidenfeld & Nicolson, 1957) by Donald Mclachlan, and *Geoffrey Dawson and Our Times* (Hutchinson, 1955) by John Evelyn Wrench. The only comparable biography based on an editor's private papers is that of *Garvin of the Observer* by David Ayerst (Croom Helm, Melbourne/London, 1985).

II Complete Bibliography

(All books cited below were published in London unless otherwise stated.)

1 Contemporary Records, Memoirs and Diaries

Vernon Bartlett, *And Now, Tomorrow* (Chatto & Windus, 1960).
Viscount Camrose, *British Newspapers and Their Controllers* (Cassell, 1947).
E. H. Carr, *The Twenty Year Crisis* (Macmillan, 1939).
Cassandra (Sir William Connor), *The English at War* (Secker & Warburg, 1941).
Cassandra (Sir William Connor), *Reflections in a Mirror* (Secker & Warburg, 1969).
Cato (Michael Foot and Frank Owen), *Guilty Men* (Gollancz, 1940).
Arthur Christiansen, *Headlines All My Life* (William Heinemann, 1961).
Sir Walter Citrine, *Men and Work* (Hutchinson, 1964).
Sir Walter Citrine, *Two Careers* (Hutchinson, 1967).
Claud Cockburn, *I Claud* (Penguin, 1967).
Patricia Cockburn, *The Years of The Week* (Macdonald, 1968).
Sir John Colville, *The Fringes of Power: Downing Street Diaries 1939 to October 1941*,
    vol.1 (Sceptre Books, 1986).
Sir Edward Cook, *The Press in War-time. With Some Account of the Official Press
    Bureau. An Essay*, ed. A. M. Cook (Macmillan, 1920).
Duff Cooper, *Old Men Forget* (Rupert Hart-Davis, 1953).
Colin Coote, *Editorial* (Eyre & Spottiswoode, 1965).
Hugh Cudlipp, *Publish and Be Damned: The Story of the Daily Mirror* (Andrew
    Davers, 1953).
Hugh Cudlipp, *Walking on the Water* (Bodley Head, 1976).
David Dilks (ed.), *The Diaries of Sir Alexander Cadogan* (Cassell, 1971).
Tom Driberg, *Beaverbrook: A Study in Power and Frustration* (Weidenfeld & Nicol-
    son, 1946).
Tom Driberg, *Ruling Passions* (Jonathan Cape, 1977).
Anthony Eden, *Facing the Dictators* (Cassell, 1960).
Anthony Eden, *The Reckoning* (Cassell, 1962).
Paul Einzig, *In the Centre of Things* (Hutchinson, 1960).
Victor Gollancz and others, *The Betrayal of the Left* (Gollancz, 1941).
W. W. Hadley, *Munich: Before and After* (Cassell, 1944).
Wilson Harris, *The Daily Press* (Cambridge University Press, Cambridge, 1943).
John Harvey (ed.), *The Diplomatic Diaries of Oliver Harvey* (Collins, 1970).
Tom Hopkinson (ed.), *Picture Post* (Penguin Books, 1970).
Tom Hopkinson, *Of This Our Time* (Hutchinson, 1982).
Sebastian Haffner, *Offensive against Germany* (Searchlight Books, 1941).
Edward Hulton, *New Age* (George Allen & Unwin, 1943).
Douglas Jay, *Change and Fortune* (Hutchinson, 1980).
Cecil King, *Strictly Personal* (Weidenfeld & Nicolson, 1969).
Cecil King, *With Malice Toward None: A War Diary* (Sidgwick & Jackson, 1970).
Sir David Low, *Autobiography* (Michael Joseph, 1956).

Iverach McDonald, *A Man of The Times* (Hamish Hamilton, 1976).

James Margach, *The Abuse of Power: The War between Downing Street and the Media from Lloyd George to Callaghan* (W. H. Allen, 1978).

James Margach, *The Anatomy of Power: An Enquiry into the Personality of Leadership* (W. H. Allen, 1979).

Kingsley Martin, *Editor: A Second Volume of Autobiography, 1931–45* (Penguin Books, 1945).

Kingsley Martin, *Truth and the Public* (Watts, 1945).

Kingsley Martin, *The Press the Public Wants* (Hogarth Press, 1947).

Mass-Observation, *Weekly Intelligence Service.*

Mass-Observation, *War Begins at Home* (Mass-Observation, 1940).

R. J. Minney (ed.), *The Private Papers of Hore-Belisha* (Weidenfeld & Nicolson, 1960).

Nigel Nicolson (ed.), *The Diaries and Letters of Harold Nicolson*, vol. 1 (Collins, 1966), vol. 2 (Collins, 1967).

Ben Pimlott (ed.), *The Second World War Diary of Hugh Dalton* (Jonathan Cape, 1984).

Ben Pimlott (ed.), *The Political Diary of Hugh Dalton, 1918–40, 1945–60* (Jonathan Cape, 1986).

J. W. Reith, *Into the Wind* (Hodder & Stoughton, 1949).

Robert Rhodes James (ed.), *Chips: The Diaries of Sir Henry Channon* (Weidenfeld & Nicolson, 1967).

Robert Rhodes James (ed.), *Memoirs of a Conservative: J. C. C. Davidson's Memoirs and Papers, 1910–1937* (Weidenfeld & Nicolson, 1969).

Viscount Rothermere, *My Fight to Re-arm Britain* (Eyre & Spottiswoode, 1939).

Viscount Rothermere, *Warnings and Predictions* (Eyre & Spottiswoode, 1939).

Royal Commission on the Press, 1947 to 1949 (HMSO, 1949).

Wickham Steed, *The Press* (Penguin Special, 1938).

Viscount Templewood, *Nine Troubled Years* (Collins, 1954).

Admiral G. P. Thomson, *Blue Pencil Admiral* (Sampson Low, 1947).

Ronald Tree, *When the Moon Was High: Memoirs of Peace and War, 1896–1942* (Macmillan, 1972).

Sir Robert Vansittart, *The Mist Procession* (Hutchinson, 1958).

Francis Williams, *Press, Parliament and People* (William Heinemann, 1946).

Francis Williams, *Dangerous Estate* (Arrow Books, 1955).

Francis Williams, *Nothing So Strange: An Autobiography* (Cassell, 1970).

2 Secondary and Other Works

Anthony Adamthwaite, 'The British Government and the Media, 1937–1938'. *Journal of Contemporary History*, Vol. 18, no. 1, 1983).

Paul Addison, *The Road to 1945* (Quartet Books, 1982).

Christopher Andrew, *Secret Service: The Making of the British Intelligence Community* (William Heinemann, 1985).

David Ayerst, *Guardian: Biography of a Newspaper* (Collins, 1971).

David Ayerst, *Garvin of the Observer* (Croom Helm, Melbourne/London, 1985).

Correlli Barnett, *The Audit of War* (Papermac, 1987).

Frank Beckwith and Mildred Gibb, *The Yorkshire Post: Two Centuries* (Yorkshire Conservative Newspaper Company, 1954).

Earl of Birkenhead, *Halifax: The Life of Lord Halifax* (Hamish Hamilton, 1965).

Earl of Birkenhead, *The Life of Viscount Walter Monckton of Brenchley* (Weidenfeld & Nicolson, 1969).

Asa Briggs, *The History of Broadcasting in the United Kingdom*, vol. 2: *The Golden Age of Wireless* (Oxford University Press, 1965).

Asa Briggs, *The BBC: The First Fifty Years* (Oxford University Press, Oxford, 1985).

Alan Bullock, *The Life and Times of Ernest Bevin*, vol. 2 (William Heinemann, 1967).

Churchill–Roosevelt: Complete Correspondence, vols 1 and 2, ed. Warren F. Kimball (Princeton University Press, Princeton, 1984).

R. B. Cockett, 'Sir Joseph Ball, Neville Chamberlain and the Secret Control of "Truth": An Exercise in Power Without Responsibility', *The Historical Journal*, March 1989.

R. B. Cockett, 'The Government, Press and Politics in Britain, 1937–1945' (unpublished Ph.D. thesis, University of London, 1988).

Ian Colvin, *Vansittart in Office. An Historical Survey of the Second World War Based on the Papers of Sir Robert Vansittart* (Gollancz, 1965).

J. A. Cross, *Sir Samuel Hoare: A Political Biography* (Jonathan Cape, 1977).

Dictionary of National Biography, 1961–70 (Oxford University Press, Oxford, 1981).

Documents on German Foreign Policy 1918–1945: From the Archives of the German Foreign Ministry. Series D: 1937–1945 (HMSO, 1950).

Maurice Edelman, *The Mirror: A Political History* (Hamish Hamilton, 1966).

David Farrer, *G for God Almighty: A Personal Memoir of Lord Beaverbrook* (Weidenfeld & Nicolson, 1969).

Sir Keith Feiling, *The Life of Neville Chamberlain* (Macmillan, 1946).

Michael Foot, *Aneurin Bevan: A Biography*, vol. 1 (McGibbon & Kee, 1962).

Foreign Relations of the United States, Diplomatic Papers 1938, vol. I.

Larry William Fuchser, *Neville Chamberlain and Appeasement: A Study in the Politics of History* (Norton, New York/London, 1982).

F. R. Gannon, *The British Press and Germany, 1936–1939* (Clarendon Press, Oxford, 1971).

J. Edward Gerald, *British Press Under Economic Controls* (University of Minnesota Press, Minnesota, 1956).

Martin Gilbert, *The Roots of Appeasement* (Weidenfeld & Nicolson, 1966).

Martin Gilbert, *Winston S. Churchill,* vol. 5: *1922–1939* (William Heinemann, 1976).

Martin Gilbert, *Finest Hour: Winston S. Churchill 1939–1941* (William Heinemann, 1983).

Martin Gilbert, *Road to Victory: Winston S. Churchill 1941–1945* (William Heinemann, 1986).

Martin Gilbert and Richard Gott, *The Appeasers* (Weidenfeld & Nicolson, 1963).

V. Gorodetsky, *Stafford Cripps's Mission to Moscow* (Cambridge University Press, Cambridge, 1983).

José Harris, *Beveridge: A Biography* (Clarendon Press, Oxford, 1977).

Nevile Henderson, *Failure of a Mission* (London, 1940).

Anthony Howard, *RAB: The Life of R. A. Butler* (Jonathan Cape, 1987).

David Hubback, *No Ordinary Press Baron: A Life of Walter Layton* (Weidenfeld & Nicolson, 1985).

Stephen Koss, *The Rise and Fall of the Political Press in Britain*, vol. 2: *The Twentieth Century* (Hamish Hamilton, 1984).

John Lawrenson and Lionel Barber, *Reuters: The Price of Truth* (Sphere Books, 1986).

Charles Lysaght, *Brendan Bracken* (Allen Lane, 1980).

R. B. McCallum and Alison Redman, *The British General Election of 1945* (Oxford University Press, Oxford, 1947).

Iverach McDonald, *The History of The Times: Struggles in War and Peace, 1939–1966* (Times Books, 1984).

Donald Mclachlan, *In the Chair: Barrington-Ward of The Times, 1927–1948* (Weidenfeld & Nicolson, 1957).

Ian Mclaine, *Ministry of Morale: Home Front Morale and the Ministry of Information in World War II* (George Allen & Unwin, 1979).

Ian Macleod, *Neville Chamberlain* (Frederick Muller, 1961).

Keith Middlemas and John Barnes, *Baldwin* (Weidenfeld & Nicolson, 1969).

R. J. Minney, *Viscount Southwood* (Cassell, 1954).

Political and Economic Planning, *Report on the British Press* (PEP, 1938).

John Ramsden, *The Making of Conservative Party Policy* (Longman, 1980).

Anthony Read and David Fisher, *Colonel Z: The Life and Times of a Master Spy* (Hodder & Stoughton, 1984).

Robert Rhodes James, *Anthony Eden* (Weidenfeld & Nicolson, 1986).

Harold Robson and Phillip Knightley, *The Pearl of Days: An Intimate Memoir of the Sunday Times* (Hamish Hamilton, 1972).

Norman Rose, *Vansittart: A Study of a Diplomatist* (William Heinemann, 1978).

A. L. Rowse, *All Souls and Appeasement* (Macmillan, 1961).

Colin Seymour-Ure, *The Press, Politics and the Public: An Essay on the Role of the National Press in the British Political System* (Methuen, 1968).

Colin Seymour-Ure and Jim Schloff, *David Low* (Secker & Warburg, 1985).

John Stubbs, 'Appearance and Reality: A Case Study of the Observer and J. L. Garvin, 1914–1942', in J. Curran and G. Boyle (eds), *Newspaper History: From the 17th Century to the Present Day* (London, 1978).

Christopher Sykes, *Nancy: The Life of Lady Astor* (Collins, 1972).

A. J. P. Taylor, *English History, 1914–45* (Clarendon Press, Oxford, 1966).

A. J. P. Taylor, *Beaverbrook* (Hamish Hamilton, 1972).

George Malcolm Thomson, *Vote of Censure* (Secker & Warburg, 1968).

Neville Thompson, *The Anti-Appeasers: Conservative Opposition to Appeasement in the 1930s* (Clarendon Press, Oxford, 1977).

Richard Thurlow, *Fascism in Britain: A History 1918–1985* (Basil Blackwell, 1987).

History of the Times, vol. 4, part 2: *1921–1948* (written and published at the Office of *The Times*, 1952).

John Turner, *Lloyd George's Secretariat* (Cambridge University Press, Cambridge, 1980).

W. J. West, *Truth Betrayed* (Duckworth, 1987).

Sir John Wheeler-Bennett, *Munich: Prologue to Tragedy* (Macmillan, 1948).

Temple Willcox, 'Projection of Publicity: Rival Concepts in the Pre-War Planning of the British Ministry of Information', *Journal of Contemporary History*, vol. 18, no. 2, 1983).

John Evelyn Wrench, *Geoffrey Dawson and Our Times* (Hutchinson, 1955).

References

Manuscript collections cited below:

Lord Astor Papers (Astor Papers) – The University Library, Reading.

Stanley Baldwin Papers (Baldwin Papers) – Cambridge University Library.

Lord Beaverbrook Papers (Beaverbrook Papers) – House of Lords Record Office, London.

Sir William Beveridge Papers (Beveridge Papers) – British Library of Political and Economic Science, London.

Neville Chamberlain Papers (Chamberlain Papers) – The University Library, Birmingham.

Sir Walter Citrine Papers (Citrine Papers) – British Library of Political and Economic Science, London.

Sir Stafford Cripps Papers (Cripps Papers) – Nuffield College, Oxford.

W. P. Crozier Political Interviews (Crozier Political Interviews) – Deansgate Library, Manchester.

Daily Herald Archive of the Trades Union Congress (*Daily Herald* Archive) – Congress House, London.

Geoffrey Dawson Papers (Dawson Papers) – Bodleian Library, Oxford.

J. L. Garvin Papers (Garvin Papers) – Harry Ranson Humanities Research Center, University of Texas at Austin, Texas.

Sir Edward Grigg Papers (Grigg Papers) – Bodleian Library, Oxford.

Lord Halifax Papers (Halifax Papers) – Churchill College, Cambridge.

Commander King-Hall Papers (King-Hall Papers) – In the private possession of Miss Anne King-Hall.

Sir Walter Layton Papers (Layton Papers) – Trinity College, Cambridge.

Manchester Guardian Archive (MGA) – John Rylands University Library of Manchester.

Arthur Mann Papers (Mann Papers) – In the private possession of Mr Peter Wright, Washington DC.

Public Record Office (PRO) – Premier Files (PREM), Ministry of Information Files (INF), Cabinet Files (CAB), Foreign Office Files (FO).

Templewood Papers, formerly Sir Samuel Hoare (Templewood Papers) – Cambridge University Library.

203

The Times Archive (*The Times* Archive) – Gray's Inn Road, London.
Sir Robert Vansittart Papers (Vansittart Papers) Churchill College, Cambridge.

(All books cited below were published in London unless otherwise stated.)

Chapter 1: Whitehall and the Press

1. Jeremy Turnstall, *The Westminster Lobby Correspondents: A Sociological Study of National Political Journalism* (Routledge & Kegan Paul, 1970), p. 94.
2. A. P. Waterfield's conversation with George Steward on 25 July 1939; PRO INF 1/156.
3. James Margach, *The Anatomy of Power: An Enquiry into the Personality of Leadership* (W. H. Allen, 1979), p. 137.
4. From the Annual Reports of the Lobby, 1931 and 1932; quoted in James Margach, *The Anatomy of Power*, pp. 137–8.
5. Quoted by James Margach, *The Abuse of Power: The War Between Downing Street and the Media from Lloyd George to Callaghan* (W. H. Allen, 1978), p. 51.
6. Maurice Webb to Sir Samuel Hoare, 15 May 1940; Templewood Papers Box XII.
7. *Lobby Rules*, quoted in Turnstall, *The Westminster Lobby Correspondents*, p. 124.
8. Sir Robert Armstrong quoted in the *Guardian* 9 December 1986.
9. James Margach, *The Anatomy of Power*, p. 129.
10. James Margach, *The Anatomy of Power*, p. 129.
11. Recorded by Harold Nicolson: *The Diaries and Letters of Harold Nicolson*, ed. Nigel Nicolson (Collins, 1966–8), vol. 1, 11 April 1939.
12. James Margach, *The Abuse of Power*, p. 51.
13. James Margach, *The Abuse of Power*, p. 53.
14. Larry William Fuchser, *Neville Chamberlain and Appeasement: A Study in the Politics of History* (Norton, New York/London, 1982), p. 58.
15. James Margach, *The Abuse of Power*, p. 51.
16. *Dictionary of National Biography: 1961–70* (Oxford University Press, Oxford, 1981), p. 68.
17. *Memoirs of a Conservative: J. C. C. Davidson's Memoirs and Papers, 1910–1937*, ed. Robert Rhodes James (Weidenfeld & Nicolson, 1969), p. 272.
18. Christopher Andrew, *Secret Service: The Making of the British Secret Service* (William Heinemann, 1985), p. 340.
19. John Ramsden, *The Making of Conservative Party Policy* (Longman, 1980), p. 66.
20. John Ramsden, *The Making of Conservative Party Policy*, p. 87.
21. Sir Joseph Ball to Baldwin, 6 December 1935; Baldwin Papers.
22. Memorandum on 'The Control of the Newspaper Truth'; Vansittart Papers 11 2/31.
23. Neville Chamberlain to Ida Chamberlain, 23 July 1939; Chamberlain Papers 18/1/1108.
24. 'Report on Truth and Truth Publishing Company Ltd.'; Vansittart Papers 11 2/32.
25. *The Diaries and Letters of Harold Nicolson*, vol. 2, 28 July, 1941.

26. Sir Joseph Ball to Neville Chamberlain, undated (but probably August/September 1940); Chamberlain Papers 7/11/33/19.
27. German Ambassador to German Foreign Ministry, 18 November 1937; *Documents on German Foreign Policy* (hereafter D G F P), Series D, (HMSO, 1950) vol. 1, p. 52.
28. Leo Amery, *Unforgiving Years* (Hutchinson, 1955), p. 225.
29. Quoted in John Ramsden, *The Making of Conservative Party Policy*, p. 66.
30. James Margach, *The Abuse of Power*, p. 50.
31. Memorandum by Leeper on 'The British Press and Foreign Affairs', July 1939; PRO FO 395/553 PN56.
32. Undated memorandum by Leeper: quoted in Philip Taylor, *The Projection of Britain: British Overseas Publicity and Propaganda* (Cambridge University Press, Cambridge, 1981), p. 297.
33. PRO FO 395/553 PN56.
34. Minute by I. Kirkpatrick, 23 February 1939; PRO FO 371/2298.222.
35. Report by A. Rumbold, 10 February 1937; PRO FO 371/2076.1242.
36. PRO FO 371/21158.2376.
37. Iverach McDonald, *Man of The Times* (Hamish Hamilton, 1976), p. 55.
38. Robert Dell to W.P. Crozier, 9 August 1935; *Manchester Guardian* Archive (hereafter MGA), 214.
39. Dell to Crozier, 25 March 1935; MGA 213.
40. Dell to Crozier, 25 March 1935, MGA 213.
41. Dell to Crozier, 25 March 1935, MGA 213.
42. F. A. Voigt to Crozier, 11 December 1935, MGA 214.
43. Crozier to Dell, 2 March 1935; MGA 213.
44. Voigt to Crozier, 11 December 1935, MGA 214.
45. Dell to Crozier, 2 March 1935, MGA 213.
46. This account given in Ian Colvin, *Vansittart in Office: An Historical Survey of the Second World War Based on the Papers of Sir Robert Vansittart* (Gollancz, 1965), pp. 44–6.
47. Martin Gilbert, *Winston S. Churchill*, vol. 5: *1922–1939* (William Heinemann, 1976), p. 639.
48. Voigt to Crozier, 11 December 1935; MGA 214.
49. Ian Colvin, *Vansittart in Office*, p. 49.
50. *The Diaries of Sir Alexander Cadogan*, ed. David Dilks (Cassell, 1971), 7 May 1938.
51. PRO FO 371/21158.2376.
52. Leeper memorandum and Vansittart minute in PRO FO 395/538 and FO 395/541; quoted by Martin Gilbert, *Winston S. Churchill*, vol. 5: *1922–1939*, pp. 725–6.
53. Neville Chamberlain to Hilda Chamberlain, 12 September 1937; Chamberlain Papers 18/1/1020.
54. Neville Chamberlain to Hilda Chamberlain, 18 August 1937; Chamberlain Papers 18/1/1014.
55. J. L. Garvin to Lord Astor, 19 July 1937; Astor Papers 1310.
56. Lord Astor to Garvin, 16 May 1937; Garvin Papers, Astor File.

57. Garvin to Leo Amery, 9 March 1937; Garvin Papers, Amery File.
58. Garvin article, the *Observer* 28 February 1937.
59. Larry William Fuchser, *Neville Chamberlain and Appeasement*, p. 49.
60. *History of The Times*, vol. 4, part 2: *1921 to 1948*, (written and published at the offices of *The Times*, 1952), p. 915.
61. Quoted by R. S. Bennett in Bennett to Neville Chamberlain, 28 March 1938; Chamberlain Papers 7/11/31/13.
62. Dawson to H. G. Daniels, 23 May 1937; *The Times* Archive.
63. Lord Astor to Garvin, 8 May 1937; Garvin Papers, Astor File.
64. PRO FO 371/20736.7232.
65. *The Diplomatic Diaries of Oliver Harvey, 1937–1940*, ed. John Harvey (Collins, 1970), 23 April 1937.
66. Lord Astor to Garvin, 26 October 1937; Garvin Papers, Astor File.
67. As summarized by William Strang; PRO FO 371/20/36.7905.
68. Lord Astor to Garvin, 26 October 1937; Garvin Papers, Astor File.
69. Lord Astor to Garvin, 26 October 1937; Garvin Papers, Astor File.
70. *The Political Diary of Hugh Dalton, 1918–40/1945–1960*, ed. Ben Pimlott (Jonathan Cape, 1986), 4 November 1937.
71. Sir Horace Wilson to John Evelyn Wrench, 10 June 1953; Dawson Papers.
72. *The Diplomatic Diaries of Oliver Harvey*, 23 September 1937.
73. Minutes in PRO FO 371/2042.5137 and 1495.

Chapter 2: The Road to Munich

1. Neville Chamberlain to Hilda Chamberlain, 24 October 1937; Chamberlain Papers 18/1/1025.
2. Neville Chamberlain to Ida Chamberlain, 14 November 1937; Chamberlain Papers 18/1/1028.
3. Sir Nevile Henderson to Foreign Office, 13 November 1937; PRO FO 371/2076.7799.
4. Henderson to Foreign Office, 14 November 1937, No. 286; Halifax Papers, Microfilm 1, A4.410.3.3.
5. Henderson to Foreign Office, 14 November 1937; PRO FO 371/20751.7324.
6. *The Diplomatic Diaries of Oliver Harvey*, 16 November 1937.
7. Neville Chamberlain to Ida Chamberlain, 14 November 1937; Chamberlain Papers 18/1/1028.
8. Henderson to Foreign Office, 15 November 1937; Halifax Papers, Microfilm 1, A4.410.3.3.
9. German Embassy in London to Foreign Ministry, Telegram A4980, 18 November 1937; DGFP, vol. 1, Series D, p. 52.
10. Henderson to Foreign Office, 14 November 1937; PRO FO 371/20751.7828.
11. German Embassy in London to Foreign Ministry, Telegram A4980, 18 November 1937; DGFP, vol. 1, Series D, p. 52.

12. Henderson to Foreign Office, 15 November 1937; PRO FO 371/20751.7828.
13. Vansittart to Henderson, 15 November 1937; PRO FO 371/20751.7828.
14. Dell to Crozier, 12 January 1938; MGA 219.
15. Voigt to Crozier, 17 November 1937; MGA 218.
16. Patricia Cockburn, *The Years of The Week* (Macdonald, 1968), p. 232.
17. Voigt to Crozier, 17 November 1937; MGA 218.
18. *The Diplomatic Diaries of Oliver Harvey*, 16 November 1937.
19. Lord Astor to Garvin, 17 November 1937; Garvin Papers, Astor File.
20. Lord Astor to Garvin, 15 December 1937; Garvin Papers, Astor File.
21. 'Lord Halifax's Diary: Visit of the Lord President to Germany', pp. 11–13, 'Meeting with Hitler', 19 November 1937; Halifax Papers, Microfilm 1, A4.410.3.3.
22. PRO FO 371/20736.8094.
23. Memorandum by Henderson; PRO FO 371/2076.245.
24. 'Memorandum by His Majesty's Ambassador on a Conversation between Lord Halifax and Dr. Goebbels on November 21st 1937; Halifax Papers, Microfilm 1, A4.410.3.3.
25. Halifax to Henderson, 24 November 1937; Halifax Papers, Microfilm 1, A4.410.3.2.
26. Account of conversation with Steward given by Halifax to Henderson, 25 November 1937; Halifax Papers, Microfilm 1, A4.410.3.2.
27. Henderson to Halifax, 2 December 1937; Halifax Papers, Microfilm 1, A4.410.3.2.
28. Henderson to Halifax, 2 December 1937; Halifax Papers, Microfilm 1, A4.410.3.2.
29. Basil Newton to Anthony Eden; PRO FO 371/22326.160.
30. Lord Astor to Garvin, 19 November 1937; Garvin Papers, Astor File.
31. Halifax to Henderson, 25 November 1937, Halifax Papers, Microfilm 1, A4.410.3.2.
32. Unpublished draft of 'Layton Memoirs'; Layton Papers Box 26.
33. Halifax to Lord Southwood, 1 December 1937, and Southwood to Halifax, 2 December 1937; Halifax Papers, Microfilm 1, A4.410.3.2.
34. Halifax to Henderson, 3 December 1937; Halifax Papers, Microfilm 1, A4.410.3.2.
35. *The Political Diary of Hugh Dalton*, 5 June 1938.
36. Douglas Jay, *Change and Fortune* (Hutchinson, 1980), p. 71.
37. I am indebted to Lord Jay for pointing this episode out to me.
38. Halifax to Henderson, 9 December 1937; Halifax Papers, Microfilm 1, A4.410.3.2.
39. Colin Seymour-Smith and Jim Schoff, *David Low* (Secker & Warburg 1985), pp. 54–5.
40. Larry William Fuchser, *Neville Chamberlain and Appeasement*, p. 96.
41. Halifax to Eden, 2 December 1937; Halifax Papers, Microfilm 1, A4.410.3.4.
42. Larry William Fuchser, *Neville Chamberlain and Appeasement*, p. 90.

43. Henderson to Halifax, 7 December 1937; Halifax Papers, Microfilm 1, A4.410.3.2.
44. Halifax to Henderson, 9 December 1937; Halifax Papers, Microfilm 1, A4.410.3.2.
45. Eden to Halifax, 10 December 1937; Halifax Papers, Microfilm 1, A4.410.3.2.
46. Typed notes by Hoare, p. 8; Templewood Papers Box x(5).
47. *The Diplomatic Diaries of Oliver Harvey*, 17 November 1937.
48. Neville Chamberlain to Ida Chamberlain, 12 December 1937; Chamberlain Papers 18/1/1031.
49. As told to Oliver Harvey, *The Diplomatic Diaries of Oliver Harvey*, 9 March 1937.
50. *The Diplomatic Diaries of Oliver Harvey*, 1 January 1938.
51. *The Diplomatic Diaries of Oliver Harvey*, 9 February 1938.
52. *The Diplomatic Diaries of Oliver Harvey*, 14 February 1938.
53. *The Diplomatic Diaries of Oliver Harvey*, 9 February 1938.
54. *The Diaries of Sir Alexander Cadogan*, 14 February 1938.
55. *The Diplomatic Diaries of Oliver Harvey*, 12 February 1938.
56. Sir Joseph Ball to Neville Chamberlain, 21 February 1938; Chamberlain Papers 7/11/31/10.
57. *The Diplomatic Diaries of Oliver Harvey*, 23 February 1938.
58. John Ramsden, *The Making of Conservative Party Policy*, p. 87.
59. Robert Rhodes James, *Anthony Eden* (Weidenfeld & Nicolson, 1986), p. 193.
60. Henderson to Foreign Office, 24 February 1938; PRO FO 371/21709.1279.
61. Peake minute; PRO FO 371/21709.1372.
62. Minutes in PRO FO 371/21709.1431.
63. Anthony Adamthwaite, 'The British Government and the Media', *Journal of Contemporary History*, 1983, p. 282.
64. Draft by Leeper in PRO FO 371/21709.1431. Text of message in PRO FO 395/561.1259.
65. Voigt to Crozier, 23 February 1938; MGA 219.
66. Example in telegram from Henderson to Foreign Office; PRO FO 371/21709.1372.
67. Vienna correspondent to Dawson, 16 March 1938, quoted in *History of The Times*, vol. 4, part 2, p. 917.
68. Dell to Crozier, 19 February 1938; MGA 219.
69. Crozier interview with Vansittart, 11 March 1938; Crozier Political Interviews.
70. Alexander Werth to Crozier, 15 March 1938; MGA 219.
71. Quotations from the Kennedy Journal, 15, 16 and 18 March 1938; *The Times* Archive.
72. Lord Beaverbrook to Halifax, 14 November 1938; Beaverbrook Papers C/152.
73. J. A. Cross, *Sir Samuel Hoare: A Political Biography* (Jonathan Cape, 1977), p. 63.
74. J. A. Cross, *Sir Samuel Hoare: A Political Biography*, p. 64.
75. *Chips: The Diaries of Sir Henry Channon*, ed. Robert Rhodes James (Weidenfeld & Nicolson, 1967), 2 June 1938.
76. Beaverbrook to Hoare, 22 November 1938; Templewood Papers Box x(3).

77. J. A. Cross, *Sir Samuel Hoare: A Political Biography*, p. 293.
78. Hoare to Beaverbrook, 15 February 1943; Beaverbrook Papers C/299.
79. *News Chronicle* Policy Conference no. 5; 17 June 1938; Layton Papers Box 26.
80. Francis Williams oral evidence, Royal Commission on the Press, 1947 to 1949 (HMSO, 1949), 15 October 1947.
81. *The Political Diaries of Hugh Dalton*, 5 June 1938.
82. David Hubback, *No Ordinary Press Baron* (Weidenfeld & Nicolson, 1985), p. 159.
83. *News Chronicle* Policy Conference no. 2, 18 February 1938; Layton Papers Box 26.
84. 'Observer and Its Future: Discussions with Lord Astor', September 1937; Garvin Papers.
85. 'Notes on Advertising and the Sunday Times', January/February 1938; Garvin Papers.
86. Arthur Mann to Stanley Baldwin, 27 December 1923; Mann Papers.
87. Broadcast entitled 'The Editor's Job', for the BBC series *The Press Today*; text in Mann Papers.
88. Arthur Mann to Rupert Beckett, 9 November 1938; Mann Papers.
89. Rupert Beckett to Arthur Mann, 23 March 1938; Mann Papers.
90. 'Interview with Neville Chamberlain', 27 March 1938; Mann Papers.
91. Beckett to Mann, October (undated) 1939; Mann Papers.
92. Interview with Chamberlain, 27 March 1938; Mann Papers.
93. Garvin to Lord Astor, 30 August 1938; Garvin Papers, Astor File.
94. Lord Astor to Garvin, 6 May 1938; Garvin Papers, Astor File.
95. *The Diaries of Sir Alexander Cadogan*, 7 May 1938.
96. Quoted in Iverach McDonald, *Man of The Times*, p. 48.
97. PRO FO 371/21709.1607.
98. PRO FO 371/21709.
99. Quoted in Larry William Fuchser, *Neville Chamberlain and Appeasement*, p. 134.
100. PRO FO 395/362.2404, 25 July 1938.
101. 'Memorandum by Baron von Welch ... on a conversation with Baron Hahn, Member of the D.N.B. Office in London', DGFP, vol. 11, Series D, p. 624.
102. PRO FO 395/362.2404.
103. Voigt to Crozier, 3 August 1938; MGA 219.
104. Account by Dr Hesse, 'On Probable Genesis of the Oft-Quoted Article in The Times of June 3rd', DGFP, vol. II, Series D, p. 399.
105. John Walter to Dawson, *History of The Times*, vol. 4, part 2, p. 921.
106. Kennedy Journal, 17 and 20 June, 18 July 1938; *The Times* Archive.
107. Quoted by London Office of the *Manchester Guardian* to Crozier, 28 July 1938; MGA 219.
108. PRO FO 395/362.2881.
109. Crozier to Voigt, 26 July 1938; MGA 219.
110. Crozier to Voigt, 22 July 1938; MGA 219.
111. Crozier interview with Vansittart, 11 August 1938; Crozier Political Interviews.
112. Charles Tower to Mann, 12 August 1938; Mann Papers.

113. PRO FO 371/21764.9361.
114. Kennedy Journal, 17 October 1938; *The Times* Archive.
115. Minute of 7 September 1938; PRO FO 371/21764.9356.
116. PRO FO 371/21735.9384.
117. Jan Masaryk to Lord Halifax, 7 September 1938; PRO FO 371/21764.9362.
118. PRO FO 371/21735.9415.
119. Dawson Diary, 7 September 1938; Dawson Papers.
120. Barrington-Ward note of 7 September 1938; quoted in *History of The Times*, vol. 4, part 2, p. 934.
121. *The Diplomatic Diaries of Oliver Harvey*, 8 September 1938.
122. *Chips: The Diaries of Sir Henry Channon*, 10 September 1938.
123. Kordt to German Foreign Ministry, Telegram No. 406 of 8 September 1938; DGFP, vol. II, Series D, p. 723.
124. Kordt to German Foreign Ministry, 3 October 1938; DGFP, vol. II, Series D, p. 292.
125. *The Diaries of Sir Alexander Cadogan*, 16 September 1938.
126. Beaverbrook to Halifax, 16 September 1938; Beaverbrook Papers C/152.
127. Beaverbrook to Neville Chamberlain, 16 September 1938; Beaverbrook Papers C/80.
128. *Foreign Relations of the United States: Diplomatic Papers 1938*, 1, p. 611.
129. Orme Sargent minute; PRO FO 371/21688.2367.
130. Mann to Churchill, quoted in Martin Gilbert, *Winston S. Churchill*, vol. 5: *1922–1939*, p. 969.
131. *The Diaries of Harold Nicolson*, vol. 1, 20 September 1938.
132. Crozier to Werth, 16 September 1938; MGA 219.
133. Crozier to Voigt, 14 September 1938; MGA 219.
134. Garvin to Lord Astor, 21 September 1938; Astor Papers 1310.
135. *The Diaries of Harold Nicolson*, vol. 1, 20 September 1938.
136. Halifax to British Delegation, 23 September 1938; quoted in Viscount Templewood, *Nine Troubled Years* (Collins, 1954), pp. 309–10.
137. Hoare notes 'On Munich Crisis'; Templewood Papers Box X(5).
138. Lord Rothermere to Churchill, 26 September 1938; quoted in Martin Gilbert, *Winston S. Churchill*, vol. 5: *1922–1939*, p. 974.
139. David Hubback, *No Ordinary Press Baron*, p. 158.
140. Account in a letter from Gerald Barry to Sir Walter Layton, 14 December 1944; Layton Papers Box 24.
141. Beckett to Mann, 30 September 1938; Mann Papers.
142. *Yorkshire Post* leader, 1 October 1938.
143. Barry to Layton, 14 December 1944; Layton Papers Box 24.
144. Lord Rothermere to Chamberlain, 1 October 1938; Chamberlain Papers 7/11/31/228.
145. Hoare to Beaverbrook, September (undated) 1938; Beaverbrook Papers C/299.
146. Undated Beaverbrook memo; Beaverbrook Papers G.37/Folder VIA.
147. Minutes in PRO FO 395/622.2831.
148. Viscount Templewood, *Nine Troubled Years*, p. 318.

149. Quoted in Anthony Adamthwaite, 'The British Government and the Media'.
150. Garvin notes on 'Correspondence and Documents Relating to Czechoslovakia', September 1938; Garvin Papers.
151. Lord Astor to Garvin, October (undated) 1938; Garvin Papers, Astor File.
152. W. W. Hadley, *Munich Before and After* (Cassell, 1944).

Chapter 3: Munich to War

1. *The Diaries of Sir Alexander Cadogan*, 4 October 1938.
2. Cadogan minute to Halifax, 28 November 1938; quoted in David Dilks, *The Diaries of Sir Alexander Cadogan*, p. 99.
3. *The Diplomatic Diaries of Oliver Harvey*, 24 and 29 May 1939 respectively.
4. Viscount Templewood, *Nine Troubled Years*, p. 255.
5. Von Dirksen to German Foreign Ministry, DGFP, vol. 4, Series D, p. 306.
6. Quotations from Cadogan Mss Diary of 6 December 1938; quoted in Christopher Andrew, *Secret Service*, p. 387, where a detailed account of this episode is available.
7. Hansard, vol. 34, col. 1528, 22 November 1938.
8. As quoted by Oliver Harvey; *The Diplomatic Diaries of Oliver Harvey*, 28 December 1938.
9. Arthur Mann to Forbes Adam, 30 November 1938; Mann Papers.
10. Mann to Beckett, 29 December 1938; Mann Papers.
11. Neville Chamberlain to Hilda Chamberlain, 15 October 1938; Chamberlain Papers 18/1/1072.
12. Neville Chamberlain to Ida Chamberlain, 4 December 1938; Chamberlain Papers 18/1/1091.
13. Neville Chamberlain to Hilda Chamberlain, 15 October 1938; Chamberlain Papers 18/1/1072.
14. *The Diplomatic Diaries of Oliver Harvey*, 28 December 1938.
15. All minutes and correspondence relating to the Italian visit are in PRO FO 395/363.
16. All minutes and correspondence in PRO FO 395/363.
17. J. Dundas to Halifax, 2 January 1939; PRO FO 395/363 3540/4.
18. Personal information supplied by Iverach McDonald to the author.
19. Dawson Diary, 18 January 1939; Dawson Papers.
20. As related to Dawson, recorded in the Kennedy Journal, 17 January 1939; *The Times* Archive.
21. PRO FO 371/22988.222.
22. Correspondence in PRO FO 395/623.2881.
23. Hoare to Halifax, 18 October 1938; Templewood Papers Box x(3).
24. Beaverbrook to Halifax, 24 July 1938; Beaverbrook Papers c/152.
25. Correspondence between Beaverbrook and Halifax on this matter in PRO FO 371/636.3444.

26. PRO FO 371/636.3444.
27. Quoted by Iverach McDonald, *Man of The Times*, p. 48.
28. Barrington-Ward to Dawson, 13 October 1938; *The Times* Archive.
29. Winn to Dawson, 4 October 1938; *The Times* Archive.
30. Colin Coote, *Editorial* (Eyre & Spottiswoode, 1965), p. 62.
31. Mann to Beckett, 25 November 1938; Mann Papers.
32. Beckett to Mann, 8 December 1938; Mann Papers.
33. Beckett to Mann, 10 November 1938; Mann Papers.
34. Beckett to Mann, 13 December 1938; Mann Papers.
35. Beckett to Mann, 14 December 1938; Mann Papers.
36. Beckett to Mann, 14 December 1938; Mann Papers.
37. Mann to Beckett, 18 December 1938; Mann Papers.
38. Text of the broadcast for the BBC series *The Press Today*, 24 January 1939; Mann Papers.
39. Mann to Beckett, 22 February 1939; Mann Papers.
40. Beckett to Mann, 1 February 1939; Mann Papers.
41. Hoare to Dawson, 28 February 1939; Templewood Papers Box X(4).
42. Eden to Mann, 2 March 1939; Mann Papers.
43. Layton to Chamberlain, 26 November 1938; Layton Papers Box 26.
44. Voigt to Crozier, 15 January 1939; MGA 221.
45. PRO FO 395/362.2508.
46. *The Diaries of Harold Nicolson*, vol. 1, 31 May 1939.
47. Ronald Tree, *When the Moon Was High* (Macmillan, 1972), p. 70.
48. Ronald Tree, *When the Moon Was High*, p. 71.
49. Neville Chamberlain to Hilda Chamberlain, 19 February 1939; Chamberlain Papers 18/1/1086.
50. *Chips: The Diaries of Sir Henry Channon*, 7 March 1939, p. 229.
51. Lord Astor to Garvin, 15 March 1939; Garvin Papers, Astor File.
52. *The Diplomatic Diaries of Oliver Harvey*, 10 March 1939.
53. James Margach, *The Abuse of Power*, p. 56.
54. *The Diaries of Sir Alexander Cadogan*, 10 March 1939.
55. Crozier interview with Vansittart, 28 March 1940; Crozier Political Interviews.
56. *The Diplomatic Diaries of Oliver Harvey*, 10 March 1939.
57. *The Diplomatic Diaries of Oliver Harvey*, 10 March 1939.
58. Chamberlain to Halifax, 11 March 1939; Halifax Papers, Microfilm 11, A4.410.17.1.
59. *The Diplomatic Diaries of Oliver Harvey*, 13 March 1939.
60. *The Diaries of Sir Alexander Cadogan*, 13 March 1939.
61. James Margach, *The Abuse of Power*, p. 58.
62. Crozier interview with Vansittart, 28 March 1940; Crozier Political Interviews.
63. Crozier interview with Vansittart, 28 March 1940; Crozier Political Interviews.
64. Garvin to Lord Astor, 15 March 1939; Crozier Political Interviews.
65. *Yorkshire Post*, 29 March 1939.
66. Dawson Diary, 19 March 1939; Dawson Papers.
67. *Yorkshire Post*, 29 March 1939.

68. *The Diaries of Sir Alexander Cadogan*, 30 March 1939.
69. David Dilks, *Diaries of Sir Alexander Cadogan*, p. 167.
70. Neville Chamberlain to Hilda Chamberlain, 2 April 1939; Chamberlain Papers 18/1/1092.
71. Hansard, vol. 345, col. 2501, 3 April 1939.
72. Dawson Diary, 3 April 1939; Dawson Papers.
73. James Margach, *The Abuse of Power*, p. 58.
74. *The Diplomatic Diaries of Oliver Harvey*, 3 May 1939.
75. As quoted by Voigt to Crozier, 4 May 1939; MGA 221.
76. PRO FO 371/23019.7304.
77. *The Diaries of Sir Alexander Cadogan*, 9 April 1939.
78. *The Diplomatic Diaries of Oliver Harvey*, 5 May 1939.
79. Voigt to Crozier, 4 May 1939; MGA 221.
80. Dawson Diary, 12 April 1939; Dawson Papers.
81. PRO FO 371/21701.15573.
82. PRO FO 395/663.691.
83. From George Barnes' account of this episode in the Harold Nicolson Contributor files; BBC Written Archive Centre, quoted in W.J. Werth, *Truth Betrayed*, pp. 138–40.
84. Lord Astor to Garvin, 30 June 1939; Garvin Papers, Astor File.
85. Martin Gilbert, *Winston S. Churchill*, vol. 5: *1922–1939*, p. 1083.
86. Halifax to Mann, 6 July 1939; Mann Papers.
87. *Chips: The Diaries of Sir Henry Channon*, 3 July 1939.
88. Neville Chamberlain to Hilda Chamberlain, 8 July 1939; Chamberlain Papers 18/1/1106.
89. Quoted in Martin Gilbert, *Winston S. Churchill*, vol. 5: *1922–1939*, p. 1081.
90. Neville Chamberlain to Hilda Chamberlain, 8 July 1939; Chamberlain Papers 18/1/1106.
91. Neville Chamberlain to Hilda Chamberlain, 8 July 1939; Chamberlain Papers 18/1/1106.
92. *Chips: The Diaries of Sir Henry Channon*, 3 July 1939.
93. Dawson Diary, 16 July 1939; Dawson Papers.
94. Neville Chamberlain to Hilda Chamberlain, 23 July 1939; Chamberlain Papers 18/1/1108.
95. *News Chronicle* Policy Conference, 19 May 1939; Layton Papers Box 26.
96. Dawson Diary, 22 August 1939; Dawson Papers.
97. Leo Kennedy to Charles Dilke, 9 July 1939; Dilke File, *The Times* Archive.
98. *News Chronicle* Policy Conference No. 34, 24 August 1939; Layton Papers Box 26.
99. *News Chronicle* Policy Conference No. 34, 24 August 1939; Layton Papers Box 26.
100. Garvin to Lord Astor, 21 June 1939; Astor Papers.
101. Garvin to Lord Astor, 24 July 1939; Astor Papers.
102. Garvin to Lord Astor, 24 July 1939; Astor Papers.
103. Neville Chamberlain to Hilda Chamberlain; quotations from, respectively, 30

July 1939 (Chamberlain Papers 18/1/1110) and 2 July (Chamberlain Papers 18/1/1107).

104. Account of conversation with Hitler on 27 July 1939; PRO PREM 1/332.
105. Account of conversation with Dr Rosenberg on 25 July 1939; PRO PREM 1/332.
106. PRO FO 395/666.3430.
107. Hoare notes; Templewood Papers Box x(5).
108. Hoare notes; Templewood Papers Box x(5).
109. Liddell Hart Diary, 27 August 1939; *The Times* Archive.
110. Unsigned Beaverbrook article; Beaverbrook Papers C/299.
111. James Margach, *The Abuse of Power*, p. 60.

Chapter 4: Chamberlain and the Ministry of Information

1. Mass-Observation, *Weekly Intelligence Service*, 16 March 1940.
2. Mass-Observation, *War Begins at Home* (London, 1949), p. 21.
3. King-Hall unpublished memoirs, p. 408; King-Hall Papers.
4. Henderson to Sir Lancelot Oliphant, 19 July 1939; PRO FO 3/1/665.3322.
5. *The Diplomatic Diaries of Oliver Harvey*, 13 November 1938.
6. *The Week*, 31 August 1938.
7. *King-Hall Newsletter*, 17 March 1939.
8. Wickham Steed, *The Press* (Penguin Special, 1938), p. 30.
9. Mass-Observation, *War Begins at Home*, p. 23.
10. *King-Hall Newsletter*, 17 March 1939.
11. Beckett to Mann, October (undated) 1939; Mann Papers.
12. Arthur Mann, *Memo on Business*, 2 October 1939; Mann Papers.
13. Arthur Mann to Brendan Bracken, 5 September 1941; Garvin Papers, Bracken File.
14. Temple Wilcox, 'Projection or Propaganda? Rival Concepts in the Pre-War Planning of the British Ministry of Information', *Journal of Contemporary History*, 1983.
15. Admiral G. P. Thomson, *Blue Pencil Admiral* (Sampson Low, 1947), p. 2.
16. Dawson Diary, entries of 5, 6, 16 and 25 September 1939; Dawson Papers.
17. Hoare Diary, 13 September 1939; Templewood Papers Box XI.
18. Quoted in Ian Mclaine, *Ministry of Morale*, p. 40.
19. Edward Cadbury to Sir Walter Layton, 6 September 1939; Layton Papers Box 26.
20. Press Committee of the MOI to the Prime Minister, 28 September 1939; PRO PREM 1/391.
21. Hoare Diary Notes, 14 September 1939; Templewood Papers Box XI.
22. Lobby Journalists Committee to the Prime Minister, 21 September 1939; PRO PREM 1/391.
23. Press Committee of the MOI to the Prime Minister, 28 September 1939; PRO PREM 1/391.

24. Paper describing a conversation between the Lobby journalists and Sir Horace Wilson, 29 September 1939; PRO PREM 1/392.
25. Lord Macmillan to Chamberlain, 30 September 1939; PRO PREM 1/392.
26. Ian Mclaine, *Ministry of Morale*, p. 41.
27. A. P. Waterfield to Mr Woodburn, 25 July 1939; PRO INF 1/156.
28. Memo by Wing Commander Heald, 11 June 1941; PRO AIR 2/5322.
29. Notes of meeting held at MOI on 23 February 1940; PRO INF 1/529.
30. PRO FO 371/28692.12439.
31. Minute by Charles Peake, 28 December 1939; PRO FO 3/1/23788.12122.
32. PRO FO 371/28692.12439.
33. PRO FO 371/23788.12122.
34. PRO FO 371/23787.7955.
35. Minute of 11 November 1941; PRO FO 371/23/88.12122.
36. Lord Perth to P. Nichols, 15 December 1939; PRO FO 371/23788.11657.
37. Perth to Nichols, 15 December 1939; PRO FO 371/23788.11657.
38. Perth to Frank Owen, 1 January 1940; PRO FO 371/24949.3269.
39. Hoare to Beaverbrook, 6 September 1940; Beaverbrook Papers C/308.
40. Beaverbrook to Hoare, letters of 30 August and 18 July 1940 respectively; Beaverbrook Papers C/308.
41. Correspondence in PRO FO 3/1/24510.5548.
42. PRO FO 371/24512.11441.

Chapter 5: The Final Act

1. Dawson Diary, 2 September 1939; Dawson Papers.
2. Leo Amery to Dawson, 4 September 1939; Dawson Papers.
3. Dawson to Leo Amery, 4 September 1939; Dawson Papers.
4. Dawson Diary, 17 September 1939; Dawson Papers.
5. Liddell Hart to Barrington-Ward, 28 October 1939; Liddell Hart File, *The Times* Archive.
6. Barrington-Ward Diary, 2 October 1939; quoted in *History of The Times*, vol. 5, p. 45.
7. Lord Astor to Mrs Carolyn Martin, 28 May 1938; Astor Papers, Box 118 (General Correspondence).
8. Lord Astor to John Stewart Bryan, 1 November 1939; Astor Papers, Box 120.
9. Lord Astor to Garvin, 21 September 1938; Garvin Papers, Astor File.
10. Lord Astor to Garvin, 28 June 1939; Garvin Papers, Astor File.
11. Lord Astor to Garvin, 24 March 1939; Garvin Papers, Astor File.
12. Lord Astor to Dawson, 4 October 1939; Astor Papers, Box 119 (General Correspondence).
13. *The Diaries and Letters of Harold Nicolson*, vol. 2, 3 October 1939.
14. Lord Astor to Garvin, 3 October 1939; Garvin Papers, Astor File.
15. Lord Astor to Garvin, 3 January 1940; Garvin Papers, Astor File.

16. Garvin to Lord Astor, 24 January 1940; Astor Papers 1310.
17. Garvin to Lord Astor, 3 November 1938; Astor Papers 1310.
18. Garvin to Lord Astor, 10 July 1939; Garvin Papers, Astor File.
19. Memorandum by Lord Astor, 23 October 1941; Astor Papers 1236.
20. Lord Astor to Garvin, 3 May 1940; Garvin Papers, Astor File.
21. Garvin to Sir Edward Grigg, 3 January 1940; Grigg Papers Ms. Film 1005.
22. Garvin to Lord Astor, 12 February 1940; Garvin Papers, Astor File.
23. Ivor Brown to Arthur Mann, 5 October 1942; Mann Papers.
24. Leo Amery to Dawson, 19 November 1940; Dawson Papers.
25. Dawson to Leo Amery, 3 December 1939; Dawson Papers.
26. Leo Amery, 'The Case for a War Cabinet', Dawson Papers.
27. Beveridge paper on 'Co-ordination in War', 17 September 1939; Layton Papers Box 5.
28. Beveridge to Sir Herbert Morgan, 4 October 1939; Beveridge Papers 11b 39/1.
29. 'Report of a Meeting of the Trade Union Side of the National Advisory Council to the Ministry of Labour with Mr. J. M. Keynes on January 24th, 1940'; Citrine Papers.
30. A. J. Cummings in *News Chronicle* Policy Conference No. 42, 23 November 1939; Layton Papers Box 26.
31. Layton memorandum 'Notes on Some War Problems', 5 December 1939; Layton Papers Box 5.
32. Crozier interview with Vansittart, 19 January 1940; Crozier Political Interviews.
33. Crozier interview with Churchill, 18 January 1940; Crozier Political Interviews.
34. Crozier interview with Churchill, 29 March 1940; Crozier Political Interviews.
35. Crozier interview with Brendan Bracken, 18 January 1940; Crozier Political Interviews.
36. Mr Nelsey to Sir Stafford Cripps, 13 October 1939; Cripps Papers.
37. 'Memo on the Post-War Bureau', 28 November 1939; Beveridge Papers 11b 39/111.
38. Sir Walter Citrine to Francis Williams, 2 November 1939; *Daily Herald* Archive, 558/790.3.
39. Williams to Citrine, 6 November 1939; *Daily Herald* Archive, 558/790.3.
40. Francis Williams, *Nothing So Strange* (Cassell, 1970), p. 131.
41. Francis Williams, oral evidence to the Royal Commission on the Press, 15 October 1947.
42. Memorandum on 'A National Debate', 17 January 1940; *Daily Herald* 558/790.
43. Laurence Cadbury to Sir Walter Layton, 9 October 1939; Layton Papers Box 26.
44. *News Chronicle* Policy Conference No. 36, 12 October 1939; Layton Papers Box 26.
45. *News Chronicle* Policy Conference No. 36, 12 October 1939, Layton Papers Box 26.
46. *News Chronicle* Policy Conference No. 40, 9 November 1939; Layton Papers Box 26.
47. Laurence Cadbury to Sir Walter Layton, 11 July 1939; Layton Papers Box 26.

48. Laurence Cadbury to Sir Walter Layton, 4 December 1939; Layton Papers Box 26.
49. A. J. P. Taylor, *Beaverbrook* (Hamish Hamilton, 1972), p. 398.
50. Neville Chamberlain to Ida Chamberlain, 27 January 1940; Chamberlain Papers 1/1/1140.
51. H. Boardman to 'S. B.' April (undated) 1940; MGA 145/40.
52. Hoare to Chamberlain, 10 January 1940; Chamberlain Papers 7/11/32/131.
53. Stokes to Beaverbrook, 18 March 1940; Beaverbrook Papers D/405.
54. Beaverbrook to Stokes, 16 March 1940; Beaverbrook Papers D/405.
55. Beaverbrook to Stokes, 29 March 1940; Beaverbrook Papers D/405.
56. Garvin to Lord Astor, 4 January 1940; Astor Papers 1310.
57. Hugh Cudlipp, *Publish and Be Damned: The Story of the Daily Mirror* (Andrew Davers, 1953), p. 136.
58. Beveridge to Viscount Bledistone, 18 December 1939; Beveridge Papers 11b 39/111.
59. *News Chronicle* Policy Conference No. 45, 14 December 1939; Layton Papers Box 26.
60. Dawson to Beveridge, 13 December 1939; Beveridge Papers 1xa.
61. Beveridge to Sir Horace Wilson, 7 October 1939; Beveridge Papers 11b 39/1.
62. Sir John Simon to Garvin, 2 February 1940; Garvin Papers, Simon File.
63. Lord Astor to Garvin, 29 November 1939; Garvin Papers, Astor File.
64. Neville Chamberlain to Hilda Chamberlain, 10 September 1939; Chamberlain Papers 18/1/1116.
65. Dawson Diary, 24 September 1939; Dawson Papers.
66. *News Chronicle* Policy Conference No. 40, 9 November 1939; Layton Papers Box 26.
67. Crozier to Fodor, 21 December 1939; MGA 221.
68. Hoare to Lord Lothian, 12 November 1939; Templewood Papers XI.
69. Neville Chamberlain to Ida Chamberlain, 27 January 1940; Chamberlain Papers 18/1/1140.
70. *Truth*, 19 January 1940 and 19 October 1938.
71. 'Observations on the Control of Truth', September 1941; Vansittart Papers 11/31.
72. For Major-General Fuller's letter, see *Truth*, 24 November 1939.
73. John Colville, *The Fringes of Power, Downing Street Diaries*, vol. 1: *1939 to October 1941* (Sceptre Edition, 1980), 19 November 1939.
74. Lord Astor to Garvin, 10 October 1939; Garvin Papers, Astor File.
75. Garvin to Lord Astor, 26 February 1940; Astor Papers 1310.
76. Lord Astor to Garvin, 20 October 1939; Astor Papers 1310.
77. Sir Edward Grigg to Garvin, 29 December 1939; Garvin Papers, Grigg File.
78. *The Diaries and Letters of Harold Nicolson*, vol. 2, 7 January 1940.
79. As related by Hore-Belisha to Crozier on 20 January 1940; Crozier Political Interviews.
80. Neville Chamberlain to Ida Chamberlain, 20 January 1940; Chamberlain Papers 18/1/1139.

217

81. *The Diaries of Sir Alexander Cadogan*, 8 January 1940.
82. Dawson Diary, 5 January 1940; Dawson Papers.
83. *The Diaries and Letters of Harold Nicolson*, vol. 2, 7 January 1940.
84. Lord Astor to Garvin, 9 January 1940; Garvin Papers, Astor File.
85. Dawson Diary, 6 January 1940; Dawson Papers.
86. Cecil King, *With Malice Toward None* (Sidgwick & Jackson, 1970), 13 January 1940.
87. Lord Astor to Garvin, 17 January 1940; Garvin Papers, Astor File.
88. Cecil King, *With Malice Toward None*, 17 January 1940.
89. Neville Chamberlain to Ida Chamberlain, 20 January 1940; Chamberlain Papers 18/1/1139.
90. Cecil King, *With Malice Toward None*, 31 January 1940.
91. Neville Chamberlain to Ida Chamberlain, 20 January 1940; Chamberlain Papers 19/1/1139.
92. 'Report on Truth and Truth Publishing Company Limited'; Vansittart Papers 11 2/32.
93. Lord Astor to Garvin, 17 March 1940; Garvin Papers, Astor File.
94. *The Diplomatic Diaries of Oliver Harvey*, 4 April 1940.
95. Lord Astor to Garvin, 4 April 1940; Garvin Papers, Astor File.
96. John Colville, *The Fringes of Power*, 4 April 1940.
97. *The Diplomatic Diaries of Oliver Harvey*, 4 April 1940.
98. Dawson Diary, 17 April 1940; Dawson Papers.
99. *Chips: The Diaries of Sir Henry Channon*, 16 April 1940.
100. Lord Astor to Garvin, 14 April 1940; Garvin Papers, Astor File.
101. Lord Astor to Garvin, 3 May 1940; Garvin Papers, Astor File.
102. Crozier interview with Brendan Bracken, 29 March 1940; Crozier Political Interviews.
103. Hoare Diary Notes, (March) 1940; Templewood Papers XI.
104. Hoare to Lord Lothian, 13 February 1940; Templewood Papers XI.
105. Neville Chamberlain to Hilda Chamberlain, 10 March 1940; Chamberlain Papers 18/1/1146.
106. Hoare to Rothermere, 5 April 1940; Templewood Papers XII.
107. Garvin to Lord Astor, 3 April 1940; Astor Papers 1310.
108. J. R. S. Scott to Crozier, 24 April 1940; MGA 145/90.
109. *The Diaries and Letters of Harold Nicolson*, vol. 2, 30 April 1940.
110. *The Diaries and Letters of Harold Nicolson*, vol. 2, 30 April 1940.
111. Crozier interview with Churchill, 1 May 1940; Crozier Political Interviews.
112. Cecil King, *With Malice Toward None*, 1 May 1940.
113. *Chips: The Diaries of Sir Henry Channon*, 5 May 1940.
114. Chamberlain to Beaverbrook, 6 May 1940; Beaverbrook Papers C/80.
115. Rothermere to Chamberlain, telegrams of 7 May and 8 May respectively; Chamberlain Papers 11/33/144 and 11/33/145.
116. Lord Kemsley to Chamberlain, 9 May 1940; Chamberlain Papers 7/11/33/117.
117. Chamberlain Diary; Chamberlain Papers NC2/24A.

Epilogue

1. Lord Astor to Garvin, 9 May 1940; Garvin Papers, Astor File.
2. Lord Astor to Garvin, 11 May 1940; Garvin Papers, Astor File.
3. *News Chronicle* Policy Conference No. 52, 9 May 1940; Layton Papers Box 26.
4. *Chips: The Diaries of Sir Henry Channon*, 11 May 1940.
5. Lord Astor to Garvin, 11 May 1940; Garvin Papers, Astor File.
6. Lord Astor to Garvin, 4 October 1940; Garvin Papers, Astor File.
7. Lord Astor to Garvin, 4 September 1940, Garvin Papers, Astor File.
8. Dawson Diary, 13 May 1940; Dawson Papers.
9. Dawson Diary, 26 February 1941; Dawson Papers.
10. Dawson Diary, 23 December 1940; Dawson Papers.
11. Cecil King, *With Malice Toward None*, 12 May 1940.
12. Correlli Barnett, *The Audit of War* (Papermac, 1987), p. 11.
13. See R. B. Cockett, 'The Government, the Press and Politics in Britain, 1937–1945' (unpublished Ph.D. thesis, University of London, 1988), for a fuller account of these developments in the press during the war.
14. In the same context, A. J. P. Taylor, Beaverbrook's biographer, also wrote the standard historical account of the period in *Oxford History of England, 1914 to 1945*.
15. Chamberlain Diary; Chamberlain Papers NC2/24A.
16. Sir Joseph Ball to Neville Chamberlain, undated (probably August or September) 1940; Chamberlain Papers 7/11/33/19.
17. For the debate on *Truth*, see Hansard, vol. 374, cols 1454–62.
18. 'Report on *Truth*', p. 15; Vansittart Papers 11/32.
19. Anthony Howard, RAB: *The Life of R. A. Butler* (Jonathan Cape, 1987), p. 152.

Conclusion

1. Cranbourne to Arthur Mann, 13 August 1940; Mann Papers.
2. Hoare interview with Sir Horace Wilson, 5 March 1947; Templewood Papers XIX (B)5.

Index

223